PRAIRIE TIME

PRAIRIE TIME
THE LEOPOLD RESERVE REVISITED

JOHN ROSS & BETH ROSS

THE UNIVERSITY OF WISCONSIN PRESS

A North Coast Book

The University of Wisconsin Press
2537 Daniels Street
Madison, Wisconsin 53718

3 Henrietta Street
London, WC2E 8LU, England

5   4   3   2   1

Printed in Canada

Photographs on pages i, iii, x, xxii, 8, 11, 14, 25, 33, 42, 45, 51, 54, 58, 60, 63, 66, 68, 74, 78, 80, 84, 88, 90, 93, 96, 102, 106, 114, 127, 129, 193: © 1998 by John E. Ross.
Photographs on pages xix, 1, 17, 18, 21, 23, 27, 29, 38, 81, 100, 117: © 1998 by Elizabeth B. Ross.

The authors and the publisher gratefully acknowledge permission from the Aldo Leopold Foundation and Oxford University Press to reprint the quotations from Aldo Leopold, *A Sand County Almanac and Sketches Here and There,* © 1949 by Oxford University Press, Inc., that appear on the following pages (numbers in parentheses refer to the pages on which the passages occur in *A Sand County Almanac*): xi (103), xxiii (41), 5 (79), 12 (18), 13 (95), 19 (78), 20 (51), 25 (45), 26 (53), 32 (59–61), 37 (66), 43 (102), 44 (66), 52 (20), 53 (105), 61 (204), 62 (52), 72 (173), 73 (112), 82 (69), 83 (55), 95 (111), 95–96 (188), 98 (6–7), 106 (132–33), 107 (109–10), 118 (82), 119 (200), 128 (vii).

The quotation on p. 91 is reprinted from "Wilderness," in Aldo Leopold, *The River of the Mother of God and Other Essays,* edited by Susan L. Flader and J. Baird Callicott (Madison: The University of Wisconsin Press, 1991), p. 229.

Library of Congress Cataloging-in-Publication Data
Ross, John (John Elton), 1926–
   Prairie time : the Leopold Reserve revisited / John Ross and Beth Ross.
      254 p.   cm.
   "A North Coast book."
   Includes index.
   ISBN 0-299-15660-5 (cloth : alk. paper)
   1. Natural history—Wisconsin—Aldo Leopold Memorial Reserve.   2. Phenology—Wisconsin—Aldo Leopold Memorial Reserve.   3. Prairie ecology—Wisconsin—Aldo Leopold Memorial Reserve.   I. Ross, Beth, 1927–   .   II. Title.
QH105.W6R67   1998
508.775'76—dc21   97-5268

Title page photograph: Bottle gentian

To Charles and Nina Bradley

CONTENTS

PREFACE

This book represents a collaborative effort. John Ross is the author of the prologue, the essays, and the glossarial notes in this volume. John and Beth Ross are the photographers. Beth also wrote the species descriptions for "Citizens of the Prairie and Savanna"; their content is rooted in the phenological data collected by Aldo Leopold in the 1930s and 1940s and Charles Bradley and Nina Leopold Bradley in the 1970s, 80s, and 90s.

The Aldo Leopold Memorial Reserve, near Baraboo, Wisconsin, is the site for our explorations. Charles and Nina Bradley are the inspiration for many of the events described in the essays.

The land in the reserve is being restored to its natural vegetation. The project is a monument to the concept that environmental quality can be achieved not only by preservation and protection of remnants of natural flora and fauna, but also through actual restoration of the natural beauty of the land. The aim is to promote ecological restoration as a means of sustaining the diversity of life on Earth and reestablishing an ecologically healthy relationship between nature and culture.

The authors acknowledge with gratitude the contributions of the Bradleys to this volume. We are indebted to Virginia Kline, as well, for her spirited review of the species descriptions. The staff of the University of Wisconsin Press has given us unbounded support. We are particularly grateful to Allen Fitchen, Elizabeth Steinberg, Mark Crawford, and Laura Moss Gottlieb, who made the index. We are also grateful to the Aldo Leopold Foundation and Oxford University Press for allowing us to include quotations from *A Sand County Almanac* which occur at the beginning and end of each essay and elsewhere in the text.

Dried Compass Plant

PROLOGUE

There are other plants who seem to ask of this world not riches but room. Such is the little sandwort that throws a white-lace cap over the poorest hilltops just before the lupines splash them with blue. Sandworts simply refuse to live on a good farm, even on a very good farm, complete with rock garden and begonias. And then there is the little Linaria, so small, so slender, and so blue that you don't even see it until it is directly underfoot; who ever saw a Linaria except on a sandblow?

PRAIRIE TIME

Aldo Leopold's words set the stage for this volume about life as shaped by the prairies, the sandy savannas, and the woodlands in south-central Wisconsin.

The land about which we are writing lies within the transition zone between the native eastern forests, dense and deciduous, and the western grasslands, so fully open to the sky. Here, the natural expression is that of sweeps of prairie with oak openings. Grasses and forbs fill the prairies. Clusters of oaks create the "openings." Before settlement, it was one of the major prairie/savanna regions of the world. Today, with cultivation and urbanization, only classic, natural remnants remain of this vast expanse. But they do remain.

The volume includes a series of essays, species descriptions, and photographs inspired by the Aldo Leopold Memorial Reserve in Sauk County, Wisconsin.

The essays are written in four phases:

they (1) explore the seasons of the year, (2) explore the relationships of life in the area to the underlying physical forces of land, water, ice, and fire, (3) return to a longer than seasonal consideration of time and roots, and (4) conclude with a metaphorical story about the efforts of a sentient species on another planet that goes to infinite lengths to control its environment.

The species descriptions provide intimate glimpses of many of the inhabitants of this region, and describe how humans have recognized their values.

Scenic photographs give a general sense of the area; other photographs focus in close on individual species.

THE PHENOLOGY OF THE PRAIRIE

Time and place are the framework for this book. Phenological expressions in the prairie are a unifying focus.

Phenology is the study of periodic

biological phenomena such as flowering, breeding, and migration as related to geology and climate. The root *pheno* means "showing" or "displaying."

Phenology requires the patient tabulation, across the years, of the dates of these events. This was undertaken in a singular location by Aldo Leopold, the wildlife ecologist and land ethicist, in the 1930s and 1940s, and has been continued by Charles Bradley, the geologist and climatologist, and by Nina Leopold Bradley, the botanist/ecologist, starting in the 1970s. Their work lies behind what is expressed here.

They have tabulated dozens of phenomena, including when the pasque flower blooms in the harshness of early spring, the autumn frost first coats the big bluestem with cloaks of silver, and the geese depart.

There is also the search for the meaning of why things happen when they do. The dimension of time becomes the second pathway in this journey of discovery, because the biological mix, climate, and even geological conditions change over time.

The changing patterns of expressions are most obviously pulsed by the seasons. The seasonal changes are an integrated expression of the physical and biological worlds. At this latitude, near 45° North, the celebratory days are the equinoxes of spring and autumn, the solstices of winter and summer.

With some knowledge of last year and the years before that, the phenologist becomes intimate with how those changes persist or change over the decades. The 60-year time span, between 1930 and 1990, does offer biological evidence suggestive of a warming trend. But more than that, there evolves a deeper understanding of the web of life that preceded today's community, and how life here has continuously adjusted to the sandy terrain, weather and climate patterns, moving continents, and even the astronomical journey of Earth.

The relationships between the physical and biological worlds so exquisitely expressed in this land become more apparent through careful study. There is also the possibility of understanding what this land could be like in the future—or not be like.

In spite of the full-throated expression of nature's timetable, phenologists do use a human contraption called the calendar to document the flow of dates. They note the date of the earliest blizzard in December. They date the return of the first sandhill crane in late March, the first bloom of the sandwort in the middle of May, and the bloom of linaria very near to June 16.

The expressions of the plants and animals are dated on the calendar, but the sensory impressions given by the plants and animals seem more like a chorale prelude on a pipe organ than a demarcation on a calendar. The calendar is based in Earth's astronomy, but it also gives a sense of regularity, even security, in the face of natural forces that are always shifting under our feet. Humans are well served to search for a sense of time and place in nature's documentations, because the phenological expressions do respond to the long-term changes as well as the seasonal ones. With observations of long-term changes, theories of climate change and of the sweep of evolution on the land gain specificity. There is also an understanding of the intrinsic meaning of the long reaches of time. But more than that, there is an understanding of how the web of natural structure is a safety net for all species—including humans. We even begin to sense our own phenological expressions.

If we humans are wise enough to track the changes from the past, we find a rationale for the calendar that is deeper than today's appointments or next week's openings in our schedules. We can hear more clearly the higher and lower tones in nature's pipe organ.

But even more than that, we gain a deeper sense of our own destiny than could ever be provided alone by a philosophy myopically centered on the calendar.

LIFE ON THE BORDER

The underlying physics of Earth as a planet—its orbit and rotation around the sun—is the basic framework for all of Earth's life, whether at the equator, the poles, or in between. The land of which we speak in this book lies in between, at about 44° North Latitude and 89° West Longitude, almost halfway to the North Pole, and deep within the vast North American continent.

The earth has an elliptical orbit and rotates on a tilted axis. The orbit and rotation at this latitude bring a constantly revolving pattern of night and day, spring and autumn, and long-term orbital cycles that are the source of climatic rhythms. This country is the junction between the tropics and the arctic. Summer is tropical. Winter is polar.

But that is just the underlying astronomical basis for our neighborhood. There is another related element that is geologically recent. This middle ground is located where glaciers stopped advancing about 11,000 years ago. On one side the terrain is shaped by hills of glacial sand and "drift"; the other side is unglaciated and driftless.

Glaciation comes and goes on a scale of about 100,000 years, but there are warmer intervals within these major cycles as the earth's seas, continents, and atmosphere work to exchange in-flowing energy from the sun (direct at the equator, oblique at the poles). Climatologists now assert that "glacial climates" ebb and flow in shorter time spans than glacial epochs, as little as hundreds of years or even decades. The major Wisconsin period of glaciation phased away between 12,000 and 13,000 years ago. But sometime between 11,000 and 12,000 years ago, glacial climates returned for about 600 years in a period called the Younger Dryas.

The cooler and warmer periods, with shifts in amounts and distribution of rainfall, give advantages and disadvantages to different complexes of plants and animals over time. As the glaciers advanced over the millennia, the animals and the plants migrated south, but were persistent enough to return time and again over the two million years of the Pleistocene. Some perished to extinction as the ice advanced. Other species became finely tuned to the short-run climate changes embedded in that broader design—adjustments are evident now, even from year to year. The seasonal changes of the plants and animals reflect year-to-year variations in the environment, but are also related to longer-term events. We just need to be clever enough to observe them!

The seasonal changes in this land are dramatic. Temperatures can range from -30°F in winter to 100°F in summer. Blizzards can rage in January, and humidity in July can be as dense as in the tropics. Rainfall now averages about 31 inches a year, but there can be multiyear droughts at half that, or summer deluges measured in inches of rain in hours. Within all this tumult, are days, weeks, and seasons of great temperance. Human residents here often complain about the climate, but we really have developed an affinity to both the tumult and the temperance. Our migrations, to the south in winter and to the north in summer, tend to be on the order of a week or so—but then we return in time for the warming days of spring and the golden days of autumn.

THE GREAT OAK SAVANNA

Biologically, this land is within the broad, dynamic continental ecotone, or transition zone, between eastern deciduous forests and western grasslands. Before the land was settled and cultivated extensively, the ecotone was an oak savanna complex that stretched from southwestern Texas through the American Midwest to central Manitoba in Canada—with ideal conditions for savanna and tall-grass prairies here in the Upper Midwest. There were expanses of prairie and clusters of oak openings, as a function of soil conditions and fire. The sandy terrain at our specific location is a result of glacial out-wash. Farther east, mixed hardwoods and brush occupied the deciduous forests. The western grasslands were more dominated by short-grass prairies and had few trees, mostly cottonwoods along the water courses. Settlement has radically changed the biology on the land, but the underlying physical conditions persist.

The boreal forest lies some 300 miles away to the northeast and stretches another 1,200 miles before giving way to tundra. There has been less settlement impact there. The vast sweep of the tall-grass prairies started just southwest of what is now the Leopold Reserve and spanned 500 miles to the land of short-grass prairies; in another 500 miles the prairies gave way to the desert. Due south and east were the wet mesic prairies of Illinois. To the east were the dense deciduous woods of the North Atlantic states, the Middle South, then the swamps and estuaries of the coastal plains.

The oak savanna ecotone covered some 30 million acres before settlement. In Wisconsin, oak savanna occurred naturally on an estimated six million acres. The sandier parts of the Wisconsin savanna tended toward pine barrens that contained primarily jack pine, but also oak and patches of white pine in cooler microclimates. Now only about 5,000 acres of prime oak savanna, and remnant patches of prairie, remain in Wisconsin.

Ecologists agree that distribution of natural vegetation is largely structured by climate, along with influences from fire, geological features, and the general elevation above the sea. The oak savanna/prairie complex defined a boundary between the humid regions of the east and the more arid and higher regions of the west.

The transition zone is the larger biological resolution for these essays. Using a finer resolution, we have focused on a boundary within the savanna—that is, the edge of the Wisconsin glaciation.

THE EDGE OF THE GLACIER

The dominant features in this more local terrain are the recessional and terminal moraines, overlain with savanna, prairie, wetlands, and the Wisconsin River floodplain. Moraines are hills and ridges of sand, gravel, and boulders left behind by retreating glaciers. This terrain forms a diagonal belt across Wisconsin, with glaciated land to the northeast, and driftless, unglaciated land to the southwest.

Before settlement, fires regularly swept across the landscape. The fires generally moved from west to east with the prevailing winds. They could be momentarily intense, but really only brushed the surface and hop-skipped over the landscape. Plant communities bounded on the west by water or wetlands were somewhat protected. Thus, forests tended to develop on less frequently burned sites. Prairies, barrens, and savannas occupied the areas subject to frequent fires. Their abundance supported grazing and browsing animals—first Ice Age mammals, and later bison and elk. In turn, grazing served to maintain the plant cover.

In spite of the extremes, even because of them, biodiversity of the natural savanna communities was extraordinarily high, because this was a community of mixed vegetation formed by the overlapping of adjoining communities. Biodiversity was greatest in classic savanna areas, rather than in the pockets of prairies, wetlands, or forests.

In this ecotone, both forest and prairie species existed. Many species, such as the bur oak or the sandhill crane, were adapted to the niches created by the ecotone itself. There was a reliance on uncertainty. There were opportunities for both residents and migrators. Life was on the move in tune to a moving earth.

In roughly the last two million years, the climates of the glacial Pleistocene Epoch are the most obvious definers of the ecotone. But there are vast reaches of earlier time worthy of consideration in the quest to really understand the land, and those earlier ages do appear in this narrative, if only partly understood. They speak of the Pliocene, a warmer time. They also speak of the dinosaurs in the Mesozoic Era (65–245 million years ago) and the flourishing of mammals in the late Cretaceous Period about 80 million years ago. They speak of vast, shallow, tropical seas that covered this land as far back as 500 million years ago.

OF SANDY SOIL

There is a physical commonality here that reaches across the ages. Life in this borderland has obviously developed a toughness that is rooted in sandy soils. Quartz is the dominant soil material. Chemically, quartz is silicon dioxide, inert and stubbornly bound together. An important molecule in the condensation of the earth over four billion years ago, silicon dioxide has been detected as an ingredient of cosmic dust.

However, the actual crystals of quartz we see at our feet are no longer identifiable as cosmic dust. The crystals are descendants from geologic changes on this planet, including magma that erupted from deep layers at least two billion years ago. About 140 million years ago a single land mass began to break into parts. These continents separated and floated northward on Earth's mantle, from tropical to temperate zones. North and South America were once joined to Antarctica. As the continents moved, the crystals of quartz eroded from mountains to sandy beaches, where they were buried and recast as quartzite. In relatively recent times, the quartzite and other rocks were ground into sand by those repeated glaciations.

Through the 100 centuries or so since the last glaciation, the quartz sand in the moraines and the braided levees northeast of here has spread out in the glacial outwash to the southwest. On the glacial side of the border, the sand is mixed with deposits of erratic granite boulders in the moraines, and the sand yields to pockets of clay in the sedge meadows and potholes. On the unglaciated side of the border, outcroppings of ancient limestone, sandstone, and occasionally shale, rise like sentinels above the outwash of glacial sand. Just to the south is a very ancient outcropping of quartzite, over one billion years old, that partially escaped the rub of glaciers. Farther to the south are the rich loess prairies, also a product of glaciation.

So glaciation created the sandy conditions of the moraines and the barrens just to the north. Some of the silicon dioxide in the sand was already here in the quartzite rock. Granite boulders and more quartz sand came from the great continental peneplain that lies some 300 miles to the north.

THE ALDO LEOPOLD MEMORIAL RESERVE

In 1935, Aldo Leopold bought 80 acres of this sandy terrain beside the Wisconsin River floodplain for eight dollars an acre, a purchase that his daughter Nina describes as "a considerable investment at the time." Leopold had asked Ed Ochsner, a Sauk County real estate agent, to "find me some acreage." Thus, putting down roots at this specific site by the Leopold family was somewhat circumstantial. First, Leopold rented the land for two weeks, then decided it was fine, and bought it.

The land had been farmed for corn and buckwheat, perhaps for only a decade or two, but it was described as "corned to death." The farmer's house had burned. The fences were down, and neighborhood cows roamed the moraines. Most of the white pine had been logged by the end of the nineteenth century.

Still on the property was a chicken house complete with perch and waist-high manure. With a leap of faith that the lice had been frozen out, the family set out on a shack restoration project, as Nina says, "without spending any money." Modeling their project after Thoreau's house of driftwood, they hiked along the riverbank looking for cottonwood planks. They found windows in a junkyard, but no screens. One summer evening, with mosquitoes thick in the air, they moved into a Baraboo motel for the weekend. But by the next weekend, they had located screens. Almost immediately the Leopold family started tree-planting, savanna and prairie restoration, and their phenological journals.

Today, a privately owned area of 1,400 acres is known as the Aldo Leopold Memorial Reserve. It is located where the Wisconsin River and its floodplain cut a swath through the moraines and wetlands north of the Baraboo Range.

The glaciation, wind erosion, and fluvial actions of the Wisconsin River have molded the reserve's surface features. The acreage is covered with a mantle of sediments and till laid down by a series of glacial advances, the last being the Green Bay Lobe of the Woodfordian age, which reached its maximum advance into the area before 13,000 years ago.

As the glacier melted, an extension of glacial Lake Wisconsin formed to the east of the terminal moraine. The north-south-trending ridges in the reserve were probably formed during this time as deltas in the lake and at the ice margin. There are locally at least three of these ridges, composed of sand, gravel, and clay. In between the ridges are wet mesic prairies, sloughs, and old river courses. The lake existed in the area until the ice margin cleared the east end of the resistant quartzite hills in the Baraboo Range, thus allowing vast outpourings of water to escape near present-day Portage.

The lake drained through the Portage outlet, establishing the present course of the Wisconsin River. Subsequently, the river eroded the north ends of the ridges. Later processes reworked both the glacial and modern sediments to form sand blows and dunes, resulting in today's topography.

Fire, fluctuating water levels, and siltation influenced the changing composition of plant communities on the land that is now the reserve. Presently about two-thirds of the area is floodplain forest and marshland, dotted with ponds and river sloughs. The

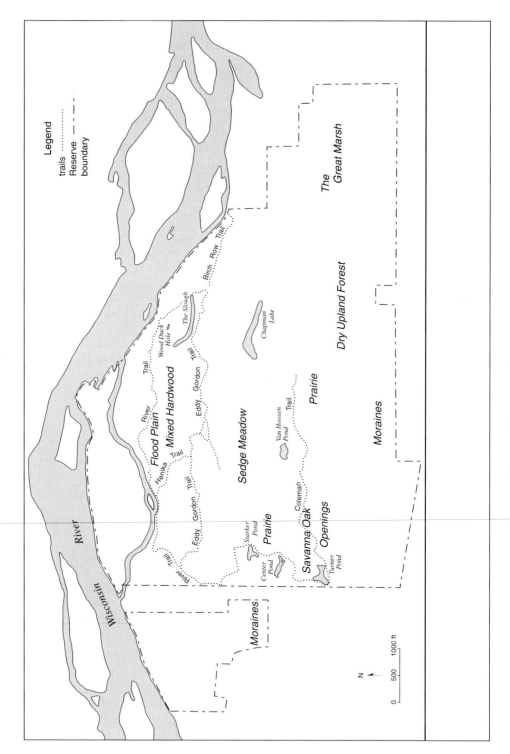

The Leopold Memorial Reserve, with Presettlement Features

remainder is hilly moraine that has recently been covered by a mixed oak-hickory-pine forest and broken by a few fields still under cultivation. A sandy substrate underlays the entire reserve and produces an easily eroded soil of low fertility.

European immigrants settled the area in the 1840s. At that time oak savanna, abetted by fires, was the dominant regional ecotype. Lumbering, cultivation, drainage of wetlands, grazing, mowing, and fire suppression in the nineteenth and early twentieth centuries caused rapid change in the vegetative cover. Farming reached its peak in the mid-1920s. During the drought and depression of the 1930s many farms were abandoned to brush, weeds, wind,

and weather. Corn, it seems, is not well adapted to the vagaries of drought or the market. Corn is a creature of economic subsidies as much as cultivation. It is certainly not phenologically adjusted to this land and climate.

On the northern slopes, there still remain relic flora of the glaciers now found mostly in Canada, typically including trilliums, Indian pipe, and prince's pine. Winter's ice can persist until May or June in cold pockets in the Baraboo Range. Along the edge of the river, where the terrain takes on desert conditions, there are indicator species of sandburs, switchgrass, and annual wild-rye. In the oak savanna areas there are puccoon, penstemon, and prairie dropseed. Tiny wisps of

Prairie Smoke

rose-colored flowers once again emerge in late April. They are aptly named prairie smoke.

Restoration management on the reserve has brought the savanna back. Now there are patches of reestablished prairie with waves of big bluestem as tall as a person on a horse. Fire management is being used, and the woodlands are rapidly taking on the form of the natural savanna. The multitude and diversity of the prairie and savanna species are increasing. A redefinition of human relationships with this land has produced a notable change in a short period of 60 years. But one additional element seems unchanging: On summer evenings, the mosquitoes are still thick enough to swallow.

AN EARLY MORNING HIKE

The four of us, Nina and Charles, Beth and I, will start our personal journey with an early morning hike along the river. Since it is late November now, we can see the landforms that have emerged from the dense cover of summer foliage. The trail leads us from the floodplain forests, where the sloughs and levees are now starkly obvious, to the sedge meadows, over the wet mesic prairie, up and across the steep-sided recessional moraine that edges the floodplain, and to the woods, where tree thinning is restoring the savanna. All of this land is bound by the seasonal changes, the sandy topography, and seasonal and annual variations in the moisture supply.

Because this tumbled terrain changes quickly, we hike through all of these areas in a few hours. We reach the bench, hand-hewn by Aldo Leopold over 50 years ago, and pour a morning cup of coffee from the thermos. The hot coffee will challenge the winter chill in the air, as the first, big snowstorm is gathering energy down in Missouri. The winter storm roared in from the Pacific Ocean, jumped the Cascades and Rockies, and gathered strength over the Oklahoma plains before it closed down the Missouri highways.

Life is hunkering down for winter—at the river's edge, in the slough, the sedge meadow, the savanna, and in the deeper woods. It is at the edge of the woods that we will finish our coffee before it cools off, absorb the intimacies of life at our elbow, and imagine the root cellars of the prairie plants near our feet with their ample stores of carbohydrates. Then—we will contemplate the ridge of the moraine, listen to the rustle of the November wind in the grasses, and sniff the wind for the smell of the advancing snow. And that will remind us of the glaciers.

THE HOLOCENE

But what we imagine is just a short chapter in a long history. On our hike, we had pulled up our coat collars and pulled down our wool caps and talked about the glaciers. Many scientists now assume that the Pleistocene is over and have labeled the newest geological age the Holocene. *Holo* refers to "whole" or "entire" in Greek. In the minds of the Greeks, *holo* meant the emergence of civilizations, which, they assumed, gave a sense of completeness to Earth. *Cene* refers to "recent" and is used to identify those recent epochs of geologic time, such as the Pleistocene, preceded by the Pliocene, Miocene, Oligocene, Eocene, and Paleocene that lead us all the way back through the Tertiary Period—a span of nearly 70 million years. The term "tertiary" itself means recent or modern—in geological terms.

There is a touch of irony in such assumptions and such terms. The Pleistocene, the epoch just preceding "our time," means "the most complete record of fossils." Some have concluded that there were more species to be preserved from the Pleistocene than from previous ages—with the assumption that evolution, through speciation, inevitably increases the branches on the evolutionary tree. Others, with a touch of cynicism, believe more fossils survived from the Pleistocene only because they were more recently deposited.

In the not-too-distant future, say 100,000 years from now, it could be too late for such human cynicism. A scattering of paleontologists may then conclude that the Pleistocene, with its myriad of species, was a more biologically generous age than its successor, the Holocene. Through the coming millennia, the fossil deposits will almost surely reveal a period of accelerating extinctions from the pervasive impact of humans. A deeper irony could be that the Holocene may merely be an extension of the Pleistocene Epoch of repeated glaciations, and not a new age at all. The mammals that survive the next round of glaciation, perhaps including some paleontologists, will also be known as Ice Age mammals.

In our hike across the hours of morning, we have been reminded how humans modified this land—with fire, spears and atlatls, ax and plow, muzzle loaders, and bulldozers to build levees. But now, with some arduous restoration, these little patches of prairie and savanna are regaining a foothold.

But the coffee is getting cool, and Charles declares he is ready to sip a glass of sherry in front of the oak fire, so the three of them start out. I am not quite ready to go in.

THE ISSUE OF EDGES

It is difficult to maintain a focus on monumental spans of time both past and future, as I sit huddled on the bench, and so my thoughts turn to my own early roots "out west."

I can see the winter storms flowing eastward over the Cascade volcanoes and sweeping across the high desert that was my childhood home. I can smell the pungent odors of sage and juniper after the first warm rain in March. I can look "all the way west," across the violent breakers of the ocean. These sensory images are rooted somewhere deep in my mind.

Sitting here, I decide that phenologically the Wisconsin prairies and savannas, in their own way, are just as bold. Here I can imagine the grinding and moulding ice cliff, studded with big granite boulders and crystals of quartz. I can see streams of water pouring from its face—with great fans of roaring, braided rivers, depositing thick layers of sand.

It is true that here in this place I now rely more on subtle senses of sound and smell and touch. My view to the west is blocked by the crest of the moraine, and I must sense the approaching winter storm by a veil of thin cirrus clouds and sun dogs on both sides of an anemic sun. In close, I can see that the clumps of prairie dropseed are bowing down to the approaching winter. I can anticipate a parting of the winter clouds so that the sun will shine behind the stiff, black lace of oak trees on the moraine at the moment of winter solstice. And I imagine that I may someday see a pair of whooping cranes, leaving for the Texas coast.

I remember how I sat on this bench a few short months ago and gazed straight down at the earth around my feet to really sense the subtleties and complexities of this land—how I lay flat on my belly in mid-April sand to see the hairy stem of the pasque flower, or got down on my hands and knees to see the white spider with a yellow beak in the butter-yellow center of the trillium in May. And how, in late September, I parted the tall prairie grasses to examine the deep blue serrations of the fringed gentian.

Here, place and time seem more condensed, as if gravity has more hold on me here than it would "out west." And I am certainly less likely to get cheatgrass stickers in my socks, or alkali dust in my nose.

Whether here or there, inevitably, land is a woven tapestry of our sensory impressions. And in my mind's eye the fabric becomes a metaphor for the undefinable emotions that surge in my chest, year after year, as the seasons change.

If I sit here long enough, the minutiae of the prairie and savanna will become etched in my mind, and I will absorb the sounds and smells as if my mind were a dry parchment designed to soak up nature's imprints. But maybe I've sat here too long, because the coffee in my cup is cold. So I hustle

Fringed Gentian

up the path in the face of a fitful patter of snow, its crystals as fine as the sand under my feet.

LEOPOLD'S PHILOSOPHY

The story in this book is rooted in the records kept by Aldo Leopold and by Charles and Nina Bradley.

However, this is not the classic guidebook to be tucked in a side pocket of your day pack. We suggest you examine it while seated on a bench in the prairie or in front of a good oak fire on a November afternoon. We write about the "why," "what," "where," "who," and "when" of this land—but the fundamental emphasis is on "why." Why are things the way they are? But remember, our understanding of it is continuing to unfold, because the weaver is still at work. After all, that is the nature of nature.

Words, data, and even photographs cannot capture the whole experience. The authors can rhetorically examine the roots of the prairie. We can be analytical in our pursuit of an understanding of the natural history of this place.

We can approximate the sounds and smells with photographs and words, and philosophize about this land. We can even create human judgments about the value of the land, and therein conceptualize a land ethic and a land culture.

But, inevitably, the words, the photographs, and the ethic are not enough.

I think you must walk the trails and then sit alone on the bench—to really understand. If you are lucky, sometime in the next day or so, you will witness the exodus of the geese. That storm over the horizon will dump eight inches of snow. The river and the ponds will still be open, but the geese will get nervous with the cornfields covered. And, on a foggy morning, they will take off, long streams of them above the clouds, as they head southwest toward the Mississippi bottoms.

To begin to understand, it takes a lot of sitting on the bench, or in front of an oak fire, looking at life, listening to the departing geese, and soaking in the ether of a winter night as new snow sparkles in the starlight.

. . . at daybreak I am the sole owner of all the acres I can walk over. It is not only boundaries that disappear, but also the thought of being bounded. Expanses unknown to deed or map are known to every dawn, and solitude, supposed no longer to exist in any county, extends on every hand as far as the dew can reach.

LAND & THE SEASONS

Preceding page: Indiangrass

These pages will take us on a hike through the prairie and savanna at the spring and autumn equinoxes, and the summer and winter solstices. These dates—March 21, September 21, June 21, and December 21—are the seminal, natural festival dates of the year, marking as they do astronomical turning points of the seasons. They are nature's benchmarks for each year, and we should start any hike from benchmarks.

The arrival of the equinoxes and solstices can be predicted with confidence, even a thousand years from now. The four dates are precise pivots in the Earth-Sun choreography and their timely arrival assures us that our planet remains on course in its elliptical and inclined orbit.

Averaged over time, there is also a determined gradation in solar radiation from the equator to the pole. The sun is most directly over the equator and here the stream of photons is the most intense. If the earth rotated at a right angle to the sun there would be no seasons. The earth is off-center in relation to the sun. Because of that, the ratio of night to day changes more rapidly at the time of the equinoxes at the poles, and also here in our middle latitudes. And it seems so obvious on the prairie. The solstices seem steadfast, while the equinoxes reveal accelerating change. Life here does feel the pulse of the earth's astronomical cycle.

We need the assurance that comes from clocking sunrise and sunset on the pivotal solstice dates. We need the assurance of where we are on Earth with the precision of latitude and longitude.

There are other physical boundaries that change over the long reaches of time, but that are relatively fixed in our time, such as the latitude of the continent in this era, the elevation above or below sea level, the character of the soil, and the average annual precipitation.

There are also more random forces at work: examples include the amount of light that reaches the surface as a function of cloudiness, the ambient or surrounding temperature, the amount of moisture this year, the supply of available nutrients, and fires and storms.

Here in the middle latitudes, both fixed and random conditions change from deep winter to high summer, from the flush of spring to the mellow confidence of autumn.

The phenological records that reveal the biological responses to these various conditions are our field guide. But there will always be surprises in plant and animal expressions from year to year, because individuals and species experiment with their allotments of time.

Assurances derived from an understanding of such varying and fixed parameters are a good thing to have in mind when charting the biological expressions, but curiosity spurs us on. We can partly satisfy our curiosity by observing "what" and "when," but the real challenge is understanding "why" things happen. Why are some flowers blue and others yellow? Why are some creatures predators and others prey? Why do some creatures migrate and others stay? Why are some years so bountiful and others so parsimonious? Why do some creatures prosper and others falter? Is it the amount of light or the weather patterns, or some combination of both, that frames the timing of migrations?

There's something else important beyond all of this. The quest also provides a reason to get outdoors, away from thermostats, light bulbs, and humidifiers. There is the chance to see, hear, smell, and feel. Ultimately, feeling is what provides our sense of balance. Let us begin our hike.

WINTER SOLSTICE

The fresh tracks of three deer, clear in yesterday's snow, pass through our woods. I follow the tracks backward and find a cluster of three beds, clear of snow, in the big willow thicket on the sandbar.

THE MOMENT OF CHANGE

The December clouds hang thick and dark from rim to rim across the sky bowl. The cold, aggressive wind from the east has finally subsided, and has shifted quietly to the northwest.

Clouds have persisted over much of the last seven weeks. The Wisconsin state climatologist reported only 32.8 hours of sunshine in all of November, which tied an all-time record low for sunshine in the month of November set in 1944. Oh, for some winter sunshine! December has been a little brighter. In the first three weeks there were 68.8 hours of sunshine. But, we could have used three times as much!

Now, after the zenith of this short winter day, the clouds seem to be thinner and to be giving way. I hope that the weather is changing, as this is an auspicious date. The end of winter's shortest day is fast approaching. There is a need to get outside and break this spell of cabin fever with a long trek through the woods and across the prairie.

So the four of us bundle up, snap on our skis, and push off together through eight inches of new snow. Across Levee Road we pause in our trek, on the edge of the woods, and examine the western sky. Sunset is just a couple of hours away. With the collars of our jackets turned up and our wool hats pulled down over our ears, we rest on our ski poles here in the chill and wonder if we shall glimpse the sun. Perhaps the Arctic high moving toward us from the west will reach us in time for the moment of sunset on the winter solstice.

A big bird slides into view just above the tree line. Is it the rough-legged hawk? He's been around for a week. No! It is a bald eagle, gaining altitude. Then another eagle appears, and veers toward the first. The two eagles feint and circle and soar, etched against the clouds, working slowly west and then returning in a swoop directly overhead, so close we can see the glints in their eyes. Two more eagles appear, and they join in the wild choreography. The eagles fly low along the edge of the prairie and the woods, rise high in the air, hanging nearly motionless, soar downwind in sweeping parabolas, and then disappear behind the dark line of trees. Are they still out there? High enough to see a break in the clouds? Do they see the sun?

And then, to the west, we see an amber light in the clouds, strong enough to cast a halo on the tips of the white pines. There are windows of pale blue in the sky, the first hint of real sunshine in a week, as we head deeper into the woods. We hear and then we see a single goose low in the sky. A month ago the geese, by the thousands in their afternoon flight, were a pulsating and noisy sky-carpet just below the cloud ceiling—now only this one remains. Is it searching for a mate it will not find? Winter closed in as December arrived, and, in the face of an advancing storm, the geese took off, just below the clouds. We could see them forming and reforming their arrows. As they disappeared in the clouds we could hear their receding calls from far down the flyway.

There is a shadow of loneliness on a winter evening, as the geese leave.

SIGNS OF WINTER

The shadow does not linger for long. There is much to see on this winter hike. There are partridge and turkey tracks in the snow. The partridge have, in their droppings, left the purple stain of elderberry and the red of buckthorn. The turkeys have scratched away at the snow. The turkeys and partridges themselves were furtive this

afternoon, but they'll be bolder in April. Tracks of the white-tailed deer criss-cross the snow in a pattern that would frustrate any city planner.

Sometime around January 18, the chickadees will call from within the woods, and around February 11, the cardinals will sing from the highest limbs. This week, the week of the solstice, the cardinals are here, vivid, silent splashes in the cedar branches. Today, the red-breasted nuthatches are in pursuit of food and ignore our presence.

The deer, in their nocturnal way, have been working on the white pine on the moraine. According to Leopold's phenological records for December, the deer will also have been working on the sumac and the bur oak twigs. By March they'll still be chewing the tender tips of white pine branches, but also feeding on the jack pine and the Norway pine. A lot of plants must be tastier to the deer in the spring, because their March diet will include red cedar, chokecherry, aspen, and willow. By June, they'll be feeding on black oak, black cherry, flowering spurge, Solomon's seal, veronica, trillium, and wood nettle. They would also be chewing on American elm trees in June if any had survived the plague of Dutch elm disease in the 1950s and 1960s.

We move on under the bulging arms of a giant white oak that must be older than 200 years. From below, its limbs fill our view. When the tree sprouted late in the eighteenth century, around the time of the American Revolution, this hillside was a savanna. The sapling oak stood in a waving sea of little bluestem, side-oats grama, big bluestem, and Indiangrass.

The dense stand of red and black oaks and black cherry now occupying the hillside are, in nature's terms, new-comers in this community, dominating this recessional moraine in only the last 100 years. However, one of the cherry trees, already grown up and grown old, collapsed during the first big winter storm, blocking our trail with a long solid trunk that is a prime candidate for the sawyer.

As we take off our skis to climb over the fallen tree, we debate its destiny. We could make a hand-hewn bench with a plank from the cherry and tapered legs of jack pine. Or we could burn it in the fireplace, mixed with oak. But perhaps we should just leave it here, and a decade later the log will be rotting where it fell.

Near the end of our loop through the woods we pause at the edge of Turner Pond. Ice crystals hang in the air. The beavers have opened a hole in the ice at the edge of the pond, and are working on a stand of aspen, dragging limbs to their cache under the ice. In one night's effort they have toppled trees up to 10 inches thick. My grandpa used to chide me to be "as busy as a beaver." From the looks of it, these beavers gave in to the lazy days of autumn, and didn't stock up enough for this unusually cold winter. Only hunger would force them to break through the ice in the middle of such a winter to replenish a depleted pantry.

As we ski east onto the prairie, we talk about the dormant vitality under the crusted snow. As we circle west again, our anticipation is growing. The end of the shortest day approaches.

I have been resisting looking at my watch, trying to close my mind to the precision of minutes. But the habits of civilization are strong, and, at 4:15 on this twenty-first day of December, the clouds are starting to dissipate. Ten minutes later a broad band of winter blue can be seen as the red edges of the sun flare as it sinks behind the frozen hill, just when it was supposed to.

The clouds of November and December are quickly dissolving, and time seems to stand still for a moment as the amber glow diffuses up and across the zenith. But then Earth moves on, and the sky darkens into a royal purple cave. We had ceased our phenological chatter as the sun broke through the clouds, and stood alone in the evening glory, silent in Earth's dominating presence.

There is nothing more to say or see this evening. Earth is dark, and we are drowsy. Tomorrow, December 22, will be a better day to think about the astronomical rationality of the solstice and its phenological displays on our sandy land.

PRAIRIE ANALYSIS

At dawn, on December 22, this "official" first day of winter, the sun arrived to a crystal world. The sunlight created long blue shadows toward the west all morning, and the shadows rapidly shifted to the east as the sun passed the zenith. Now, as the winter light clears my head, I can be analytical—for a moment or two—before I get philosophical (or drowsy) again.

The winter solstice and summer solstice are pivot points of Earth's annual cycle. They are the points on Earth's clock, where the astronomical hands converge at a precise moment and the yearly cycle moves into the next season.

A solstice is one of the two points in the ecliptic orbit of Earth at which the sun's distance from the celestial equator is greatest and which is reached by Earth "about" December 21 and June 21 each year. The actual moment varies, because Earth's orbit changes in a determined way.

Our mystical attachment to yesterday afternoon's sunset as the exact moment of the solstice was technically incorrect if one wants to be precise about it. We were influenced, no doubt, by our trek through the woods and prairie and by our hope for a glance at the sun at the end of the shortest day. However, this year, the exact moment of solstice was really at 2:26 P.M., a solid two hours before the sun crossed the horizon. The solstice this coming summer will occur on June 21 at precisely 3 A.M. A year ago the winter solstice occurred at 8:43 A.M. on December 21 and the summer solstice at 9:14 P.M.

The time varies from year to year because of the astronomical nature of

Winter Solstice

the cycle. The forces at work include the elliptical nature of the earth's orbit and the extra quarter-day each year in our calendar of 365 annual days. Precession, the torque in Earth's rotation, and inclination, the tilt of Earth's angle in relation to the sun, also figure mathematically into the cycle.

If I took the Latin definitions of winter and summer solstices seriously, I would conclude that there is a pause in this annual cycle of movement between Earth and Sun. "Solstice" is derived from *sol,* meaning "sun," and *sistere,* "to pause."

When I imagined that the earth stood still at the moment the sun broke through and touched the horizon yesterday afternoon, and that even time stood still for a moment, it was not totally emotional. The Romans must have known. There is a fleeting sensation of physical pause by the earth as viewed from our position down here at the bottom of things, although I must admit that the actual pause had occurred a couple of hours before sunset this year.

Although Earth and time do not literally stop, our planet does appear to pause in its orbit. It is more obvious if you plot the changing length of days on a graph. The trace of increasing and decreasing day length falls on a parabolic curve. The equinoxes are on the slopes of the curve and the solstices occupy the peaks and valleys. The relationship between day and night changes more rapidly in spring and fall than it does in winter and summer.

I admit a sense of mysticism at these moments—reality is sometimes in the eye of the beholder. Life does seem to catch its breath along with Earth, at the height of summer and the depth of winter.

SEASONS AND LIFE

The calendar is an analog predictor of the natural cycles stated in explicit units of time. I can say that December 21, or thereabouts, is the predicted date of the solstice. I could be off by 24 hours, more or less, because the calendar does not account for the complexity in our planet's orbit and rotation.

The calendar is an even cruder analog for the realities of life on our landscape. It gives us a target date in tracking the timing of natural events on the land. But the bull's-eye on the target keeps shifting.

Living creatures do shape their behavior around the solstices and the equinoxes, because life responds to the different amounts of sunlight that reach Earth in the different seasons. Life is biochemically and behaviorally sensitive to photons, those quantums of energy that flash our way from the sun at phenomenal speeds. It is a rare Earth species that is adapted to total darkness, although life in the depths of the oceans may still hold some surprises for us. Life at the surface is certainly sensitive to the changes in weather that track the seasonal shift in the energy budget.

While biological calendars are not as precisely timed as the astronomical clock, let alone the calendar, life does fit within the sunlight and weather boundaries marked by the solstices and equinoxes. Weather's seasonal patterns change more rapidly during spring and autumn than during summer and winter. Individual winter and summer storms can grab our attention, but spring and fall are the seasons of change. This is a fundamental lesson that all life has learned, even the modest *Homo sapiens*. Ironically, it seems that "intellectual" humans have to keep relearning this fundamental aspect of nature the hard way.

Because life is adapted and conditioned to both Earth's astronomical movements and the seasonal changes in weather, we can predict its phenological expressions with some degree of accuracy. But there is more to it than just predicting a date of change. The plants and animals "know" in advance. But how? How, for example, do the migrating birds know when to start their journeys?

The birds that migrate long distances are clearly more responsive to the astronomical calendars than to variations in weather. The arrivals of the migrators to our prairie are more precisely on target than the seasonal behavior of the local inhabitants. The locals seem more responsive to weather variations than to astronomical rhythms, and certainly adjust to the impact of fire and to competition from others.

For us, predicting how the actors behave from year to year here under our sky-tent becomes a three-ring circus, an inner ring surrounded by wider rings. In the center are the quite predictable solstices and equinoxes and the inevitable responses of life to changing seasons. Surrounding that are the vagaries of day-to-day weather. Sometimes we achieve the prediction of tomorrow's weather, and often we do not. Immediate cause and effect, some of it random, creates an urgency in the changes we observe. And beyond the vagaries of weather, the third ring consists of the patterns of coexistence among the species.

But in phenology, there are no business appointments that humans must absolutely keep—in spite of the fact that we try to plant the corn when the leaves on the bur oak are the size of a squirrel's ear.

Phenology expresses a natural economy, but it is not an econometric discipline. With "restoration management," humans can give a nudge to the reestablishment of a prairie. Once relaunched, the prairie is really on its own, because we cannot change the earth in its orbit, nor can we change the climate. Thus our role in phenology is to observe and ask why. For me, it's a relief to be content with observation and questions, because I can then take that incoming storm in stride and not worry about whether the driveway gets plowed by 8 A.M. tomorrow morning. Later on, however, I may fret about "the worst winter on record."

THE QUESTION OF VARIATION

What then do I observe about the natural course of events—with confidence?

I check the charts and see that tomorrow the sun will set at exactly 4:26 P.M.

On January 1 it will set at 4:33 P.M., and on March 21, the day of the spring equinox, it will set at 6:10 P.M.

I observe that last November was so cloudy that it tied the old record for lack of sunshine. But why? The meteorologists said that it could be attributed in part to the continuation of a weather pattern from nearly a year ago. This pattern is often seen in an El Niño year and involves a split in the upper-level jet stream. The result is an increase in relatively warm, moist air arriving over the continent from the Pacific, leading to cloudy conditions rather than the usual clear and frigid weather associated with Arctic highs. But they aren't absolutely sure about the reason. And who knows, for sure, about this November?

I do predict, with some confidence, that the chickadees will sing their two-note territorial song sometime between the first week in January and the first week in February. The cardinal's first song will be heard sometime during the first two weeks of February, but there are surprises. Five years ago, I heard a cardinal sing on December 21 in Madison, 50 miles south of the Leopold Reserve, on the morning of the winter solstice. But I am not sure what motivated such a song on the shortest day.

The skunk cabbage may be more reliable than the cardinal. It will be in pollen by mid-March and the Canada geese and the woodcock should arrive by March 22. The pasque flower should be in bloom in early April.

The upland plover will arrive sometime between April 17 and 19, having

Pasque Flower

flown all the way from Argentina. How did the plover know exactly when to leave Argentina, or navigate the storms along the Andean coast? Did it recognize a different pattern in El Niño? Did it taunt the monsoons in Mexico, the dust storms of the "blue northers" of Texas in January, and the spring tornadoes of Oklahoma—to arrive so precisely here? And why did it struggle on such a monumental journey at all? Is the memory of a warmer Pliocene in its genes? Has the plover been able to integrate the declining flow of photons in a southern hemisphere autumn with the increasing flow in a northern hemisphere spring so sensitively that it can tell the change from day to day? It must appreciate sunshine to put out all that effort! But did it migrate so far during the last glaciation?

The pasque flowers, without any migration at all, will be stirring on the south side of the sand moraine when the plover arrives, even if the temperature plunges to 20°F. But maybe their emergence will be a week after the plover gets here. I will have to wait and see.

I am assured this evening that winter inevitably follows autumn. But spring pulls apart the shrouds of winter. In March and April, the subtropical convergence, moving up from the equator, will be in a raging contest with the circumpolar vortex, reluctant to retreat toward the polar regions. I will flinch as the tornadic fronts approach us here at the margin, and maybe I'll head for the basement. But, I've always wanted to "see" a tornado.

In between the big storms, I will enjoy the gentle rains of the westerlies and soar in the warm sunshine. I will soar with the plover, up the flyways of spring. Cabin fever? Not a chance! I'm content waiting for spring.

A cardinal, whistling spring to a thaw but later finding himself mistaken, can retrieve his error by resuming his winter silence. A chipmunk, emerging for a sun-bath but finding a blizzard, has only to go back to bed. But a migrating goose, staking two hundred miles of black night on the chance of finding a hole in the lake, has no easy chance for retreat. His arrival carries the conviction of a prophet who has burned his bridges.

VERNAL EQUINOX

A dawn wind stirs on the great marsh. With almost imperceptible slowness it rolls a bank of fog across the wide morass. Like the white ghost of a glacier the mists advance, riding over phalanxes of tamarack, sliding across bog-meadows heavy with dew. A single silence hangs from horizon to horizon.

Out of some far recess of the sky a tinkling of bells falls soft upon the listening land. Then again silence. Now comes a baying of some sweet-throated hound, soon the clamor of a responding pack. Then a far clear blast of hunting horns, out of the sky into the fog.

High horns, low horns, silence, and finally a pandemonium of trumpets, rattles, croaks, and cries that almost shakes the bog with its nearness, but without yet disclosing whence it comes. At last a glint of sun reveals the approach of a great echelon of birds. On motionless wing they emerge from the lifting mists, sweep a final arc of sky, and settle in clangorous descending spirals to their feeding grounds. A new day has begun on the crane marsh.

THE CRANES AND THE GEESE COME BACK

The phenological records show that the sandhill cranes will arrive back in Fairfield Township in Aldo Leopold's sand county on an average date of March 10. Last year they showed up on March 5 and this year March 16. I'll grant them a margin of error of 11 days without complaining. What human ever won an argument with a sandhill crane regarding the arrival of spring? The Canada geese will arrive sometime between March 1 and March 22. This year the first skein arrived at midday today, on March 19. The wild songs of the cranes and the geese bound and rebound across the land.

With the cranes and the geese on hand, there is solid evidence that spring is on the way. However, the astronomers and even some theologians will maintain it is winter until the equinox arrives on the twenty-first of March.

The geese, with no particular concern for precision or dogma, flew in low over the moraine with wild cries of intention. They brought a marsh hawk off his perch in the river birch at the edge of the sedge meadow. The marsh hawk returned a week ago. He seems well fed. His response only momentarily silenced the geese, and he settled back into the trees. The geese will be able to find a place to rest this evening. Center Pond and Helland Slough are still frozen solid, but there are holes in the ice on the river.

An early-arriving male robin perched morosely on a bare limb of the black cherry tree this morning, his feathers puffed out against the cold. He's here, well ahead of the females, to stake out territory.

The radio reports that a line of thunderstorms is drenching the big prairie country 700 miles southwest of here with wild, warm rain. But, closer to home, along the Illinois border, the edge of that same storm is coating the oak limbs with ice. The red oaks and the black oaks will lose some big limbs to the ice, but the bur oaks will shrug it off.

With a cold wind blowing from the northeast, there is fitful snow. The wind is buffeting low-flying clouds. Snow is coming in intermittent gusts—flurries that bluster and then back off. A patch of pale sky appears in the west. Then, in the fading light, the clouds and snow return.

Geese Landing

A week ago, in a burst of warm air, the ground turned soft enough to cake my boot cleats with clay and sand. That warm air must have encouraged the geese. It also encouraged the year-round residents. Down along the edge of the slough, at an intersection created by the comings and goings of the animals in the willow thicket, the four of us had seen the tracks of skunk, red fox, raccoon, and possum.

But now the surface is frozen again, and the snow is piling up in the hollows among the matted thatch of prairie grasses, and it is covering again the clumps of sodden leaves.

The prairie grasses had stood tall until the big Thanksgiving Day storm four months ago, which bent them in disarray under eight inches of snow, with only shreds of them poking above the snow. The snowfall had created opportunity for the animals underneath the grasses. The ruffed grouse found hideaways. Within days, the mice and the voles had settled into dens and elaborate passageways, secure against the next storm. But the shrews would pursue the mice in the alleys under the snow all winter long. And the weasels, on many a cold morning in January, would emerge with mice dangling from their jaws, leaving trails of fresh red blood in the white snow.

With the first burst of warm air a week ago, the ice on Center Pond turned green and sodden, and we thought winter was giving way. The woodchuck ambled out and yawned, and the first killdeer arrived. But this evening, the ice on the pond is as solid

as bedrock. Under the ice, at the bottom of the pond, most of the turtles and frogs are still buried in the clay, but they must sense that the days are longer now. In fact, the first leopard frog appeared on land two days ago, well ahead of its usual appearance around April 14. Did he make a mistake?

The extended family of beavers has been working on the aspen beside Turner Pond since the time of the winter solstice, emerging from a hole at the edge of the pond. But the beavers get restless as soon as the ice gets mushy. Breeding occurred in early January. Gestation is 120 days, so the pups will be due in another month. The den will be even more crowded then, and it will be time for some of the colony to move on. Beavers are monogamous, with close family ties, but fate can intervene. If he loses his mate, the old widower will be the first to leave. He will be followed by any mature bachelors in the lodge. Finally, with spring on the move, the two-year-olds will be evicted. There's already a set of tracks leading away from the pond in the spring snow—a one-way set of tracks. I imagine a big, old male paused, halfway up the hill and reluctantly looked back. But he will not return to the lodge on Turner Pond.

WHEN WILL THE RIVER OPEN?

The ice on the main channel of the river has been banging around as great chunks break loose. Surges of water buffet the trunks of the cottonwoods at the upper edge of the sandbar. The phenological records for the freezing over of the river reveal the complexity of our fluctuating climate. Freeze-over is defined as a person's being able to walk across the river at this location. The average date of freeze-over in this century is around January 25, and the average opening date is March 2. In 1978 the river froze over on March 22, a disconcerting thing when you are longing for spring.

The dates given here for the years from 1979 to 1987 show the wide range in the opening of the river:

1979	March 18
1980	March 9
1981	January 30
1982	March 13
1983	stays open
1984	February 19
1985	February 28
1986	March 15
1987	February 14

There's some satisfaction when the river opens early in March. I like winter, but by March it really is time to move on. And so it seems this year.

In recent days, downy, hairy, and red-bellied woodpeckers have been feeding more aggressively on the suet hanging in a net on the deck. A week ago, when the temperature reached 50°F, a flicker called from the woods. That's unusually early, and he obviously hasn't been convinced by the phenological records. The goldfinches are on the move, and the cranes are calling hoarsely from the wet meadow.

THE MOMENT OF THE EQUINOX

Just two days from now, on March 21, the sun will be directly over the equator. The equator is a line on the map as thin as a pencil mark, and the sun will be directly over it for only a second. Although the equinox will not be particularly noticeable at the equator, here it is the epiphany of the prairie, illuminating the approaching reality of spring. For the animals, the sensations of smells will come alive again. Chemistry is the most ubiquitous means of communication for the animal kingdom, and the air will soon be full of trillions of molecules signaling accelerating change.

Earth itself seems to be a little mixed up. The sun is setting now at 6:08 P.M. and tomorrow morning will rise at 6:01 A.M. So, we've already passed that pencil line when night and day are exactly equal. It would seem that even daytime is as anxious for spring as we are, unwilling to wait for the exact moment when the sun crosses the equator to dish out equal quotas of day and night.

The astronomers can be precise in predicting the vernal equinox, but the gradual arrival of spring on the land is always filled with hesitation and is spread over many weeks. Winter seems as reluctant to leave as the widower beaver. The weatherman predicts that tomorrow should be sunny with the temperature again in the 50s. If that happens, the snowdrifts will soften and the meltwater will erase the grime on

Skunk Cabbage

the retreating snowbanks. A huge flock of crows, flying in and out of the cottonwoods, will argue loudly at dawn, and the cardinal will sing across the morning. The male robin will preen his feathers, and when the female robins arrive, he will sing from the topmost limb in the black cherry tree. The sky in the west will be hazy and wisps of cirrus clouds will float high overhead.

When the astronomical equinox does officially arrive, we may be lucky and get a tempest. The sky could be alive with lighting and great, black, rolling clouds, the limbs of the white oak in a wild dance. We do surely deserve gusts of wind and rain in the night, melting the frost from the ground. We deserve a tempest worthy of the equinox.

A SETBACK

Well—we expected a tempest, but what we got was the March 22 snowstorm. Winds blew strongly from the northeast and the storm left behind another six inches of heavy, wet snow. The deer that had been working the white pines at the edge of the woods all winter hunkered down during the storm. So did we, in front of a good oak fire.

In front of the fire, you can always dream of spring, of the freshness of the grasses that will poke up within days after the first big, warm storm, and of the prairie violets, biding their time.

As the white-hot coals warm your shins, you can imagine what the prairie would look like from the vantage point of another planet. If I were a citizen of that planet, with my telescope focused on this earthly latitude for the next four weeks, I would observe and record the inevitable lengthening of the days. I would detect the slow retreat of win-

Marsh Marigold

ter's blue shadows and the shift to green. If I lived on a planet that had a circular orbit perpendicular to its sun, I would have no memory of spring.

Observing Earth, I would wonder about the meaning of that shift to green on that little planet way out on an arm of the Milky Way.

The wild things that live on my farm are reluctant to tell me, in so many words, how much of my township is included within their daily or nightly beat. I am curious about this, for it gives me the ratio between the size of their universe and the size of mine, and it conveniently begs the much more important question, who is the more thoroughly acquainted with the world in which he lives?

Like people, my animals frequently disclose by their actions what they decline to divulge in words. It is difficult to predict when and how one of these disclosures will come to light.

SUMMER SOLSTICE

I know a painting so evanescent that it is seldom viewed at all, except by some wandering deer. It is a river who wields the brush, and it is the same river who, before I can bring my friends to view his work, erases it forever from human view. After that it exists only in my mind's eye.

Like other artists, my river is temperamental; there is no predicting when the mood to paint will come upon him, or how long it will last. But in midsummer, when the great white fleets cruise the sky for day after flawless day, it is worth strolling down to the sandbars just to see whether he has been at work.

CROSSING THE BORDER

We crossed the astronomical border into summer last night at exactly 3 A.M. I was deep in a midsummer night's sleep. Just an hour earlier I had been awake, peering into the black night wall to assess the progress of a storm approaching from the west.

It came closer now. I could hear the rushing wind and cracks of thunder—simultaneous flash and crack, the sort that jolts your spine. Violet lightning danced within a giant cumulus cloud as the main storm line veered to the south. Then the leaves on the black oak just outside the bedroom window were motionless. The air was damp and op-pressive, and mists filled the swale be-hind the oak. Sleepy and with an ache in my knee, I kicked off my pajamas, slumped back onto the bed, pushed aside the cotton sheet, and fell asleep.

There is no regret in missing the moment of solstice on such a night. Besides, the solstice would seem more real at sunrise, and sunrise was not far away.

The astronomical chart indicated that the sun would cross the horizon at 5:18 A.M., but it was hidden by the receding storm clouds in the eastern sky. By 6:30 A.M. the sun had risen over the bank of clouds, blood-red, with foreground vapors rising over the woods and Center Pond.

The spiderwort was heavy with drops of moisture, and the spike lobelia nodded in a whisper of a breeze. Under the alders, sweet Cicely was opening to the morning sunshine, with its tiny white blooms and scent of anise. The very first blooms of the compass plant were yellow-rayed at the

Compass Plant

top of five-foot stalks. The morning grew increasingly muggy.

The deciduous woods had become, once again, lush and waxy, jungles of green canopies and wet understories. The afternoon light filtered through the layers of leaves at every level of the woods. High overhead, scattered white clouds sailed east, trying to keep up with the storm of the night. From the floor of the woods to the limbs in the highest canopy, the air was filled with the buzzing of insects, activated by this photosynthetic summit. The afternoon stretched on and on, as the light persisted, and the hum of summer on the prairie continued.

The sun set at 8:41 P.M. and disappeared into an amber horizon. Steamy as the day was, the sun had shone through, for a total of 923 minutes. All that sunshine and moisture had made it a frantically metabolic day for plants and insects.

After sundown, the shadows of summer lingered for another hour. A cricket started to sing. The mosquitoes had been on the move all day, and now increased the intensity of their attacks. Waves of little brown bats emerged from a hole in the eaves to feast on the mosquitoes.

We sat on the porch in the velvet evening, watching the bats soar and dive and a swollen moon rise in the east. Only later did it occur to me that the sun hadn't really risen this morning, nor had it sunk in the west. More accurately, if less romantically, I realized that the earth is spinning around the sun in its elliptical orbit. From our perspective the sun only seemed to rise on our horizon and to disappear in the west. Earth is the one on the move. The moon did not really rise in the east, because it is in a locked rotation with Earth, though it lags behind about an hour a day. And we humans are tourists along for the ride. But I remain confident that the sun will show up again tomorrow. I had wished we could hang on to at least one more hour of the longest day of the year, but the earth will give us a shorter day tomorrow. And I will happily ride along.

A WET ONE

The climatological summary in the newspaper this morning reported that we have had 20.15 inches of rain since the first of January. Normal for this date is 12.78 inches. A cool, wet, and biologically late spring is turning into an unusually humid summer. And the river is very restless in its bed, remaking it on a daily basis.

By June 21, the circumpolar vortex and the jet stream, so indebted to Earth's rotation and orbit, would normally have retreated at least as far north as the Canadian border, maybe even farther north into the taiga forests beyond Lake Superior, but not this year. There is a blocked meridional flow, an unusual condition for this time of year, and the jet stream hasn't completed its summer northward migration yet.

The climatologists are debating the

reason. Maybe it's a lingering, cooling effect from a volcanic eruption half-way round the globe. Add to that the warm El Niño surface temperatures of the ocean in the southern Pacific. Such forces could have combined to give us more than our normal share of tropical moisture. Maybe it's a counter-reaction to a worldwide warming that is expressed in the earth's albedo and atmospheric circulation. Or maybe it's a short-run cyclical effect that climatologists have not discovered.

Whatever the reasons (and there must be reasons), June has been overcast 64 percent of the daylight hours. A normal June is about 50 percent overcast. In fact, this June is turning out to be the third-cloudiest on record. No wonder the plants responded vigorously to this day of sunshine.

Leading up to the solstice this year, growing conditions have favored some plants and seemed downright hostile to others. Queen of the prairie, probably at the northern edge of its natural range, has given up, its roots rotting in the soggy soil. On the other hand, spiderwort appears more lush than it has been in years. Blue-eyed grass and yellow-eyed grass are also doing well. The lupine showed great promise for a spectacular bloom a month ago, but the deer ate the masses of budding flowers. The interaction between soil and climate, and plants and animals, is certainly providing us with plenty to observe this year.

Such moisture conditions may not be repeated in a hundred years. The

Blue-eyed Grass

plants adjust in subtle and even dramatic ways to the extremes. However, our land is on a climatic boundary and thus in a biological tension zone. This tension zone is a decisive line that coincides with the southern edge of former glaciation. Its latitude results in distinct seasonal variations in sunlight and a short frost-free growing season. Thus, year-to-year variations in climate, including our record wet summer, are superimposed upon these more basic geographic influences. But maybe, for the balance of the summer, we'll have a beautiful stretch of those flawless, clear days.

The plants in our savanna and prairie terrain have adapted to the soil types, the range in moisture, and the seasonal extremes. The species in any given location will be different from those just over the hill because of neighborhood variations. Some plants, such as turtle head, thrive locally in marshy areas. Others—spiderworts, lupines, and paint brushes—tolerate a wide range of conditions. Spiderworts range across the eastern deciduous biome, and lupines and paint brushes across the continent. They must have special abilities to speciate in different geographic locations. It's worth a wager that next year, and the year following, the plants who like dry feet, such as the coneflowers and the lead plant, will temporarily retreat from the edge of the pond. They will return if rainfall is less in following years.

The prairie perennial grasses, with their deep roots, can canvass the soil for moisture. Their food reserves are protected from seasonal aboveground extremes, and individuals will persist for a long time, resisting climatic variations from season to season. So will the bur, black, and white oaks, unless the climate really takes a turn, or the sawyer returns.

Because of this wet year we should be watching for extremes from the phenological averages, and perhaps even a major shift in the composition of species. But it should be remem-bered that the rainfall statistics Charles has tabulated this year are only a moment in the geological, climatolog-ical, and genetic fabric of the prairie. Resilience to change and to even extreme variations from normal con-ditions has not come quickly. The ancestors of these prairie residents have persisted through decades of wet years and decades of drought.

TOMORROW AND TOMORROW

The clock will prove that tomorrow will be 24 hours long, just as today was. But daytime will be two minutes short-er than today.

The summer solstice has quickly come and gone. With the last flicker of the solstice sun on the western hori-zon, the year suddenly seems middle-aged. It leans, ever so slightly and with a tinge of melancholy for me, away from its June flush of enthusiasm.

The spring-blooming forbs retreated over a month ago, their gentle colors bold against the weather—the pasque flower and prairie smoke, out in the sunshine, and the trilliums, bluebells and violets on the edge of the woods. The gaudy prairie gypsies—spiderwort and bergamot, purple prairie-clover and liatris, asters and coneflowers— are dancing now. They swirl wildly to the brassy sounds of a symphonic summer storm, and then nod demure-ly in unison as the wind lessens to a minuet of breezes. Their blooms dom-inate the mind's eye, but we also sense in the landscape that the days are getting shorter.

The robins have yet to admit to the change in seasons. At dawn, their territorial calls were as strong as in April. But this morning they did not seem to persist in their singing quite as long as yesterday, and they certainly weren't awake quite as early as a month ago.

In the meantime, we can drink a toast of fine red wine to approaching July. Earth has crossed the magical line into summer. And we waltz along.

Purple Coneflower

. . . this yard-square relic of original Wisconsin gives birth, each July, to a man-high stalk of compass plant or cutleaf Silphium, spangled with saucer-sized yellow blooms resembling sunflowers. . . . What a thousand acres of Silphiums looked like when they tickled the bellies of the buffalo is a question never again to be answered, and perhaps not even asked.

AUTUMNAL EQUINOX

By September, the day breaks with little help from birds. A song sparrow may give a single half-hearted song, a woodcock may twitter overhead en route to his daytime thicket, a barred owl may terminate the night's argument with one last wavering call, but few other birds have anything to say or sing about. . . .

It is on some, but not all, of these misty autumn daybreaks that one may hear the chorus of the quail. The silence is suddenly broken by a dozen contralto voices, no longer able to restrain their praise of the day to come.

THE GRAVITY OF AN AUTUMN DAY

The blackbirds are flocking in the sky this morning like black ink stirred into a pool of blue water. A thousand or more of the birds are bound silently together in the sky by a subliminal communication, the flock parting to flow up and around an old black oak, flowing together again, responding to a social gravity that I simply do not sense.

A breeze ripples a branch of crimson leaves showing amongst the green in the maple, and both are reflected on Center Pond. The leaves rustle softly, the only sound here on the moraine on this autumn morning. The blackbirds have been silent the day long. They did not sing their hormonal calls of spring and summer early this morning, from perches on dried cattails in the marsh. Now, still locked together, they swoop over the moraine and out of sight, as quiet as the morning.

The solitude is suddenly broken by the rattling calls of a trio of kingfishers flashing just above the waterline on the far side of the pond. They're after the mud minnows lying in the shallows.

And then I hear the geese from the other side of the river—sudden cries of alarm. Maybe they were flushed off the water by a coyote, slouching down, curling his lips, and twitching his tail on the bank.

The geese rise into view above the alders, and it seems there is more than just alarm in their voices. There is a note of anxiety, like a memory of harsh winds and crusted snow. As the geese circle low overhead they glance to the left and right—their eyes are not yet fixed toward the south.

Frost formed at the base of the prairie grasses last night. Below the big bluestem and the Indiangrass it

Autumn Grasses

resembled cuffs of lace on the brown collars of the prairie dropseed and the side-oats grama. There was the thinnest skim of ice on the edge of the slough. It's too early, isn't it, for a killing frost?

A midmorning breeze picks up, and microthermals begin to rise from the prairie. I can feel the warmth on the back of my neck. The seed heads of the big bluestem, a full three feet taller than I, are nodding against the cloudless sky, right and left, backward and forward.

The green of the grasses is giving way to the torches of autumn. The Indiangrass reflects bronze when I look at it with my back to the sun. But if I turn around to face the sun, the same grass reflects a silver-gray. The little bluestem is cast in an ultraviolet glow. The unruly shocks of prairie dropseed are green to golden brown. Perhaps the different colors in the grass reflect the remaining traces of sugars, each opaque to different parts of the spectrum.

The baptisia is also silver-gray, more reminiscent of death than any of the other species. But it was silver-gray with its yellow spring blooms in May, and silver-gray as it developed its big, purple seed pods near the end of summer. Why is it gray? I don't know.

The flowers of the helianthus persist into September, butter-yellow, pleated skirts against the sky, brown centers as intense and large as the eye of a bison. The gentians have waited all summer for their moment in the sun, and now there are pools of blue, deep in the grasses, down near the pond where the soil is wet. The fringed gentian is past its prime, but the bottle, downy, and stiff gentians are lush and full—defying, it seems, impending winter.

All the grasses have been moving their nutrients from the blades to the roots, a savings account that they will draw on next spring. But the waving seeds are their other strategy, the security deposit against a spate of unfavorable years. Today, their seed heads have halos in the morning sun, with the gleam of brightly polished gold.

Most of the little brown bats left their roost in the loft a week ago, for caves along the Mississippi River in southern Missouri, where the insect populations have not declined. Only a few of the bats remain. Maybe these laggards sense some fleeting opportunity we do not; maybe they anticipate a late hatch of mosquitoes; maybe they are just reluctant to leave this blue, northern air behind.

The swallows also departed as the insects declined. As the supply of nectar disappeared, so did the hummingbirds. For a day or two, the black cherry trees pulsated with catbirds, cedar waxwings, warblers, and kinglets, as noisy as a crowded barroom. They stayed until they had stripped the trees clean of the fermenting fruit. The kingfishers will be around here until ice freezes on the kettles and sloughs, and then will leave for Louisiana or Mexico.

The skunks have been working the edge of the sedge meadow, digging up seedlings. The deer have been feeding on the silphium. For them, it must seem like dessert after a summer-long meal loaded with carbohydrates. They're fat and ruddy as the autumn rut approaches. The mud turtles and painted turtles have dug into the bottom of the pond. So too have the green and leopard frogs. The gray tree frogs on the edge of the woods have stopped their singing. Just weeks ago, the leopard frogs were jumping out of the sedges, soaring like arrows. Coming back from a fungus disease, the frogs displayed a population binge this year. Now they're settling in for a long winter nap in the mud.

The eagles, ospreys, red-tailed hawks, and harriers have been circling high among the thermals over Gumz Marsh. The tamaracks in the marsh are just taking on the autumn dress Aldo Leopold described as "smoky gold." The ring-billed gulls have been making their determined evening flights just high enough to catch the fading sunlight, and the nighthawks have gathered in flocks to soar in the darkening sky.

A pair of young sandhill cranes has been dancing erotically in the wet meadows, behavior that is out of synch with the crane's mating season in the spring. Perhaps their juvenile hormones tell them something the old folks have forgotten. The turkeys, quail, and partridge have been gorging on the translucent seeds of the partridge pea.

Summer is over and autumn is here. We are moving down the trail toward winter. The plants and creatures of the prairie know about winter—about the long nights and frigid mornings. Soon the blackbirds will leave the neighborhood, and, on a stormy November day, the geese will move out. The coyote, skunk, and deer will stay in the neighborhood. So will the big bluestem and gentians, their leaves and stalks brown and bent. But even the grasses moved south when glaciers occupied this land long ago.

Am I sad now that autumn has arrived? Does the autumnal equinox cast a shadow of anxiety on my brow, on this glorious morning? Maybe it is the sense that, once again, night is overtaking day, and the oncoming night brings to mind my own inevitable signs of age.

THEY SAY THAT NIGHT AND DAY ARE EQUAL

The word "equinox" comes from the Latin *aequus* for "equal," and *nox* for "night." This is the time on the celestial sphere when the ecliptic intersects the celestial equator, in spring and again in autumn. At that time the sun is crossing the equator and the length of day and night are indeed equal.

I know they're equal in length, but,

Smoky Gold Tamaracks

29

in a broader sense, that is not really so. Night is not the same as day. Day brings clarity to the local scenery, but a clear autumn night brings clarity to the three dimensions of space and the fourth dimension of time. Night also brings a fifth dimension into play—the spiritual.

I think there is a reason why night is a spiritual time. Night obscures our ability to see the immediate surroundings. But we do fill the loss of vision with our sharpened senses of hearing, smell, and touch. We round out what we sense with our imaginations. And we amplify what we cannot see. It is the time for the reflections of our imaginations.

Sometimes, fear takes hold. There's even something threatening in the use of *nox* in "equinox." Equinox is an analytical term, and *nox* means night and darkness. However, to us "nox" can also mean noxious, something to avoid. Is it the spirits of the night we fear?

Does the time and space of the cosmos overwhelm us? Or is there a memory deep in our brain stem of the glaciers and the struggles to survive in unheated caves in competition with larger and more powerful carnivores?

It seems we search for the fountain of youth in the increasing daylight of spring, and security in the longest day in summer. A day in spring is but a fairy ring of prairie violets and a summer day is a passing thunderstorm. The prairie tells us, when we really look and listen and smell, that security is more than the anticipations of spring and the satisfactions of summer. Security also comes from the shortening days of autumn. Even more so, though harder to accept, security comes from the climatic cycles long ago in our interglacial past.

The diurnal changes, the seasonal changes, the glacial changes on this land, force ingenuity and strength from species in competition—but they also force cooperation. From the sum of competition and cooperation come the possibilities inherent in seasons. And our real security is rooted in the sand. There is also security in the night.

Is it really worth our time, on this autumn evening, to contemplate what this landscape will look like a thousand years from now, or fifty thousand? Is it too much to ask of us to stretch our minds at a time when it's so easy to just sit and soak it in? There's enough solar energy stored in the woodpile for the most rugged winter. Let the first big snow come.

WE ARE CAUGHT IN THE WEB

Ecologists have accepted the fundamental precept that living individuals and the species they represent are embedded in a web of interrelationships. Earth scientists are beginning to accept the precept that the physical earth is affected by biological processes as well as the other way around. For example, eons of bacterial action have produced the abundance of free oxygen in our contemporary atmosphere.

As the theories of ecologists evolve, they weave the physical and the biological earth together in seasonal tapestries. In an autumn tapestry of flickering light and golden leaves, it is possible to conclude that cause becomes effect and effect becomes cause. Our world is more than the three dimensions of space plus the linear dimension of time. It is more than a line of passing generations. It has dimensions of energy and matter that are integrated with space and time. There's room here for philosophers as well, because a spiritual dimension in perception also exists. How humans imagine the world is part of the fabric. Autumn is an apt time to contemplate our layered depths of perception.

The physical fact is that the equinox would exist without humans to perceive it. I can accept this analytical and precise equality of day and night in the astronomical definition. The earth in its rotation and orbit resonates with equality. The clock and the calendar we have created to understand its precision also resonate with equality, although we might improve the calendar by making it round instead of linear.

But such precision is not enough for the human psyche. Humans add the spiritual dimension that makes a September day and a September night appear unequal. With that nip of frost, we crossed a line from the translucent vitality of summer to the transparent clarity of winter. This is the prairie aesthetic.

The autumn days drift slowly by, like cumulonimbus clouds in the afternoon sky. But that black bumblebee, who seems immobilized on a nearby blue New England aster, had better soon locate a winter home—two nights ago was the first nip of frost. The bumblebee will survive, I think.

THE MIDDLE OF A SEPTEMBER NIGHT

Last night, at 2 A.M., I lay wide awake, enjoying insomnia, tuning my ears to the world outside the bedroom wall and beyond the screened porch. At first, I heard the drone of trucks, those sleepless pachyderms on the highway. But then I heard the screech owl in the oaks. After a series of punctuated, single cries and a shrill descending warble, I then heard a second owl down the way. For a moment the owls interrupted the crickets, who fell silent. But the crickets quickly resumed and settled into unison after just a handful of discordant chirps. I heard a rustle in the tree, and thought the owl must have left his perch. What did the owl see, in the middle of the night?

Then, from the corner of my eye, I saw flashes of light that flickered and died. Far too late in the season for the last firefly of the year. And then another flash. Lightning! Too far away to hear the thunder. Off to the west, another warm front from the south is clashing with our cooler northern air. But this is surely a rear-guard action for the humid air.

I heard a light breeze rustle the leaves in the tree and thought that we'd get one of those scattered thunderstorms that were forecast last evening. Then, with sleep crowding in, it occurred to me that these little breezes passing in and out my window are the spirits of summer, leaving the oak grove. We'll need to get up early in the morning, just at dawn, to find out if that is really so.

Early risers feel at ease with each other, perhaps because, unlike those who sleep late, they are given to understatement of their own achievements. Orion, the most widely traveled, says literally nothing. The coffee pot, from its first soft gurgle, underclaims the virtues of what simmers within. The owl, in his trisyllabic commentary, plays down the story of the night's murders. The goose on the bar, rising briefly to a point of order in some inaudible anserine debate, lets fall no hint that he speaks with the authority of all the far hills and the sea.

FABRIC OF THE LAND

Preceding page: Savanna and Woods

We have just seen how nature's expression changes dramatically from season to season in this border country. The obvious reason lies in Earth's elliptical trek around the sun—with hesitant springs, when we ache for more sunshine and "growing weather"—with resonant autumns, when we soak up the mellow air, content with nature's harvests as we store our own. We travel like a comet through the changes. But there is more to it than the celestial trail and the progression of the seasons—much more.

We will now explore the physical and the biological infrastructure of the land. The first four essays deal with the physical structure. Titles of some of the essays—sand, fire, and water—have intentional allusions to the Greek philosophers. Some might say that the Greeks' categorization is no longer sophisticated in a "scientific age." But it is also possible that we are now underestimating their philosophical contributions.

Using our own categories, sand represents soil, and also geology. Ice is a symbol for glaciation. Fire represents itself, but deserves to be conceptually revived for its fundamental role in prairie and savanna ecology. Fires, either natural or human-induced, have been suppressed in the last 200 years, resulting in profound changes to the landscape. Water is separated from glaciation because glaciers have had a fundamental impact over long intervals, while water has an ongoing and contemporary impact.

As we examine the physical forces that shape the prairie and the savanna, we realize that these forces underpin, but also dwarf, the seasonal changes. Some of the physical changes occur precipitously, as with the braided levees down in the floodplain. Others change so slowly that we scarcely notice, as in the recessional moraines.

It is interesting that humans have sought to manipulate both the physical forces and the seasonal changes. We have built levees along the flood plain. We have developed short-season corn to avoid early frosts. We use drip irrigation in our garden. They do give us a margin of error. But a question we tend to ignore, as we rapidly expand our exploitation of nature, is whether we understand nature's margins of error.

The last two essays comment on the persistence of life on the prairies and savannas in this naturally sandy terrain. Plants and animals have myriad ways to adapt to changes in their environment; an analysis of them could fill many volumes. In the first of these two essays, the behavior of roots and seeds is used to represent nature's capabilities for survival. An examination of their roots and seeds does reveal how plant species relate to the environment and to each other. That examination requires a very local view of things—at your feet, on your elbows, on eye level. Reality is there, at the level of the senses.

In the second essay, we find that phenology tells us about variation from year to year, and something more. It becomes the aperture through which we can see the relationships between the physical and the biological worlds played out in the kaleidoscopic changes. Again, the phenological tabulations force us to become intimately local. To measure such expressions, you must put down your own roots, in one place and over time. More than that, you must let nature come to you. You must develop a sense of place.

As we look intimately at the expressions and behaviors of plants and animals, it becomes clear that populations fluctuate in the environment; in fact, they fluctuate radically from season to season, from year to year. There is no steady state and there are no straight-line trends. Security lies not in an unchanging environment, but in a dynamic one. Given enough time, even co-evolution rages back and forth across the land.

With an overview of the physical and biological forces, a series of questions about humankind begins to emerge. How does a cognitive species fit in? What are the consequences as we seek to form the land and design the biota? Do we play with fire? Do we synthesize our environment, ranging from habitat to food supply, to health and longevity? Do we eliminate all our perceived competitors, including micro-organisms? Do we synthesize ourselves, our very genes? We may not really know the answers to such questions until "after the fact."

We should not, however, dodge the question of the costs of synthesis. We should start our search for understanding with the underpinnings in the prairie and the savanna.

SAND

On the sandbar there is only wind, and the river sliding seaward.
Every wisp of grass is drawing circles on the sand.

GETTING READY
FOR WINTER

On this afternoon in late October, as I stand submerged in their domain, the seed heads of the big bluestem and the Indiangrass wave above my head. A gusty, southerly wind blows across the land. The topaz sunlight rebounds among the grasses.

Although the temperature is in the 80s, leaves from the sugar maple on the edge of the moraine and from the cottonwoods on the sandbar skitter off the trees and land on the water. All around the deciduous trees are undressing for winter.

The grasses bow before the wind, but even a gale would not dislodge them from the prairie. A severe winter storm might uproot the 200-year-old bur oak up on the hill, but it would not dislodge the grasses. Nor could a herd of a thousand bison. It would take a glacier or a moldboard plow to uproot the grasses.

I grab the dried, brown head of a gray-headed coneflower and rub it between my palms. It has the smell of ripe citrus and the grit of sand. I toss the seeds up into the wind, and they flutter aimlessly across the prairie.

By standing on tiptoe, I can see above the grasses to the nearest recessional moraine, deposited by the retreating glacier. The moraines are more obvious now than they were at the autumnal equinox a month ago, when the landforms were still obscured by summer foliage. Now I can see that the moraines are a series of rounded ridges lying between here and the floodplain. Made mostly of sand and granite boulders, they have retained their location and shape for the last 10 to 12 thousand years. Along the floodplain, the contours have changed from year to year in a constantly shifting pattern as the sand, moved by spring floods, has braided and rebraided the channels and levees.

The terminal moraine, formed at the southwestern front of the glacier, is the farthest away and highest above the floodplain. A phalanx of white oaks, like Roman soldiers, now dominates the ridge of that moraine. The trees on the next lower moraine are a mixed lot of black cherry, hackberry, ironwood, and hickory. On the third moraine are river birch, basswood, and aspen. Finally, along the river and the chan-

Big Bluestem

nel sandbars, the cottonwoods hang on to the bank, resisting the tear of the river.

I can identify the species of the trees by their form, the texture of their bark, and the shape of their leaves, but the autumn light also reflects differently from their leaves. The foliage on the higher moraines tends toward the regal, ultraviolet end of the spectrum. From the lower moraines, the colors are the gypsy yellows and infrared, in sharp contrast to the blue currents and brown eddies of the river.

This array of species occurs within a mile. Perhaps a varying intensity of fires over the centuries has helped align their rank and file. Fires on the higher and drier moraines might have been hotter and more frequent. But perhaps the sorting out of the trees is also defined by the level of the ground-water or availability of nutrients to the roots.

There is some variation in the soil among the moraines, but it is predom-inantly sand. And the mineral in the sand is mostly quartz.

I reach down and grab a pinch of the sand and rub it between my fingers. And then, on impulse, I rub it against my elbow until I scratch the surface of my skin and tiny drops of blood appear and glisten like garnets.

THE ORIGINS OF OUR SAND

What is this sand that is the founda-tion for these trees and grasses and forbs?

Quartz is a hard, crystalline, glassy mineral that is common in the earth's crust. It originally formed in igneous rocks like granite—major components of our continent's bedrock. Quartz is also part of metamorphic and sedi-mentary rocks, such as sandstone and quartzite, which are nearly all quartz.

Quartz can form in beautiful crystals, or be very dense and fine-grained, such as agate, chalcedony, chert, and flint. Opal is formed from a hydrated silica gel. Silica glass, or obsidian, is quartz that solidified from a lava that rapidly cooled. All forms of quartz are nearly inert and highly resistant to change.

This prairie sand must be very old. My experiment on my elbow proved that it is abrasive. I look at the sand again, this time more closely, and hold the tiny angular grains in the palm of my hand so that they catch the after-noon light. The quartz sand glistens like opals or golden topaz. In all there is the sheen of ultraviolet.

THE JOURNEY OF THE MORAINAL QUARTZ

But why is the quartz here in these moraines? The first answer is easy. We know the glacier brought sand here during the last 100,000 years and transported much of the quartz over long distances. By 10,000 years ago the glaciers had retreated 500 miles north, as far away as the northern shore of Lake Superior, back toward the bed-rock platform where they originated. The glaciers had the power to trans-port the quartz sand and the granite boulders here. But they did not form the granite and quartz, sandstone, or quartzite. All of these are products of the underworld, not the surface dredgings of a glacier.

If the quartz crystals I hold in my hand were formed deep in the earth, it had to have been in a very ancient age, eons and eons ago. Some geologists say a billion years ago; others argue more than that. They probably formed off a volcanic chain then located south of the equator.

The quartz, along with granite, crystallized out in a huge underground batholith—a mass of molten rock that cooled slowly deep in the earth, forming crystals of quartz and other minerals.

It will never be possible to directly observe the formation of a batholith. These rocks require the uninterrupted, slow cooling of molten magma under high pressures and temperatures over millions of years. It seems impossible that we would ever be able to control such a process.

If you try to lift a block of granite the size of a pumpkin protruding from the moraine, you will quickly conclude that it is very dense. But granite is, in fact, somewhat lighter than average crystal rock, and granitic magmas can rise in the earth's crust. After it hardens, the rock is exposed through the tectonic processes of mountain-building. Other processes can form quartz as white veins and streaks in cracks in the crystal rock, which sometimes carry gold and other rare elements. Granitic moun-

tains resist erosion and tend to be ancient. But they cannot resist forever.

Granites form in geologically active areas around the world. Our sand is on a stable, inactive part of the continental crust. We must look deep into the past for a time of such creation.

The highland of northern Wisconsin provides unequivocal evidence. It is now a peneplain—a surface made by the wearing down of ancient mountains followed by a more gentle upward warping. The roots of those mountains, now at the surface, comprise a mixture of igneous, sedimentary, and metamorphic rocks ranging from 700 million to billions of years in age. For comparison, Earth is estimated to be 4.5 billion years old.

Some geologists believe that these ancient mountains were at one time part of a vast, mountainous continent abutted by tropical seas. There is also evidence that a mountain chain now located in Antarctica may actually have been joined to these highlands. Continental drift broke this continental mass apart.

The ancient mountains eroded to provide the materials for the sedimentary layers of sandstone and limestone now exposed in the unglaciated areas west of here. The sedimentary rocks were laid down throughout Paleozoic times from about 250 to 470 million years ago, a reach of over 200 million years.

Just east of our local sandy prairies is a dramatic example of limestone. It is the Niagara Escarpment, which tracks all the way across the northeastern quadrant of North America. Spiny remnants of the escarpment form the string of islands on the western shore of Lake Michigan that connect to the Door Peninsula in Wisconsin. The escarpment diagonally bisects the Wisconsin mainland, although parts of it have been heavily eroded by glaciers and by weather. A remnant still persists in the unglaciated area of southwestern Wisconsin on a hill called Blue Mounds.

The Niagara Escarpment itself dates from about 450 million years ago, the time when marine animals first began to build reefs. The limestone reef probably built up on top of a fault that was created by the stresses of a continent being torn asunder. Silurian limestone has proved durable because of its magnesium content. It was strong enough to withstand the Pleistocene glaciations in the last two million years, and even directed the flow of ice from northeast to southwest in the Green Bay lobe of the latest Pleistocene glacier.

Standing below an old limestone outcrop in the Driftless Area just west of here, it is difficult to imagine such spans of time. What is now limestone was once a reef teeming with life. Pick up a slab of it now, and it shows the pores from burrowing worms and the marks of shells.

Much earlier, and well back in the Cambrian Period, about 500 to 750 million years ago, the mountains would not have had the life forms we recognize today. We know now that they were not bare of bacteria and other single-celled creatures. Recent fossil discoveries reveal that single-celled life existed in the seas and perhaps on land well before the Cambrian. These primitive forms would have emerged when there was little atmospheric oxygen at the surface and no ozone in the lower stratosphere. They were exposed to intense ultraviolet sunlight. There were no savannas, prairies, forests and tundras.

Much of life today is based on the calcified bones of the ages. But there is more than bones. We are direct descendants of the early eukaryotes and of the Cambrian invertebrates.

The modest Baraboo Range, rising up in violet haze on the horizon just to the south, is quartzite rock. Those hills have a much older origin than the peneplain and the reefs. The quartz grains were eroded from a batholith, perhaps two billion years ago. I can imagine quartz sand being eroded down to beaches and then periodically sliding deep into an ocean trench just offshore. Or maybe the sand built up in deep layers in a shallow coastal zone, and an earthquake or tremor triggered a slide that carried the sand into a deeper trench. This sand was buried and recrystallized into quartzite perhaps about 1.4 billion years ago.

Emerging at the surface in Precambrian times, the quartzite has survived eons of erosion to form what geologists call monadnocks, or isolated hills lying on the surface of the deeply buried granite peneplain. These monadnocks poke up through the Paleozoic sedimentary rocks in other scattered locations in southern Wisconsin.

At one time in its long history, the Baraboo Range may have appeared as a ridge of offshore islands, surrounded by limestone reefs in shallow tropical seas. The winds that whistle through the Baraboo Hills today whisper of great outwash plains of sand and tropical reefs. They whisper of the emergence of life across a span of a billion years—or more.

There has been time for mountains to rise and fall, beaches and reefs to form, continents to drift from the tropics to the temperates. There has been time for climatic temperatures to change from warm to cold and back again, and for life to weave its intricate webs.

However the landforms evolved, deep geological processes are the source of the quartz I see today. The minute little sand crystals that drew beads of blood to my elbow this afternoon have survived millions upon millions of years of tectonic shifts, the erosion of monumental mountains, the drift of continents, the coming and going of oceans, glaciation, and human culture.

That atomic bonding of three atoms to form silicon dioxide has persisted for perhaps the entire life of the planet Earth, and may even predate the condensation of Earth from cosmic dust.

Prairie Grass

The chemistry of life needs free atoms of oxygen and carbon to make delicate molecular complexes. But silicon and oxygen, so tenaciously joined in these quartz molecules, are the fulcrum on which prairie life must balance.

Our grains of sand have provided some of the boundary conditions for the emergence and growth of life we see here. The grasses on this windy autumn day dance and rustle softly, rooted here in silicon dioxide, unable to break the chemical bonds of the quartz. But they thrive in a parsimonious environment. Do they whisper anything to me?

OUR TIMES

The grasses are bronze now, as the shafts of afternoon light mingle with the shadows. The wind has subsided, and a very lonesome-sounding cricket is singing somewhere to the south. The clear air has a cold touch upon my face.

In another month ice will return to Center Pond, and by December I will be able, once again, to walk on water.

It is clear now that this ancient quartz sand limits the rates of return for all life on the savanna. The savings accounts of the species living here will always be small. And someday, the great ice sheets will again grind the summits of the Baraboo Range, eroding more of the rose and purple quartzite, and gorging Devil's Lake with icebergs for a thousand years.

This evening, an air of satisfaction settles across the land. A white-tailed doe hesitates at the edge of the woods, tail flicking, ears up, eyes glistening, and then she noses into the deep grass. I realize that the coming and going of the Pleistocene glacial cycles in the last two million years is really but a flutter of nature's real heartbeat. I am conscious too of the beat of my heart in my chest. There is a synchrony here.

Soil experts, likewise, would have a hard life without the Sand Counties. Where else would their podzols, gleys, and anaerobics find a living?

Social planners have, of later years, come to use the Sand Counties for a different, albeit somewhat parallel, purpose. The sandy region serves as a pale blank area, of pleasing shape and size, on those polka-dot maps where each dot represents ten bathtubs, or five women's auxiliaries, or one mile of black-top, or a share in a blooded bull. Such maps would become monotonous if stippled uniformly.

In short, the Sand Counties are poor.

I CE

The wind that makes music in November corn is in a hurry. The stalks hum, the loose husks whisk skyward in half-playful swirls, and the wind hurries on.

In the marsh, long windy waves surge across the grassy sloughs, beat against the far willows. A tree tries to argue, bare limbs waving, but there is no detaining the wind. . . .

Out of the clouds I hear a faint bark, as of a far-away dog. It is strange how the world cocks its ears at that sound, wondering. Soon it is louder: the honk of geese, invisible, but coming on.

The flock emerges from the low clouds, a tattered banner of birds, dipping and rising, blown up and blown down, blown together and blown apart, but advancing, the wind wrestling lovingly with each winnowing wing.

OUR FIRST WINTER STORM

Our first November storm started after supper on Wednesday evening. I had followed the storm on the news as it surged out of the Gulf of Alaska and whipped the Oregon coast. It dumped two feet of snow on the Cascades in Oregon, swung south across Utah, and crossed the Colorado Rockies, where the snow closed the mountain passes. Gathering energy on the high plains and moisture from the Gulf, it intensified over Missouri and swept into southern Wisconsin.

The storm started here with fine snow crystals, the way bigger storms often do. I could see the snow falling horizontally across the beam cast by the light on the garage. An inch of snow had fallen by bedtime. Not enough to shovel yet. But I stepped outside and stood for awhile in the swirling snow. How quiet the neighbors are tonight. Only the sound of the snow filling the empty spaces in the winter landscape. I went back inside to curl up under the goose down comforter and to dream of winter. I can shovel tomorrow morning.

At dawn I began to dig out. Eight inches, and the snow is heavy with that moisture from the Gulf of Mexico. The storm has departed. The sun seems faceless and as pale as a platinum disk, through the thinning clouds. And I dig some more.

GLACIATION

There was a time when digging out would have been a lot harder. Sometime around 18,000 years ago the Green Bay lobe of the glacier was inching southwestward. The Baraboo Range blocked its forward thrust, but the ice flanked both sides of the range, as if clutching at the hills with an immense forefinger and thumb. The forefinger, to the north, moved over the lower part of the range and filled the interior valley just east of the pre-

sent city of Baraboo. The thumb, to the south, followed the current course of the Wisconsin River.

The grasping palm of the hand of ice started to ascend the higher southern hills and advance across the range. Both the northern finger and the southern thumb had moved into the Devil's Lake Gorge, and were less than two miles apart. As the ice advanced, it carried away blocks of the quartzite and ground them into gleaming, rose-colored quartz crystals.

Then, the advancing glacier lost its grasp, and the skeletal ice fingers began to melt back, leaving only fragments that looked like rotten bones. The

Winter in the Woods

astronomical clock had run its course and time was running out for this round of glaciation. Left behind was an unglaciated island in the Devil's Lake Gorge. In that two-mile stretch the talus quartzite slopes survived the onslaught. They are now visible just above the lake.

Terminal moraines formed at the ice fronts. These are the moraines that now block the north and south ends of the gorge. They are ridges of glacial drift, unsorted boulders, sand, and clays— also known as till. Between the two ice fingers there had been a glacial lake, the water extending nearly a third of the way up the current bluffs. Icebergs floated in the lake. Devil's Lake today is a remnant of the glacial lake.

Before the glaciers arrived, the Wisconsin River had flowed for millennia through the Devil's Lake Gorge. The gorge was about 900 feet deep, deeper than the present gorge below Niagara Falls. About 100,000 years ago the Wisconsin River flowed through the gorge at a level 350 feet lower than the present surface. Glacial outwash and lake clay have filled more than 300 feet of the ancient gorge, and Devil's Lake sits on top of that till. The lake is now only 43 feet deep.

During the glacial period, a vast serrated lake also formed west and north of the Baraboo Range. The lake reached 70 miles north of the hills and over 40 miles to the west. Ice would have broken loose from the face of the glacier and floated out across the water. Sediments from the lake cover 1,825 square miles. The moraines today show the effects of the retreating glacier and the adjacent lake.

Just to the north, the lakebed sand is strikingly different from the Baraboo sand. It is white quartz that originated far to the north. The southern reaches of the lake include remains of the local rose-colored and golden-colored Baraboo quartzite that are tinted with iron oxides. A well drilled on the Leopold Reserve first brought up sand from the nearby hills, followed by a layer of the white sand. Thus, the quartz eroded from the Baraboos was probably deposited later than the white sand from the north.

The sandy plains that mark the lake bed were not covered by the glacier. They are the outwash carried by the vast and repeated outpourings of water. The so-called Driftless Area was, in part, buried by glacial sand that was carried by meltwater.

THE GLACIAL CYCLE

The climatologists are beginning to understand the climatic cycles that define the current boundaries for this part of the North American prairie/savanna—this land of glacial till and outwash.

They've known for decades that the terrain just east of here was buried under a mile of ice 18,000 years ago. That fact, so obvious to us now, took a long time for humans to accept, particularly for those who had come to believe that all life arrived on the scene in a spontaneous incarnation 6,000 years ago.

In the last decade or so, climatologists have identified a 100,000-year glacial cycle, that contains cold periods lasting 60,000 to 80,000 years, and interglacial warm periods lasting about 20,000 years.

A major theory argues that this cycle is produced by the astronomical relationships between the earth and the sun. There is an astronomical cycle that does repeat itself about every 100,000 years. The actual timing of the onset and then the meltdown of the glaciers displayed more complexity. Thermal mechanisms in the oceans and atmosphere were also involved in the actual timing of the changes and in how far the glaciers advanced in any given cycle.

The repeating cycles of glaciation, have persisted at least through the two million years of the recent Pleistocene. The preceding epoch, the Pliocene, seems to have been warmer. These conditions may have reached all the way back to the Paleocene 70 million years ago. But why, then, would such fundamental changes have occurred around two million years ago if the underlying forcing mechanism is astronomical? The earth didn't suddenly change its inclination and orbit at the start of the Pleistocene two million years ago. The changes that tipped the balance toward glacial cycling must have been subtle, but profound, physical and chemical mechanisms on the surface of Earth.

Some have postulated that the conditions in the Pleistocene arose because of geologic events that created mountain chains like the Himalayas. Such moun-

tains might have reached heights that would have affected atmospheric flow on a global basis.

Glacial cycles could also be framed by the location of continents drifting across different latitudes. Although such global drifting is slow indeed as measured against clocks and calendars, 70 million years of continental drift could make a significant difference in the patterns of summer and winter on a continent. The earth's position in relation to the sun would have established the right inclination for the onset of glaciers, but glacial epochs apparently need a nudge from tectonic processes.

Without contradicting the idea of continental drift, and even reinforcing it, some people have argued that the Pleistocene glacial epoch was triggered by the great lava floods on the Columbia Plateau in the Pacific Northwest and in India. Released gases could have cooled the atmosphere enough to have induced the repeated march of glaciers.

Reversals in the earth's magnetic field that have occurred about every 500,000 years could also have had an impact on climate. Extended zero interludes in the field may have resulted in intensified solar radiation at the earth's surface. There are those who argue that the earth's climatic changes are embedded in the vast rotation of the Milky Way galaxy. Such eonic rotations in the galaxy might help explain how, many millions of years ago, there were glacial periods with icebergs at sea level on the equator followed by coal-depositing tropical swamps at polar latitudes. If that is the case, then Earth may well experience a repeat of the tropical Jurassic Period in another 50 million years.

An open-minded climatologist would probably say that all these factors had potential for creating and maintaining the Pleistocene.

IN THE MEANTIME

Climatologists are continuing to document dramatic climatic shifts within the 100,000-year reach of a single ice age. During the glacial part of the cycle there have been up to 50°F ambient annual temperature increases. Over the following 1,000 years the climate drifted back to the dominating colder regime. These lurches from cold to warm occurred about every 10,000 years, within the longer glacial period.

One of the expressions of these warmer interludes is the behavior of ice during continental glaciation as revealed in ocean sediments. Vast sheets of ice built up on North America and northern Europe and froze to their earthen beds as they gathered weight and depth. One hypothesis is that the earth's fairly constant upward flux of geothermal heat brought more and more of the floor of the ice sheet to the melting point.

Eventually, the area of subglacial lubrication became so great that the ice sheet could not maintain its steep surface profile. It eventually broke down and the ice flows moved out to sea, gouging a channel hundreds of miles wide through an area such as the Hudson Bay outlet. The icebergs flowed in vast armadas into the North Atlantic. What a sound they must have made! The armada of glaciers slowly melted and deposited glacial debris on the ocean floor as far south as the Azores.

The lurches may seem but a scientific curiosity in terms of a human's life span. But that is not long at all in terms of the prairie ecology. It would be interesting to live as long as Methuselah and witness one of these shifts. One might wonder, at the age of 700, if the woodshed would hold out. On the other hand, if you really like the slow pace of autumn, you might wish for a life span that would place you on Earth in the centuries that lie ahead—as the climate cools.

Another hypothesis argues that changes in ocean currents led to a simultaneous collapse of the glaciers in North America and Northern Europe. The time it would take for a continental glacier to actually collapse is still a matter of argument. The deposition of the ocean sediment could have occurred in the space of a decade. Carbon dating of the sediments has pinpointed the timing to within a hundred-year time span.

The idea and evidence for the lurches from cold temperatures to warm during the glacial cycle seem quite plausible. But perhaps more startling to people adapted to central heating and air conditioning, there is also evidence for shifts from warm conditions to cold during the interglacials. During the present interglacial, our familiar Holocene, historians have recorded a couple of periods characterized as "little ice ages." The climatologists have yet to explain why the patterns would shift from warm to cold during the interglacial. Factors could include feedback relationships between shifting winds in the atmosphere, the earth's reflective capacity, and currents in the ocean that we do not yet fully understand.

Something else in the record brings a wrinkle to the brow. Sedimentary and ice core data suggest that climatic lurches from warm to cold occurred with more frequency during the last interglacial than during the current interglacial. The climatologists have named the last interglacial the Emian. But why would the last interglacial have been more subject to sudden spurts of cooling than this one? It is possible that the climate in our Holocene over the last 15,000 years has been unusually benign compared to the Emian, or earlier interglacials.

We do know with assurance now that climate gives us rhythms within rhythms. It is a giant chorus of thermodynamic feedback between the oceans, atmosphere, and land. But the sun sings the melody.

THE ABORIGINAL SAVANNA

I stand on the terminal moraine, looking southwest toward the hills and escarpments of the Driftless Area, with shafts of winter sunshine stretching across the land, and I can imagine an afternoon 100,000 years ago with a climate similar to today's. Herds of animals are grazing in scattered bands on the prairie openings from here to the horizon. Winter is arriving, and the geese are flying. By squinting I can imagine a family of mastodons, those North American giants, just below the crest of the far hill, with the old, matriarchal cow raising her trunk and trumpeting a warning against a sabre-toothed cat. This is the hungry season.

Then, I let my mind float forward to 50,000 years ago, and I can imagine torrents of water pouring westward from the quartzite edge of the Baraboo Range, carrying along chunks of ice, boulders, gravel, and sand in spasmodic floods that lasted for decades. Ice Age bison—*Bison crassicornis*—are lined up on a crumbling sand bank for a risky drink of water, one of them stumbling in and drowning, washed down and under in the sandy torrent. There is, however, in this melting water, the promise of spring.

The glaciers did not arrive and just sit here stolidly for a 50,000-year-long winter. The glacier pulsed and fluctuated with lurches to a warmer period and slow returns to ice. If I had been granted the privilege of witnessing the last 100,000 years, I would have seen a thousand years of advancing ice mountains and then a thousand years of torrential water, each flood carrying sparkling crystals of quartz.

If we could attach a monitor to the long arm of time in the Pleistocene, like a blood pressure cuff, we could read the rhythms of the climatic beat. On a scale of two million years, we would clearly read a systole and diastole of exquisite regularity. If we examined the 100,000 years of a single glacial cycle, we would detect rhythms within a rhythm. On a scale of 500 to 1,000 years, we would read flutterings in the pulse.

Confined by a human life span of 70 or 80 years, we tend to focus inward to the annual beat of the seasons, or perhaps the decadal cycles of drought and flood. But all these rhythms beat in the veins of the native species of the prairie. In the longer pulses, life would have advanced northward and retreated southward. Some species of insects would have advanced and retreated rapidly; plants would have moved more slowly. Some of the migrating passerines would have quickly followed the insects, but others would have waited for the migration of the fruits and nectar.

The big bluestem and the Indiangrass would have waved in the wind in our sand for a 1,000-year interlude, or a 10,000-year interlude, and then given way to taiga and tundra. The big grazing animals would have tried to survive in the tundra near the melting ice wall before migrating to the oak savannas deep in the southland.

The preparations I see for winter this year are genetic mirrors of the 100,000-year astronomical cycle, but are also shaped by the opportunities and risks that come from the warmer interludes.

Those species that prepare now for winter in this interglacial time will need the strategy of migration when the glaciers advance again. The animals, and even the plants, will yield, and then they will make opportunistic returns when those centuries of favorable springs reappear. If some of them have become too fond of the Ice Age, they may perish in a series of warm and sunny springs.

But for us, conscious now of the passage of time, there are those sudden lurches to think about. Not all of the climatologists agree about the disparity between the Holocene and the Emian. They argue about the accuracy of the data taken from the ice cores and the sediments. However, a sudden reemergence of a shift from warm to cold could upset our expectations that glowing springs will emerge after mellow autumns. Would we become accustomed to years without summers, to a killing frost in August, and snow in September? Or are we now technologically wedded to the Holocene?

The plants and animals here have genetic memories and behavioral expressions that reflect Pleistocene glacial and interglacial conditioning. The creatures have lived and survived and migrated to and from this area far longer than humans. However, genes in the somatic cells and the neurons of humans must also mirror the glacial influences that were imposed on the ancestors of Europeans and Asians. They were creatures of a colder time and often higher latitudes than we ourselves. Even our moods about the changing seasons must have millennial reflections.

WINTER IS HERE

We're settling in to winter now, with the arrival of December. Winter seems so very confident of its powers as it announces its arrival.

Last evening, just after supper, a low pressure system had moved east, ushered out by choppy winds. At bedtime, the wind had intensified, with long, low moans. It tugged hard at the last few leaves on the bur oak.

I could see through the window, in the night glow, the falling leaves skittering down the drive, dancing in wild allegroes before the wind.

A week ago, as November faded, we had dug out from that first storm. The first snow can catch you emotionally unprepared, if you are still in the mood for autumn. However, there's a thrill when I see the dust of snow in the air, late in the evening, and a satisfaction in stepping outside and smelling the snow and feeling its cold fingers on my forehead. And yet there is an underlying twinge of melancholy, a warning of deeper snows and colder nights, when the wind lays an icy hand firmly on your brow.

But now, a week later, the driveway is dry, and the leaves are free to roam. Brown and brittle, they are on the move. With the wind and the chattering leaves, our aging Golden Retriever, struggling with arthritis in his hind legs, was certainly not a happy fellow. Usually, Cheddar is deep into winter dreams on a November night, twitching and snoring, and I have to nudge him awake the next morning. But, last

Settling in to Winter

night, as the wind whistled down the chimney and shook the windows, he would drop to the floor with a thud, get up again to pace, his toenails clicking on the floor, and then yip at the shadows dancing in the oak.

What does he hear? Is it the wind? Or does an arthritic old dog hear winters past? Does he remember October sunshine from a few short weeks ago? Does his sensory world reveal to him the spirits of the season, borne on the shifting winds?

My mind flipped from pondering the nature of his insomnia, to growing irritation with his restlessness, then to enjoying the tumult of the night. Cheddar finally gave up and settled in at the foot of the bed.

As I drifted off to sleep, I thought I heard the geese calling to each other. I have made the choice not to migrate like the geese, though I could. I have made the choice to stay here and to hang on to the memories of October. I relish the thought of the second snowstorm, even with the understanding that its snow will be here until the March thaw.

It is a conspicuous fact that the corn stubbles selected by geese for feeding are usually those occupying former prairies. No man knows whether this bias for prairie corn reflects some superior nutritional value, or some ancestral tradition transmitted from generation to generation since the prairie days. Perhaps it reflects the simpler fact that prairie cornfields tend to be large. If I could understand the thunderous debates that precede and follow these daily excursions to corn, I might soon learn the reason for the prairie-bias. But I cannot, and I am well content that it should remain a mystery. What a dull world if we knew all about geese!

FIRE

All routines come to an end. This one ended with a prairie fire, which reduced the prairie plants to smoke, gas, and ashes. Phosphorus and potash atoms stayed in the ash, but the nitrogen atoms were gone with the wind. A spectator might, at this point, have predicted an early end of the biotic drama, for with fires exhausting the nitrogen, the soil might well have lost its plants and blown away.

But the prairie had two strings to its bow. Fires thinned its grasses, but they thickened its stand of leguminous herbs: prairie clover, bush clover, wild bean, vetch, lead-plant, trefoil, and Baptisia, each carrying its own bacteria housed in nodules on its rootlets. Each nodule pumped nitrogen out of the air into the plant, and then ultimately into the soil. Thus the prairie savings bank took in more nitrogen from its legumes than it paid out to its fires. That the prairie is rich is known to the humblest deer-mouse; why the prairie is rich is a question seldom asked in all the still lapse of ages.

ORANGE FLAMES
IN THE DEAD GRASS

The fire started slowly—orange flames, not more than six inches high, burned out the dead grass matted around the new spring growth.

The flames crawled north against the wind and crossed this recently abandoned farm field, now choked with quackgrass. As the fire consumed last year's detritus, curling clouds of gray smoke rose against the blue sky. Caught in the wind, the smoke swirled over our heads and toward the south. A sudden gust brought the smoke down and around me. Instinctively, I breathed in. I quickly pulled my red bandanna over my nose and up to my eyes, and my hat down to my eyebrows. But I felt a flash of wild elation as the flames accelerated in the field.

Since early this morning, April 13, the wind has been blowing across the recessional moraines from the northeast, a sure sign of changing weather. The wind has been thrashing among the trees on top of the moraine, and down here it has been rippling the silky

Fire in the Field

new grasses of spring. It has been a gusty wind all morning, but mellow for one from the northeast.

The tree swallows and the bluebirds have been banking in the wind, competing for a flush of insects and arguing over nest boxes planted in the field. The fire crew has been waiting, lying in the shade of the hedgerow.

At noon, the sweet wind shifted—for the last half hour it has been pouring over the moraines from due north. The fire crew has gotten up, stretching and grumbling, and is gathering for orders.

The wind had been blowing from due south for a week, with tempera-tures reaching the 80s. Warm air has flowed steadily northward, all the way from the Gulf of Mexico. But today, the wind has reversed and all that warm air is rushing south again.

Sometimes I wish that spring would not be so indecisive.

Until this week, the weather was wet and cool, and this year will be remembered as the one with record high water in the sloughs and kettles. The grasses and forbs of the prairie had been slow in developing until the warm air arrived, and dried the surface of the sandy soil. The ephemeral woodland flowers were almost two weeks late, but now there is a phenological rush here among the moraines. Old Sol is the great integrator of seasonal change as the increasing flow of photons inevitably reaches the face of Earth. The sun is beginning to exert its dominance again, and I can already smell the approach of summer.

Earlier this morning, when Charles and I drove through the woods and down into the abandoned field, we flushed seven sandhill cranes. As his pickup kicked up a spattering of dust on the crest of the hill, the cranes rose and soared with the wind, rose without effort on an invisible thermal and disappeared southward toward the sedge meadow. Seven cranes, flying together at this time of year, would be non-breeding singles. They are the young of a year ago, booted out by the adults, not ready to pair off and mate, but not willing to fly alone. And they were skittish when we appeared.

The cranes didn't know it then, but there is another reason for alarm: they will soon smell the fire. The fire will burn through the linear field of quackgrass in this swale between the moraines and up through the understory of the woods, licking at the trunk of the bur oak, at the white and black oaks and the birch, the maple, the old juniper, and the young white pines. The fire will consume the detritus in the prairie. It will clean out the dead leaves and brush in the woods, but will barely scorch the trees. Prairie and savanna are in the making.

The people on the fire crew know what they are doing. They've been waiting for this day with a due north wind. They strapped 60-pound cans of water on their backs and took their 30-pound tank torches in hand. Now they are fanning out around the perimeter of the field.

The wind did shift, as predicted, and at 1 P.M. the crew set the fire at the southern edge of the field to establish a firebreak. The fire slowly worked its way upwind. To accelerate the burn, the crew chief cuts straight across the field with his torch. The new fireline roars high as it catches and races downwind back toward the firebreak, the billowing smoke dimming the sun. In the sunshine the smoke was white—now, blocking the sun, it is steel gray. The fire and smoke become a wild ballet of spring. The swallows and bluebirds dart away. Some of the nest boxes catch fire. Accelerating lines of fire flow like molten lava ahead of the main line through the shallow furrows left years ago by the farmer's cultivator. My eyes smart as whirlwinds of vapors and soot spin toward us from the flames.

EMOTION AND LOGIC

My mind races back and forth between emotion and logic—from a wild fear of fire to the knowledge that fire is a natural thing, and that the plants of the prairie and savanna will have a better chance to reoccupy this quackgrass meadow.

It will be a challenge. The quackgrass has been around for some time. Quack is an aggressive invader from Eurasia, most likely a native of Mongolian sandy soils. Quack and the original wild alfalfa may have been close neighbors in Asia. Some botanists believe quack came to North America with the earliest Spaniards or Northern Europeans in the sixteenth Century, perhaps as animal bedding in the holds of ships or as stuffing in straw mattresses. If that is the case, it has had 400 years to spread from the coasts to the middle of the continent. And spread it has. It is more prolific, in biological units, than humans. The quack surely had not arrived here in the center of the continent, on this meadow, much before 1850. But it has had nearly 150 years to take hold.

Quackgrass propagates by seeds and rhizomes. In a single square meter, hugging the top soil layers, the stem-like rhizomes can generate a tangled web of shoots that has been sorted out and measured at 165 feet in total length. As many as 3,000 buds occupy a square foot, each bud capable of starting an independent plant. You'll believe these facts, without a doubt, if you have ever tried to spade it out of a garden patch by hand. Quack is a heavy feeder on nitrogen, phosphorus, and potash, capable of denying nutrients to other plants. Compared to other pasture forages, it's not much of a provider for livestock. However, the native grasses, given some relief from the plow, can crowd out the quack-grass.

THE PRAIRIE'S RETURN

In fact, there are signs that the prairie grasses and forbs have started to return to the field after just four years without cultivation. Scattered among the mass-

es of quackgrass are clumps of big bluestem, little bluestem, and a stray plant or two of side-oats grama and prairie dropseed. In only days after the fire some of the prairie forbs will bloom.

I know that these modest clumps of prairie grasses, only five to six inches tall in April, already have roots that go as far as 10 feet deep into the sand. They reach down for water, and they also establish an underground resistance to the fires that nature and aboriginal humans imposed on the land across the millennia. They have native talents the quack does not.

SPRING ARRIVES SLOWLY AT THE SURFACE

Spring arrives more slowly at the surface of the earth. The old detritus insulates the soil from the warming sun, and plant dormancy persists. In dense stands of big blue, the crown of any one plant is covered by the stems of its neighbors, which can delay spring growth by as much as three weeks. Our fire will clean out the deadfall quack and the native grasses, and accelerate the seasonal change.

The flames range in temperature from 300°F to 1100°F, and will quickly dissipate in three to four minutes. Two inches below the surface the temperature will remain less than 100°F. Within hours, the soil will be warmed enough by the sun to stimulate the tips of the plants, and then the roots.

Seeds of plants lying on the surface can tolerate a moderate fire for up to five minutes. Seeds only slightly covered can tolerate an intense fire. There is also evidence that seeds exposed to fire have a higher percentage of germination than those in nearby unburned grassland. In fact, fire removal of old litter can produce a six-fold increase in flower production of big bluestem and a 60 percent increase in plant height in the year of burning. The fire will release a flush of minerals from the dead mulch. Moisture levels are good this early in the spring, particularly this year, in spite of warm weather for a week, and the plants will quickly capitalize on the change in the temperature at the soil surface.

PRAIRIES AND FIRE

Before the crew started the fire today, I had squatted down, batted away at a swarm of aggressive mosquitoes without much impression on them, and pushed aside the dead grass. A six-inch-long angleworm, lying on the wet soil, squirmed in the sudden exposure to sunlight. I covered the angleworm, and squeezed a handful of the sandy soil, still retaining the memory of winter. There were actually crystals of frost under the detritus.

I had also brushed aside the oak leaves up in the woods and put my hand flat on the dank soil. The memory of winter was even stronger there. The bottom leaves were embedded in frost. Fire will cause more radical changes in the woods than out on the meadow, because the woods has grown accustomed to the absence of fire. The woodland shrubs have taken advantage of the interlude free of fire, and the array of trees has changed.

Two hundred miles to the west, in the tall-grass prairies, and 800 miles farther on, in the short-grass prairies, annual rainfall is too scant for the development of deciduous woods, even too scant for openings of trees in the prairie sea. Most of the trees are cottonwoods that hug the streambeds. The vast western prairies are dominated by grasses and forbs.

Here in the sand country, the postglacial climate has probably never been too dry for trees. The natural complex can provide conditions favorable to the development of savannas, but shrubs and trees will invade, dominate during a wet cycle, and then retreat during a dry cycle. Clearly, fire has worked with climate in affecting the advances and retreats of prairies, savannas, and woods in this marginal region where more rain is always possible, but never a given.

Over the centuries, the frequency of fires has probably accelerated during extended years of drought, and declined during wet cycles. There is archeological evidence that, since the last glaciation, drier periods have persisted for up to 100 years. Animal bones in the middens at Paleo-Indian habitation sites show a change in their diet from animals that would have flourished in the open prairie to animals that preferred the savannas and woodlands. In wetter years the Native Americans migrated to the high prairie swales, and in the droughts moved toward the rivers.

The changing patterns of precipitation persisted long enough to induce changes from woodlands to savanna to prairie, then back again, as rainfall actually nudged the tension zone.

Lightning was the singular, natural force for starting fires. It is hard to imagine, however, that after the arrival of humans in the last 10,000 to 15,000 years, lightning is still the major cause of brush and forest fires. Thunderstorms in this area of the continent normally occur in late spring and summer and are usually accompanied by drenching rain. On average, June is the month of heaviest rain. A bolt of lightning could strike an old tree, which

would smolder long enough for things to dry out, and then ignite a fire. In a specific location lightning-caused fires probably occurred occasionally, but not annually.

Native Americans were certainly a force in the ecological use of fire. At least some of the tribes deliberately set fires. The accelerated greening of the land, even out on the high plains, attracted elk, bison, and deer. Fires were also set to decrease the risk of circumstantial wildfires around encampments. More than a thousand years ago, Native Americans developed corn agriculture and cultivated it from Tennessee to Colorado. The corn had

Fire in the Woods

to compete successfully with prairie grasses, and those who grew it used all the technology they could muster.

Clearly then, the earliest humans in America became an integral part of the prairie/savanna ecology. They had at least 10,000 years to employ the benefits of fire, and in recent millennia the technology to grow corn. Over those thousands of years, the fires they set, along with natural fires, advanced the deeper-rooted perennials and held the deciduous woods at the edge of the prairie. Corn cultivation would require a different ecology, involving setting fires, but also protection from them.

Even with their agricultural practices, starvation was always a threat for the Paleo-Indians. Use of fire and protection from fire was a year-to-year means of adjustment. However, there was a stronger force over which they had no control—changes in climate. Manipulation of fire can affect the composition of the prairie and the savanna, but we don't know how to manipulate the arrival of spring. Humans can become impatient with nature's rhythms and pulses. We often seek to lever the forces of nature, but nature remains the stronger.

FIRE IN THE WOODS

By 2:30 P.M. the fire crew is out of the meadow and is setting backfires at the southern edge of the woods. Shortly, the crew will cut under the steep north side of the hill and start the fire downwind. The fire will sweep up the hill, burn out the dead leaves, the dogwoods, the blackberries and raspberries, and the buckthorn, another recent invader from Asia. It will also take out a generous crop of nettles, an invader from northern Europe. The goal of the managers in this part of the Aldo Leopold Memorial Reserve is to recreate the conditions of an oak savanna.

The head of the fire crew has told me to stand on the moraine to the south, but to the side of the approaching fire, so I can see it climb up the moraine toward me. And smell it. And feel it.

At first, it is a thin, orange line, licking at the understory of brush far down the hill. But it gains strength as it moves toward me, flames leaping 20 feet with the wind. The rolling smoke is caught up in the wind that curls like a reverse wave as it brushes against the hill, smoke and flames revealing the shape of the curving wave before the wind surges on.

The rising smoke is now dense at my station on top of the moraine and I feel a surge of dizzy elation, so I move closer to the fireline to avoid the rising smoke. But then, as I sense the heat, I back around the edge of the fireline and step over into the burned-out area. The chief had told me, "Keep one foot in the black!"

He calls me on the radio. "You OK?" "Sure, I'm OK." The line of flame, now beyond me, licks at the trees, but does not surge into their crowns. The smoke settles into a thick, blue veil on the lee side of the hill as the fire subsides. I kneel down to feel with the palm of my hand the temperature of the soil surface, and it is cool enough to touch.

But I am covered with soot from hat to boot, and soot stings my eyes where I rubbed them.

Then, as I reluctantly trudge off the moraine, I hear the call of a crane from the direction of the sedge meadow, a call as wild as the fire, but as sweet and clean as the north wind.

ACCEPTING FIRE

Humans in this technological age have been slow to accept the integral nature of fire in the developing of the prairie and savanna. The great fires of history become apocryphal myths. But we cover our eyes and close our minds to the idea that life can benefit from fire.

It is more than merely rising from the ashes. Fire is the releaser of stored energy from an earlier season and opens the way to this year's growing season. The prairies and the savannas

respond and adapt with great resilience. Understanding fire is to let it act, but also to sometimes light the match.

A week later, on another blue-sky day, with a gentle wind from the west, the four of us visit the burned-over moraine. At the line between the woods and the quack meadow, in a spreading carpet, rings of birdfoot violets are dancing like circles of fairies in the grass.

It's a busy day for phenologists, as the wild creatures are clearly on the move. The kinglets came in this morning. The phoebes came last week. The deer are feeding on the sumac and poison ivy.

In the woods there is a cacophony of sounds—the goldfinches, house finches, and purple finches are holding a convention. A pack of robins is work-

Birdfoot Violet

ing the grasses. The flicker sings from somewhere. The wood ducks and the crested flycatchers are showing their colors. The little brown bats should be back any day from their winter siesta along the Mississippi.

The wind is from the southwest and, as it sweeps in, there is the musty smell of spring. Last year's oak and maple leaves are silver-gray and decaying down in the slough. There is also the persistent odor of burned grasses from over the hill. The nonmigrating birds, including the chickadees, are shuffling their locations. They always seem to adjust their territories in spring. An incipient migration? Nina heard a woodcock early this morning. They've completed another successful journey.

Soon there will be scattered strands of blue-eyed grass, and the lupine will be in bud. And in the same week an isolated clump of cream baptisia will burst into bloom with fronds the color of fresh butter. Up around the scrub oaks, in a patch of bare sand, the yellow blossoms of puccoon will nod in the breeze. And then, in June, the spi-

derwort will mimic and intensify the blue summer sky.

Over on the south side of the moraine, pollen from the bur oak fills the air like gold dust floating in the sunshine. The pollen is collecting in tiny drifts around the emerging prairie grasses, some of it settling on the violet blossoms. The catkins on the oak are tossing and waving in the breeze, releasing a shower of pollen at every gust. The new leaves on the oak are about the size of a squirrel's ear and glisten gray-green on the tips of the twigs. But the leaves already show veins and lobes and already are trapping light from the sun that is streaking by the tree at 186,000 miles per second. The photons of light surely pay little heed to the oak, but the oak is storing the precious energy in carbohydrate molecules.

The grasses and forbs of the prairie, and the trees in the openings, have hung around the edges of the quack-grass meadow for more than a hundred years, waiting for their chance in the sunshine.

. . . a land ethic changes the role of Homo sapiens *from conqueror of the land-community to plain member and citizen of it. It implies respect for his fellow-members, and also respect for the community as such.*

In human history, we have learned (I hope) that the conqueror role is eventually self-defeating. Why? Because it is implicit in such a role that the conqueror knows, ex cathedra, *just what makes the community clock tick, and just what and who is valuable, and what and who is worthless, in community life. It always turns out that he knows neither, and this is why his conquests eventually defeat themselves.*

WATER

To view the painting, give the river three more weeks of solitude, and then visit the bar on some bright morning just after the sun has melted the daybreak fog. The artist has now laid his colors, and sprayed them with dew. The Eleocharis sod, greener than ever, is now spangled with blue mimulus, pink dragon-head, and the milk-white blooms of Sagittaria. Here and there a cardinal flower thrusts a red spear skyward. At the head of the bar, purple ironweeds and pale pink joe-pyes stand tall against the wall of willows. And if you have come quietly and humbly, as you should to any spot that can be beautiful only once, you may surprise a fox-red deer, standing knee-high in the garden of his delight.

Do not return for a second view of the green pasture, for there is none. Either the falling water has dried it out, or rising water has scoured the bar to its original austerity of clean sand. But in your mind you may hang up your picture, and hope that in some other summer the mood to paint may come upon the river.

MIDNIGHT STAMPEDE

The storm rode in like a herd of bison in a midnight stampede. I could feel the thunder shaking the ground as the storm front crested the moraine. With the flashes of lightning in the black night, I could see the horizontal rain lashing the prairie grasses.

For a moment, I thought I really did see the bison charging through the storm across the levees and sloughs, and then I realized I was seeing the old swamp oaks, their shaggy branches tossing in the wind. The storm unloaded two inches of rainfall, and passed as quickly as it had come.

Early this morning, the August air lies moribund around us. Mists drift across the surface of the pond, and the maturing stems of big bluestem and Indiangrass are bowed down, limp and silent. The reference book says that the blades of grass have intercepted as much as two-thirds of the precipitation. Thus not all of the rainfall from the storm will rush through the sloughs directly to the river, because the grasses will hold it until the water evaporates. Over a hundred tons of water per acre are suspended among the grasses. Each stem is decorated with strings of rainbow beads.

The storm did not usher in a northern high, as they often do this time of year, so it will be yet another muggy day as the sun climbs higher and the water evaporates. Late this afternoon or tonight, another herd of bison will probably storm over the hills.

The first cardinal flower came into bloom a week ago on August 1, earlier than expected. This morning, the outrageous *Lobelia cardinalis* sparkle low in the grasses like isolated rubies. One plant hugs the edge of the pond, and there is a perfect image of it in the still water. The cardinal flower is prolific this year. The spiderwort and the spike lobelia also seem to like wet feet.

The level of the pond is a foot higher than it was last year. However, a check of the records for precipitation since the first of the year contradicts the overwhelming impression that it has been an exceptionally wet year. Through the 1980s the average total rainfall by the end of July was 19 inches. So far this year the rainfall has totaled 19.1 inches. You couldn't get much closer to the average if you were a meteorological commander-in-chief. But with another look at the data, there appears a different twist.

The bulk of the rainfall this year has been concentrated in June and July. The recent surge of rainfall has been slow in evaporating and draining away. The

Cardinal Flower

tributaries and the rivers are swollen all the way down the valley in spite of the reservoir among the grasses. The levees and channels are reforming. Even up on the dry and sandy area among the moraines, some of the forbs are struggling with the wet soils. The puccoons thrive in drier conditions, and they're not doing well this year, except in the areas with the very best drainage, the areas of solid sand.

In the mesic prairie and the soggy

sedge meadow some of the plants usually in full summer display are also struggling. Joe-Pye weed, ironweed, and the coneflowers are in retreat. At the same time, turtle head, rare these recent years, is blooming in clusters. The silphiums, with their roots that are at least six feet deep, seem the best adjusted these past few months.

All across the land, the mosquitoes are responding vigorously. On this morning's early stroll, I made the mistake of opening my mouth and inhaled breakfast.

THE ROLE OF WATER

In a wet year, it's a good idea to ponder the role of water in the fabric of our neighborhood. It's relatively easy to observe the "what" and "how" of water. It's harder to figure out "why." Why are living things so closely interlinked with water? The question deserves a search through the archives of physics and chemistry.

Many species live submersed in liquid water all their lives, collecting oxygen through gills and other organs that process water. After all, water covers 70 percent of the earth's surface. We think of ourselves as dry-land animals with lungs adapted to the atmosphere. We relish those rare summer days of low humidity. (The relative humidity must be near 100 percent this morning—I was sweating at dawn.) The truth is that we land animals are more water-dependent that we think. Within our bodies, water constitutes 92 percent of blood plasma, and 80 percent of muscle tissue. Drowning, for land crea-

tures, is a relative, not an alien, condition.

Since we actually live in a watery environment, the "why" of water should be as familiar to us as a pair of old jeans. H_2O, simple in molecular structure, is really a very complex molecule, with characteristics that set the physical boundary conditions for our existence. Water also sets life's chemistry in motion.

What is there about a molecule of water that gives it so much authority?

Water is chemically hyperactive. It reacts with metal oxides to form bases. It reacts with oxides of nonmetals to form acids. It reacts with organic compounds to form alcohols and alkenes. Water is also a polar compound because it can have positive or negative valence states.

Water molecules can be the ultimate vehicles of transport, because water is a capacious solvent. With even a trace of dissolved compounds it is a superb conductor of electricity. Such capabilities are major planks in the platform for life, because we are creatures of chemical and electrical reactions.

But that's not all. Water has highly unusual thermal properties. It's nearly unique among the liquids in this regard. When heated from 32°F to 39°F, it contracts and becomes more dense. Most other substances expand and become less dense when heated. When water is cooled it initially expands. The expansion accelerates near and at the point of freezing. Ice is thus less dense than liquid water and floats. Life on earth, as we know it, would not exist if freezing water were more dense than liquid water and sank to the bottom of every pond and every ocean. Even on a moon of Jupiter, it is possible that life exists underneath a layer of ice.

At ordinary temperatures, the nature of the bonding between hydrogen and oxygen in water molecules is just strong enough to keep water liquid. For many another compound, such a low molecular weight would make it a gas at ordinary temperatures. We could imagine some form of life if all the water on Earth vaporized, but not our form of life.

There is another amazing characteristic of water. Water molecules can readily bond with each other to form chains of water molecules. The heat capacity of water is unusually high because of the hydrogen bonding among these multiple molecules of water. Thus the evaporation of water requires large inputs of energy to break these bonds. Condensing water vapor releases much of that energy. Water is thus a great energy bank for life on Earth.

There was enough kinetic, gravitational, and chemical energy potential in our thunderstorm last night to stampede a thousand herds of bison. However, engineers have not yet figured out how to channel and exploit the energy inherent in a thunderstorm.

Because of its thermal capacities, water serves as both a natural heat-transfer medium and a natural temperature regulator. Though humans haven't tamed nature's lightning, they have succeeded in exploiting the thermodynamic capacities of water and weather by using ice for cooling and steam for heating. They can also generate a bolt of lightning. More important than iceboxes and steam generators, the latent heat in lakes and oceans naturally tempers our climate, keeping it from the extremes we would surely experience if all the water in the world were vaporized over deserts or drained away from wetlands.

These are the physical conditions that water sets for us. There is also the direct role that water plays in the chemistry of life.

Water, carbon dioxide, and sunlight are the raw materials for photosynthesis. First, green plants use the energy of sunlight to manufacture carbohydrates from carbon dioxide and water, in the presence of chlorophyll. Water is absorbed through plant roots, and carbon dioxide is absorbed from the atmosphere. The photosynthetic process actually splits up the molecules of H_2O and CO_2, using hydrogen, oxygen and carbon to construct increasingly complex molecules that result in glucose ($C_6H_{12}O_6$), a stable organic compound. The stage is now half-ready for the chemistry of life on the prairie.

Second, the glucose holds latent energy needed for respiration. Respiration involves a series of oxidation reactions that convert organic molecules back to carbon dioxide and water.

So why is this cycle of respiration so advantageous for life? The chemical energy released in respiration propels

Oriole

the transport of substances across membranes, forms electrical impulses for internal communications within an organism, and drives protein synthesis.

Plants have the capability to trap photons and store energy. They also respirate, leading to metabolism. Animals are not capable of direct storage of solar energy in any significant amounts. Although animals must rely on the energy storage capability of plants, they have a different advantage.

The transfer of energy to animals provides the means for metabolism, which drives muscle contraction, and thus mobility. They can go to the river's edge for a drink. They can migrate in autumn. They can cut old oaks for the woodpile. They can move!

My mythical bison were certainly mobile last night. While their energy did not come directly out of a lightning bolt, the storm generated a new

supply of water, and the plants this morning are transforming H_2O into carbohydrates.

There is a third water-related condition that completes the foundation for life on the prairie, and ironically has given humans the impetus to plow it up. Under certain conditions, carbohydrates can be buried over long periods of geological time and be "reduced" to hydrocarbons, such as petroleum, coal, and natural gas. Reduction means that the oxygen is removed from the carbohydrates, leaving behind molecules composed of carbon and hydrogen, the simplest one being methane (CH_4). These fossil fuels store the latent solar energy captured in photosynthesis. When the fuels are oxidized, or burned, energy is released. The hydrocarbons are valuable to humans because they oxidize at high temperatures.

Carboniferous swamps and saline

estuaries from very ancient times have provided only a short-term bonus for humans in the water/carbon cycle. The period of consumption of the fossil fuel reserves will represent but a flicker on the geological clock, and won't really have an impact on the long-term global heat budget. However, overreliance on fossil fuels by humans becomes a major commitment to a depletable natural resource that generates carbon dioxide, water, and thermal radiation. Some of that thermal radiation will warm our earthly greenhouse, an advantage for some plants. Some of the water created by the combustion will help create a supply of hydrocarbons that could be available to the environment 500 million years from now. Too much global warming could also be catastrophic for some plant and animal species.

In the prairie, the humus built up in the 10,000 years since the last glaciation is a kind of fossil fuel for the sturdy grasses today, providing them the resilience they need to ride out a summer storm, a summer-long drought, or a frigid winter. The plants oxidize the humus at a low temperature, but there is a net gain in stored energy in the photosynthetic process. That's a process humans could apply. How could we take more advantage of the carbon, oxygen, and hydrogen cycles to generate a net gain rather than a net loss? And how could we manage to do that without destructive exploitation of the natural cycle?

Fossil fuels burn at high temperatures, and we waste much of the energy inherent in the combustion. We do need high temperatures for processes such as metallurgy, but not for other processes, including perhaps transportation. The point is that we should search for ways to perform tasks at lower temperatures and should avoid waste in the way we now use fossil fuels. It's thus much more than restraining consumption.

A more profound point is that natural elements, carbon, oxygen, nitrogen, hydrogen, and the others, move through cycles, with a time span sometimes as short as a summer night and sometimes as long as a geological age. It is the capture, storage, and release of energy in the cycles that drives the engines of Earth. We know this, but so often ignore it, as we focus on the release of energy.

WATER: ABUNDANT AND SCARCE

Water is the most abundant liquid on Earth, but there are obviously times when there's not enough around. This sand county cannot claim to be a classic desert on the scale of the Sahara, or even a classic Kansas plain. But there are seasons and years when the scarcity of rainfall limits life here, particularly on the south side of the moraines. Every year the populations of plants and animals most abundant in the dry parts of the neighborhood are very different from the ones in the sedge meadow less than a mile away.

The emergence of competition for water is no surprise—water is critical to the survival of all life, from single cells to complex organisms. Competition for a limited supply of water is a fundamental ecological characteristic. Without replenishment, organisms die. There is no more ultimate boundary, although water can be too abundant. If an animal drowns, it is because it doesn't get oxygen in its lungs and, thus, no oxygen in the brain to fuel those electrical dynamos on the top of its spinal column. There are some animals, though, that live their lives submersed. A plant "drowns" if its root system is cut off from oxygen and nutrients, though many have learned to deal with aqueous environments.

It is a delicate balance in which life prospers—a balance of optimal water. The same principles hold with photons. There can be too much light or too little. It is thus the relationship between water and sunlight that sets another basic boundary. The optimum range is much narrower than the extremes of water and energy that exist out there in the cosmos and even across Earth's environment. Living creatures are forced to develop strategies for dealing with extremes.

As summer arrives, the tall grasses shade out the ephemeral forbs of spring. But, in a wet year like this, the roots of some of the prairie forbs will drown.

Faced with a burning sun, animals,

Gray-headed Coneflower

including us, seek the shade. Because individual animals have muscles, they walk to a pond or river for a deep drink of water, even on a muggy day like this. They can also pant and sweat, and can nap in the shade of the bur oak. Around here, humans, averse to river water unless they're really thirsty, dig wells into the clean white sands.

A single plant is confined to a specific location, even though plant species can migrate widely by means of seeds and stolons to conditions of optimal water and light. They also have resident strategies. For plants, as with animals, evaporation serves as a natural process of air conditioning. On a hot day the evaporation is accelerated by the expansion of the diameter of the stomata on the bottom of a plant's leaves. But later, in the same day, the available water may not be enough to keep up with all the photosynthesis and the evapotranspiration. The stomata close and the leaves wilt.

Plants have another remarkable feature in their relationship to water and light that belies the idea of competition. A keen observer will have noted in dry years that plants such as trillium in the spring and goldenrod in the autumn thrive if they grow right beside the trunks of sugar maples, while the same species will be wilting if they are a few feet out from under the crown of the tree.

At first glance it doesn't make sense that the plants would compete successfully with the tree, even though the shade would slow evaporation. The sugar maple, with its deep roots and vast canopy, should be aggressively successful. You might expect the sandy soil under the tree to be nearly bare of plant cover. But it is not.

The tree possesses a capacity for strong hydraulic lift, drawing water up from the deeper soil layers both day and night. During the day the tree uses the water for its own photosynthesis, respiration, and thermal buffering. But during the night, it flushes water out through its shallow roots into the drier ground. A 40-foot tall maple tree can deliver between 40 and 60 gallons of water to the upper soil layer every night, water that is shared with its close neighbors.

The trillium thrives close to the maple. But there are some deep-rooted species that are aggressive in water consumption and their close neighbors do not thrive. Common ryegrass is one. Its cousin, native prairie rye, is far less aggressive. The competition and the cooperation are driven by water and light energy. Over time species prosper or decline, and out of this flows co-evolution.

So it is that living creatures exist in an inseparable union with water and light. This August morning was not the dawn of the "Age of Aquarius." Aquarius is forever.

On this day of heat and humidity it is clear that all species must deal with a wide variation in these fundamental resources. Humans spend much of their "energy" and much of nature's wealth coping with these variations in water and energy. But how good is our accounting system? What is the net gain as we seek to modify the environment? Do we overextend our budget? Does the prairie hold secrets we have not understood?

THE ARRIVAL OF NOVEMBER

The summer months have slipped away. Now it is early November again. The summer's floods receded over two months ago. Precipitation in August was slightly below normal. The maples and most of the oaks have long since shed their leaves, and the leaves are already on their way to becoming humus. I can see again the anatomy of the land, for the first time since last March. Nina suggests we go for a hike along the big moraine, across the sedge meadow, through the levees to the edge of the river, south along the river, and up over the moraine to the Shack, where we can eat lunch.

My inner reaction? "It's cold out there!" "And wet!" "We could sit here and visit by the fire."

The sun is shining, but not with a lot of enthusiasm. Charles has put on his coat, so we'll see if we can keep up with him.

It really is November. There's ice along the shadowy edges of the pond, and the ground is crusted with frost. Green leaves have given way to gray skies, brown tree trunks, and silver lichens. Now strikingly visible through the bare-limbed trees, the moraine forms a long parabolic curve that seems much too perfectly shaped to be the once-serrated edge of a retreating glacier.

The inner edge of the moraine must have been carved by the main channel of the river after the glaciers retreated. The main channel now lies a full half-mile to the east, down among the levees and sloughs. Charles points out that about 300 years ago, the channel flowed over this way. In perhaps another 300 years the river will direct its swooping course this way again and carve yet a smoother curve out of the old moraine, and maybe, in 5,000 years, will have consumed the moraine.

An arrow of noisy geese appears directly overhead, and disappears.

If I flew over the valley at about a thousand feet today, I could see that the main channel forms long meanders. If I could fly the same course 300 years from now, I might see that the westward-bending meander, now several miles upriver, had snaked its way down here. The river does undulate like a snake, but on a scale of centuries. And it will continue to do so for coming millennia.

The glacier, of course, is gone. Fifteen thousand years from now the glacier probably will have reclaimed all of the valley, and 50,000 years from now will dump its new load of rocks and quartz sand to form another series of recessional moraines.

In the meantime, the water will braid and rebraid the sand in the floodplain, in patterns that seem chaotic, but are really not so when the dynamics of the river are understood—the equation of gravity, friction, and kinetic energy that quantifies the rates of change.

LIFE ON THE FLOODPLAIN

We leave the base of the moraine and hike down through the braids, avoiding the cold muck in the sloughs whenever we can. On the first levee, the crowns of two swamp oaks rise high above the canopy. Their bark is shaggy and rough. But the trees have shed their outer layer of bark up to 10 feet from the soil line. The new bark underneath is shiny and smooth, and the tree reminds me of an old bison bull standing stolidly in the middle of its annual molt.

A scattering of white pines hugs the crests of two of the levees. They are magnificent specimens, with pontifical crowns. That's amazing, considering the lumbering history in this region over the last 150 years. Maybe the trees in the floodplain were too small for the nineteenth-century sawyers to cut. But why do the white pines occupy only two of the many levees? Why don't they cover all the levees? Perhaps the levees on which they now grow are slightly higher. Perhaps there are undetected differences in the soil. One red pine, straight and tall, stands amidst the white pines. How did the red pine get here for its solo performance? Did

the sawyers miss it? We argue about that, but come to no agreement.

Scattered among the levees and brush are pockets of prairie. This must mean that the prairie plants are able to move in fairly quickly, because the terrain and the plant cover here in the floodplain are frequently changed by flooding. Today, the grasses are brown and rustling in the November wind.

The arrival of the Europeans may have played a role in sustaining these pockets. They might have seen them as easier to bring into cultivation than the surrounding woods. At the same time, they would have settled close to the edge of the woods, because they needed logs for split-rail fences and cabins, and for firewood. They may have even, in that process, enlarged the openings and enhanced the chances for the prairie pockets that exist today. The patches of prairies would have re-emerged as the settlers gave up the struggle to grow wheat and corn on this sandy terrain. Across the way are the decaying remnants of an old fence line. I noticed it first because of a strand of barbed wire half-buried in a growing tree trunk.

Further along, the terrain takes on the savanna character, with oak openings interspersed among the grasses. The fires, set just eight months ago, cleared out much of the prickly ash, buckthorn, and dogwood. So this must be the way it looked on a November day 300 years ago.

But that is an illusion. There was a savanna ecology 300 years ago, but it flourished over there on a levee now eroded away. And real bison, not phantoms in the night, grazed on the grasses. The explorers Marquette and Joliet, just down river from here, noted them in their diaries in 1673.

The flowing river has since rebraided the floodplain many times. Water, under the irresistible pull of gravity, slowed by friction, yet propelled by kinetic energy, is the architect of our environment. Water's kinetic force is the final plank in the platform for life. Today, however, the water has settled into brown pools with lacy crystals of white ice.

Over a thousand geese rise from the marsh just south of where we stand. Something brought them off the water a few minutes ago. They swirl in tight eddies, and their calls fill the air and drown out our conversation. Groups of forty or fifty drop one wing and then the other to lose altitude. They lower both feet and sail noisily into the marsh among the willows, and their calls recede.

Is it noon already? Our timing is good. We climb up over the moraine through the pines planted by Aldo Leopold and his family (about 3,000 a year from 1935 through 1947). I scuff my feet in the pine needles coated with frost and estimate the height of the trees. One hundred feet? It's time for lunch. We sit down at the picnic table by the Shack. We've warmed up on the hike, but not because the sun was all that warm. It's that internal combustion. Now I zip up my jacket and hold my coffee cup against my cheek, then eat my sandwich. Charles says, "Let's go." My legs are getting stiff, and I realize my shoes are wet. No arguments. So we walk back up Levee Road.

We come now to another component: the perception of the natural processes by which the land and the living things upon it have achieved their characteristic forms (evolution) and by which they maintain their existence (ecology). That thing called 'nature study,' despite the shiver it brings to the spines of the elect, constitutes the first embryonic groping of the mass-mind toward perception.

Roots & Seeds

To love what was is a new thing under the sun, unknown to most people and to all pigeons. To see America as history, to conceive of destiny as a becoming, to smell a hickory tree through the still lapse of ages—all these things are possible for us, and to achieve them takes only the free sky, and the will to ply our wings.

THE CHANGING MOOD OF SUMMER

Sometime around the first of August there is a mood shift on the prairie. The passions of May, the fertility of June, and the maturity of July have evolved toward the satisfactions of a summer that is beginning to show its age. It's time to slow down. Even the plants are a bit thread-bare. And as the hot August days wear on, satisfaction is a permissible attitude. But, by the end of the month, there is a hint of anxiety in the air. Mist hovers over Center Pond in the morning, and branches on the maples begin to turn.

Some will say such talk imposes a human mood on the land, an anthropomorphic identification with the aging of the year. Perhaps it's true. I'll not argue that point of view. Consider it a concession to aesthetics. It is personally satisfying, in the August years of a human life, to walk deep into the maturing grasses, and to sit on the ground, hidden in their depths, for the closest of examinations of the smaller worlds in which we live. And

besides, the smaller things in life loom larger in August than they did in May.

Deep in the grass, you feel protected from that other world out there, that world of Interstate 90-94 just beyond the terminal moraine, though you cannot completely escape the rumble of trucks and the whine of autos racing toward the end of summer. But if you focus intently on this place, you can shut out the sounds of the highway, hear the whispers of the grasses, and the singing of the insects. There is even a sense that the grasses and insects are listening, as well as talking, remembering as well as maturing.

After you intercept the silk of a spider that is brushing across your face and gently lift the spider off your ear so that she can continue her journey in the sunshine, you can place the palm of your hand on the sandy soil and feel its warmth. It's actually hot to the touch.

Stretch if you must, but do not get up, as the grasses over your head will seem as tall as pine trees, and, from this perspective, the tops of the grasses sway like the pines in the wind, and you feel that your mind has gotten to the bottom of things as well as the top of things. Then, with a stroke of your forefinger in the sand, you can feel the cool moisture that lies just below the surface. The gradient in moisture and temperature gives a hint of something very different in the soil just below, a hint of basements and sub-basements—all of them teeming with occupants.

THE EPIDERMIS WE CALL SOIL

The specialists define soil as the unconsolidated outer layer of the earth's crust, a kind of epidermis. The crust becomes habitable for plants through the weathering of the minerals locked in the rocks on the surface, and with the addition of organic matter. Although the soil around here does have a lot of obdurate silicon dioxide, it is far from sterile. The prairie's epidermis is much more than a tough layer of inanimate crystals and lifeless detritus.

At this point in my reflections I wish I were a mole, nudging my way through the moist soil, searching out juicy grubs. I couldn't see much at all, but I could smell and feel and taste. Would the smells of cool earth seem wonderful? The mole does have advantages over those of us who must sit here under the August sun, wondering about such things.

In the level just below me, in the first

Center Pond

foot of soil, the structure is 50 percent solid minerals and 50 percent pores. At the microscopic level, it would appear as a labyrinth of tiny rooms and corridors. Air, water, and organic matter are major occupants in the complex. No wonder my seat feels more like a cushion than like concrete. However, four feet below me, the soil is about 60 percent solid, and seven feet down it is about 70 percent solid.

THE ROOTS OF THE PRAIRIE

The labyrinth has more in it than minerals, air, and water. There is a vast network of prairie roots and rhizomes. The roots probe to bring up water and nutrients. The rhizomes are stems growing just under or along the ground, sending out roots from the lower surface and leaves or shoots from the upper surface, allowing the plant to spread.

The root habits of each species, and also the community of roots, respond to the environmental conditions in their neighborhoods. The root structure, along with the stems and leaves above, reveals to the plants the fitness of the habitat in which they grow. And grow they do.

The roots of grasses and forbs probe deep into the sand, into the pockets of clay and among the boulders. The roots often extend downward five to six feet, and in some cases up to 10 feet. Great masses of roots weave a dense network of sod and fill the soil profile like tentacles of thousands of jellyfish floating together in a sargasso sea. Up

to 75 percent of the plant biomass is underground.

These networks of roots give the prairie community access to water and nutrients, but also anchor it against wind, rain, drought, snow, and fire. Late in fall, at eye level, the prairie will seem brown and dead. The roots, however, will keep the plants vibrantly alive under the snow. The roots will anchor the plants in the heat and the thrashing thunderstorms of summer.

The plants have adapted to the harsh legacy of quartz, but they are also adapted to the contemporary climatic forces that come with the seasonal changes. The vast expanses of roots express the challenges of competition among the plants for moisture and sunlight, as winter evolves into spring, then full-throated summer, then the nostalgia of autumn.

The roots also express remarkable patterns of coexistence among the species. Some plants have deep roots, others shallow. The legumes share with the grasses the nutrients from their nitrogen-fixing nodules. In the nearby woods, the maple tree draws water from deep below and shares the water with its surface-dwelling neighbors. Holding it all together are the myriad insects—those mound-builders and recyclers.

Life here is an interdependent web, competing but also cooperating.

MOISTURE IS THE DEFINER

Although on this August afternoon I found moisture just below the surface in this sandy soil, I know that grasslands indicate a water budget that is lower than in a forest and certainly lower than a marsh. Even though this midcontinental area is generally humid, conditions below the prairie grasses are drier than the surrounding woodlands, and even drier than the adjacent savanna. With more available moisture, and in the absence of fire, this landscape, in a few decades, could develop shrubs and trees that would maintain themselves with deep root systems. The shrubs and trees would probably occupy the land until they were reduced by a long period of drought or fire.

Aridity, at least in the surface of this sandy soil, is always imminent. A germinating seedling must make immediate and extensive contact with soil moisture, by spreading out or reaching down. The relationship with water is the controlling one, and the success or failure of each seedling depends largely on its ability to develop an absorbing system.

The water table here, as measured through a drilled hole, varies anywhere from 6 to 10 feet below the surface. Below that depth the soil is fully saturated unless the season has been very dry. The level of saturation is primarily a function of how much precipitation is drawn downward by gravitation and how fast the water drains away or evaporates.

In a given spot, the amount of water in the soil above the water table is affected by the capillary fringe. Water adheres to individual soil particles. Sand and gravel will not hold as much

surface water as finer-sized soil particles, like clay, do. A cubic foot of sandy soil will not hold as much water in its upper layers as a cubic foot of loess. Thus the capillary fringe is a kind of "second domain" for water in the ground.

The capillary fringe in sandy soil may extend about two inches above the water table. Clay soils might be heavily saturated nearly up to the surface. The water table and the capillary fringe across a plot of land are not flat like a kitchen table, unless the soil type is very uniform. Terrain with variable soils will have undulations in soil water content. The soils where I sit must be somewhat more sandy than the area just across the way. This spot must have an indentation in the water table; because it hasn't rained for a week, the capillary fringe must be down near the surface of the water table.

Although the prairie plants are obviously aggressive in sending their root systems out in search for water, their growth patterns will be modified by a high water table. Their roots will also be able to accommodate variations in the capillary fringe. This helps explain why some plants thrive on one spot and do not thrive 100 feet away, and why their presence will come and go with changes in precipitation. With a single wet or dry season, there will be an obvious change in the plants that flourish on a particular spot in a given year.

There is also a cybernetic relationship between the river and the level of saturation. This plot of prairie is 2,500 horizontal feet from the river, but less than 20 feet above it during normal flow. An unusual spring flush of water down the river will cause a rise in the groundwater level here over a 10-day period or longer. With the river running full in an unusually wet summer, there will be adjustments among the plants even above and beyond the immediate floodplain, because the water table will rise.

THE ROOTS ARE A PLUMBING SYSTEM

The roots and stems of the plants are a marvelous and complicated "plumbing system." The concentration of dissolved minerals within the system pulls water inward from the soil through osmotic diffusion into root cells, and then into tubes made up of xylem cells. The xylem cells themselves have died, but continue to perform as a plumbing route for the plant.

The osmotic pressures developed in root cells are not large enough to push water up through the plant in high enough amounts to sustain the plant. The driving force for the upward movement of water in the xylem tubes comes from transpiration in the leaves. As water passes out through the stomata, the vapor pressure inside the leaf falls slightly and more water molecules evaporate from the cell surfaces. The water molecules in the cells of the leaf, the xylem tubes, and the cells of the root form a continuous column of liquid water. The cohesive forces in the water column are great enough to move water to the top of even the

tallest oak on the moraine. The pressure created may be 30 times that of the surrounding air pressure.

The water molecules become raw materials for photosynthesis and supply the hydrogen used in the production of carbohydrates. They are also used in plant respiration, the regulation of internal temperature, and as a transport system for nutrients from the soil.

More than half of every prairie plant exists as roots and rhizomes to accomplish the transport of water and nutrients. The underground roots are the more permanent part of the plant, and they change their structure far less, from season to season, than the aboveground structures do. Although the root system of the perennials is sensitive to the level of the water table, as much as 90 percent of it will survive from year to year.

In this complex adaptation to above- and underground conditions, plants are more sophisticated than most animals. Relatively few animal species live both above and below Earth's epidermis. The ones that do, such as ants, appear to be among the most resistant to environmental changes and the best adapted to a wide variety of habitats. For example, some species of leaf-cutter ants have existed symbiotically with a single fungus strain for over 20 million years. The ants "farm" the fungus in their underground nests to predigest the leaves that they have cut from aboveground plants.

Root systems of plant species vary strikingly, which hints that it's not

Prairie Grasses

always a competitive "war of the underground." The variation reveals elements of accommodation in a neighborhood of niches. The root system of the big bluestem, beneath where I'm sitting this afternoon, forms a dense net of rhizomes just below the surface. The abundant roots then descend almost vertically from the base of the plant and its network of rhizomes, forming a dense sod. The larger roots can reach seven feet down, with profuse branching as they descend. Big bluestem, to support its large above-ground structure, is aggressive in its deep pursuit of water. Consequently, it is not well suited to the drier terrain on top of the sand moraine.

Prairie bunch grasses, such as needlegrass, Junegrass, little bluestem, and prairie dropseed, grow spreading showers of roots that interlock with each other. In profile, the roots of a single plant resemble the beard of a biblical patriarch. The deepest of the bunch-grass roots will be about five feet down. The bunch grasses will compete in the same location as big bluestem, but will also survive in the drier areas.

Tucked in among the more obvious grasses are the forbs, the broad-leafed, herbaceous plants. The number of species of forbs in a prairie plot is much greater than the grasses; as many as 150 species can exist in a given location. More than 90 percent of the forbs are perennial.

Root systems of the forbs also vary greatly. Some, like the liatris, have deep taproots with widely spreading branches that can go down as far as 15 to 20 feet if necessary. Others, like the snakeroot, develop branched roots with laterals in the top one to two feet. A third group, like the coneflower, have several taproots that penetrate deeply. Other forbs, like the asters, develop networks of rhizomes with root off-shoots.

THE AGGRESSIVE OAK

In sharp contrast to the root systems of the grasses and forbs is the life support system of the bur oak on the edge of the moraine. The tree is nearly 40 feet tall and the spread of its branches is about as much. Its basal trunk is probably 16 inches in diameter. Its taproot will be about 15 feet deep, and has side roots that spread out laterally for about 60 feet before turning downward for 15 feet or so. Some of these roots will have turned vertically upward and filled the surface soil with a network of rootlets. The weight of the roots and their volume will equal that of the top of the tree. It's clear that the ability of the bur oak to survive in dry conditions is directly related to its root system. It may be the toughest competitor around here.

Thus the stems and leaves and flowers of the grasses and the forbs exist in the upper floors of a tiered community. The aboveground structure is, as a rule of thumb, about half as tall as the roots are deep. For the grasses and forbs, the aboveground structure gradually ceases growth and dies with the approach of winter. Virtually all of it will yield to the changing seasons. The detritus from these dying stems and leaves will return more minerals and carbohydrates to the soil than the green plants in their photosynthetic stages have taken away. So the

prairie soil, over time, increases its store of potential energy and becomes the teeming home of bacteria, fungi, and worms. Silicon dioxide is not such an unfriendly place, after all.

SEEDS: THE SECOND STRATEGY FOR SURVIVAL

It is obvious on this August afternoon that things are slowing down for this year. The big bluestem is turning from green to purple-brown. High above my head, its seed fronds are clawing the air, and they do look like the name the pioneers gave them—turkey feet.

Although complex and persistent rooting is an obvious strategy for plant survival, the ability to produce those seeds is just as important. Seeds do have the advantage of a faster geographic mobility than roots and rhizomes, but more than that, they have genetic adaptability to changing environmental conditions that are more slow-moving than the seasons or the coming and going of generations of perennials—or even slower than the emergence and extinction of species.

Evolution has produced two major categories of seed-producing plants. The most primitive plants are the bare-seeded gymnosperms, which include not only that copse of white pine on the third levee, but also the cycads and the gingkos. The other category is the angiosperms, whose seeds are surrounded by an extra layer of fruity tissue, and often by a very durable seed coat.

Although some gymnosperms thrive

Spiderwort

here, the angiosperms are by far the more common in numbers and species. There are two chief groups of angiosperms: (1) plants with parallel-veined leaves, such as grasses, lilies, and orchids, and (2) plants with net-veined leaves, such as deciduous trees, perennial shrubs, and herbaceous forbs.

August is a good month to examine the seeds in our neighborhood, and these are some of the ones I can see from my seat down here at the bottom of things. Big bluestem is one of the more obvious. The seed heads at the tops of the long stalks branch into three parts. Indiangrass carries a single seed head that is up to eight inches tall, and the flower clusters are filled with short, soft, golden-brown hairs.

The intense blue of the spiderwort flowers faded several weeks ago. The plant put out repeated blooms atop a single stem, and clumps of seed heads now lie drooping above the ground. The bergamot still persists in blooming, but the seed heads are forming in multiple terminal clusters. The purple prairie-clover is developing long batons of seed heads on its slender and erect stalks.

Looking at the baptisia I can tell that it is a classic legume with bulbous pods. The pod can be split open to show two sides that are almost perfectly symmetrical, each with a row of eight or nine ebony seeds. Almost all the pods have been invaded by weevils. Curiously, the seeds in the pods not invaded by the insect do not appear fertile.

Prairie dropseed has a fountain of fine stalks crowned by a cluster of pin-head seeds that are waxy and smell spicy if you strip them from the stem. The individual seeds of Indiangrass, maturing in a tassel, are bronze and shiny. Butterfly weed sends out little parachutes, each containing a black seed.

The spring ephemeral forbs, their blooms so obvious four months ago, developed very different characters as the season progressed. Jack in the pulpit formed clusters of bright red fruits, and Dutchman's breeches formed fleshy fruits.

In time, and with some breathing space, the seeds will propagate and the species will spread across the land. But it is also possible to collect the seeds and give nature a boost. There are complexities in the natural processes of savannas and prairies, and humans have not learned about all of them. There are new discoveries almost every season.

Germination rates vary widely. For example, in some years germination of the coneflower may be 100 percent. Next year, it may be 50 percent. There must be a seasonal effect that remains hidden from us. Three years ago we planted a dozen bur oak seedlings in Charles's pasture. Five have survived and the foot-tall trees are growing. But

maybe that's an excellent ratio in the natural course of things.

THE SEED IS A BLUEPRINT

Within every viable seed lies hidden from direct inspection the formula for a living individual. Animals carry the formula in tiny gamete cells, but plant seeds have something animals do not. The fertilized embryo can remain dormant in the ripened seed and can thus be dispersed over great distances and survive extreme conditions of drought and cold. Recently botanists have dis-

Jack in the Pulpit

covered a noncrystalline sugar derivative in the coat of the seeds that acts as a preservative, perhaps for hundreds or even thousands of years. The pollen grains also carry a preservative. Animal sperm and even embryos have been frozen and preserved, but preservation of the gamete or the embryo is not a strategy that animals naturally use.

There is now evidence that lupine seeds have survived in dormancy under glacial conditions for over 10,000 years. Perhaps they could survive in cold storage through a glaciation of 60,000 years, and could germinate in the early stages of an interglacial. At least some plants have the capability of a millennial hibernation. A few animals can hibernate for a winter season, but most must forage through the harsh conditions, or must migrate annually. Certainly all but a very few must migrate in the face of a millennium of winters. Perhaps some animals never learn how to migrate successfully. Without rapid evolution, they would be doomed by the cycles of glaciation.

This intricate savanna blueprint is more than sand, water, and sunlight. It is more than a genetic code called up for processing and editing via electrical pulses within organisms. It is the expression of time itself. It has a tenacity that is a creation of the ages. There is a memory implicit in what I see. Do I see enough to care? That becomes a question of aesthetics as well as reason.

The birch is an abundant tree in my township and becoming more so, whereas pine is scarce and becoming scarcer; perhaps my bias is for the underdog. But what would I do if my farm were further north, where pine is abundant and red birch is scarce? I confess I don't know. My farm is here.

The pine will live for a century, the birch for half that; do I fear that my signature will fade? My neighbors have planted no pines but all have many birches; am I snobbish about having a woodlot of distinction? The pine stays green all winter, the birch punches the clock in October; do I favor the tree that, like myself, braves the winter wind?

PHENOLOGY

The tamaracks change from green to yellow when the first frosts have brought woodcock, fox sparrows, and juncos out of the north. Troops of robins are stripping the last white berries from the dogwood thickets, leaving the empty stems as a pink haze against the hill. The creekside alders have shed their leaves, exposing here and there an eyeful of holly. Brambles are aglow, lighting your footsteps grouseward.

AN EARLY DEPARTURE

At noon today, in a clear October sky, skein after skein of geese flew high and directly overhead, headed west by south. They'll likely bivouac tonight in the Mississippi River bottoms along southern Iowa. We were eating lunch and watching the nuthatches and the white-throated sparrows jostling around the feeders outside on the deck.

The geese are on the wing! Hearing them and tumbling outside, we counted a dozen long arrows between here and the horizon.

The geese were calling to each other from deep in this echo chamber, as they always do in autumn. A skein of "locals" lifted off the river. But those birds circled and returned to the water. Not all the geese are ready to leave.

There's no doubt some of them are on their way, though they could have lingered another month, or maybe even over winter. The ground and the sloughs have not frozen over. The farmers are still harvesting corn—the geese could glean the fields until snow buries the stubble, and they could crowd into open water in the main course of the river.

Maybe the cold snap has moved them out. Maybe they saw that the hunters were out scouting the marsh and repairing the blinds. Their behavior today is not what we expected.

Quite suddenly, the discipline in a skein high overhead broke down. The bird in the lead faltered. The arrow fractured as the geese argued, and they pitched into chaos. Some veered back toward the north. Others swirled in a circle. Some lost elevation. Birds in the neighboring skein saw the commotion and lost their resolution.

Then, in the next moment, a single goose, smaller than the rest, struck out again to the southwest. Indecision vanished. Within seconds, the geese reformed the arrow, and we followed them with our eyes and ears until they were dissolving dots above the hori-

Geese in the Cornfield

zon. But why are the geese leaving sooner than our phenological charts predicted they would?

A ridge of high pressure had moved in during the night behind a surge of low pressure moving now toward the east coast. In the northern hemisphere, high pressure generates a great dome of air flooding downward and then laterally outward in every direction from its center in a clockwise swirl, like water suddenly released from an overturned bell. By afternoon, the downflowing air had cleared away the turbulence of a week of stormy weather. The center of the high must have been settling in right over us at the moment

the geese had doubts. Did a downward surge of air throw the geese off course? Or was the leader attracted to a glint of water from the river?

Before the geese flew over, I had been confident that a high pressure system in autumn clears my mind as well as it clears the troposphere. But the wavering of the geese, and then their decision to continue, made me not so sure. Do the geese know something I don't know? There must be reasons for the departure of so many. Is there an anticipation of things to come? Or is it circumstantial? With this migration, we'll just have to refigure the arithmetic means in the phenological data, and compare the departure of the geese to what other gleanings we can sift out of the data.

PHENOLOGICAL EXPRESSION

Phenologists measure expressions of living creatures in relation to seasonal changes in the environment. The environment varies, but it is not chaotic. It has deterministic features that are framed by inherent physical conditions. Living creatures have a chance to experience, to experiment, to learn, and to predict within a set of physical boundaries. It is a characteristic of all species that individuals make mistakes. Sometimes entire species get out of synch with the environment as the mistakes pile up. But the chain of life on Earth goes on.

While phenology is the study of periodic biological phenomena such as flowering, breeding, and migration, the dimension of time is a vital part of the definition, because climate, and even geological conditions, do change over time. For example, Earth's magnetic field and the path of its orbit change with time. The phenological expressions respond most obviously to the seasonal changes but also to the long-term changes. Evolution is the consequence of many short-term failures, but also long-term adjustments.

The geese have memories of the glaciers deep in their brain stems. Their migration during glaciation wouldn't have been the 2,500 to 3,000 miles they fly today, because the distance from permafrost to open winters would have been shorter. And they surely have memories of the last interglacial, a time similar to this, and long annual migrations from the Arctic to the Gulf of Mexico. In this sense, their behavior seems quite predetermined when measured in the passage of millennia.

As I hear their wild cries of freedom that fill the autumn sky, I long to fly with them, but the freedom to leave winter behind is a relative thing—even for the geese. Am I really destined to stay behind, here on the prairie? I understand that winter brings competition. Why do I stay? What opportunities do I see here? Is it the opportunity implicit in competition?

Competition plays a fundamental role in the continuation of life. Adjustment to risk is the strategy for survival of the fittest. Resources are limited. There is a cause-and-effect relationship between natural resources and responses. That becomes obvious as the responses become visible through taxonomical, physiological, and phenological expressions.

Humans are now on a vast experimental journey that is, in many ways, a defiance of phenological expression. We have concluded that we can reduce the risks that are inherent in nature. A major way to do that is to reduce competition by eliminating some competitors and building barriers to others. There are also massive attempts to reduce variations in the environment.

We do not know yet if there will be enough available energy to maintain these efforts to control nature.

We do not yet know the consequences of unraveling nature's tapestries. Through science, humans are also beginning to understand the roots of phenological expression and maybe even to appreciate the value of those expressions.

PHENOLOGICAL EXPRESSION ON EARTH

The earliest prokaryotic cells may have emerged on Earth some three billion years ago. They developed the capability of responding to environmental variables. It is a strategy that has served bacteria well even to this day. Bacteria remain by far the most abundant expression of life on Earth.

Very early in the evolution of life on Earth, eukaryotic cells, containing nuclei, appeared. The nuclei allowed the cells to increase their capability for storing experience. It took about 2.5 billion years for the eukaryotic cells to develop specialization and to form complex multicellular organisms. Another 500 million years have passed, and it is only in the last two million years that *Homo sapiens* has emerged with the capabilities that flow from consciousness.

Most of the composite learning on Earth by individual cells and organisms has taken the path of fixed-action patterns. These patterns are passed along in the genes from generation to generation, whether by cloning or mating. Phenological expression is certainly rooted in these fixed-action patterns.

The fixed-action patterns in both cells and organisms are inherited and can be labeled instinctual. All of earth's prokaryotic cells, eukaryotes, and organisms, including humans, rely fundamentally on programmed instinct. But some expressions are also learned through individual experience. We don't really know whether bacteria, or for that matter plants, have the ability to learn through individual experience. However, the division between the modes of expressions—between programmed and learned—may be misleading, since no organism is independent of the physical world.

Both modes are strong. For example, all organisms carry the genes of individuality. Geneticists feel that they are nearing the point where they will be able to identify any individual through its unique genetic fingerprint—even among insects. The exception would be an individual reproduced through cloning. Philosophers and practitioners argue about the strength of nature and the influence of nurture, as if the two were somehow separable. However, reality is a complex blend of the two.

At the level of nature, it is true that any cell division has the possibility to establish a new characteristic through mutation. Mating of two gametes also produces new combinations. The mutations, however, are a fraction of the total and not enough to preclude identification through DNA analysis. Mutations introduce the possibility of experimentation. However, experimentation is always accompanied by risk. Nurture frames the risk.

Phenological expression is, accordingly, the sum of fixed-action patterns and experimentation. This is surely the boldest and most important lesson in phenology. Thus, we are committed to asking: What are the driving forces in the physical earth that create phenological expression? Why do living cells and organisms respond the way they do?

The fundamental forces lie in the universal order of atoms and molecules. There is determinism in the basic laws of physics and chemistry. That would be true on any planet. But, for life on this planet, there are also unique relationships among sunlight, water, and land. This makes Earth a phenological entity, and almost certainly unique.

The volume of sunlight reaching Earth is quantifiable and predictable. The output of the sun does not vary widely across the millennia. In another four billion years or so, however, the sun will burn out.

On the scale of a year, the seasonal changes in energy arriving at a given spot on Earth are also quite predictable. Summer does follow spring. We are assured that winter will return, even at the equator. Such a thought makes tolerable the extreme variations in weather that test the living creatures here on the prairie.

But at the next level of analysis, variation comes more strongly into play. Variations in weather from year to year occur everywhere on the surface of our planet, which is not uniform. There is a complex process of adjustment in the internal energy balance between oceans, and land, mountains and plains, and troposphere and stratosphere. The feedback mechanisms are barely understood.

In sum, there is a random display of weather, layered on a less random pattern of climate, layered on an essentially deterministic astronomical pattern.

The exquisite, complex fabric of phenology on Earth is also an extension of this planet's unique physical history. We should be humbled as we learn that this history could not possibly have been replicated on any other planet, even though the physical and chemical laws are cosmological. Perhaps planets do have common characteristics at creation, but they evolve differently.

TODAY'S AFFAIRS

To assess today's state of affairs, I must accept that I live in one place and in one time. I'll see if I can learn anything from my cohorts on the prairie and in the savanna this afternoon.

The gray squirrels are out racing around on the ground under the bur oaks, burying acorns. The red squirrel darts around them. The squirrels have worked hard this year, because the pickings have been lean.

A pair of aggressive red-breasted nuthatches, both males, are fluttering around the bird feeder on the deck. One of them is trying to drive the other away as they fly from the grape vine to the deck, snatch seeds, and fly back. The second male is persistent, and he is not going hungry. I wonder if they are siblings.

The nuthatches are fairly common winter residents in the sand country.

Hepatica

But this is the first time they have been at the feeding station this year. They obviously sense an opportunity this morning. But, they may not show up tomorrow.

The white-throated sparrows are twitting around on the outer branches of the black oak, waiting for the nuthatches to calm down. The first of them arrived from the north on September 24. At dawn we heard the three descending notes of their clear, high whistle. The sparrows summered in northern Wisconsin, along the southern shores of Lake Superior, and they will winter in the deep south— along the Gulf of Mexico. I hope they'll stick around here for a week. Maybe they won't. I cannot deduce the signals in their neurons today.

But I am relatively sure that when the white-throated sparrows come back around April 15, the hepatica should be in bloom. These adventurous little flowers will burst forth in shades of pink along the edge of the woods, showing their first bloom any time from very late March to late April. On a cloudy day, they will seem reticent, but on a magical, sunny morning, each flower will spread its petals and reveal its white stamens and yellow stigma. The sparrows will be much more predictable in the precise time of their arrival than the hepatica. Maybe the sparrows have made an advance reservation in their genes.

In spite of our wonderment about the "whens" of phenology, there are some underlying behavioral patterns. The four of us will continue our discussion about the "whys." The birds that migrate a long distance arrive close to the dates of their predicted arrival. Thus a narrow margin of error in our prediction. However, the local creatures, both plants and animals, adjust their seasonal behavior depending on the local opportunities and risks that change widely from year to year. Thus, a wider margin of error in the prediction.

To be so targeted in their migration, the white-throated sparrows must have some means of integrating the amount of sunlight across the latitudes as the season progresses.

Something also triggers the geese when they depart from the tundra breeding grounds 1,500 miles north of here in late August. Perhaps migration is set in motion by declining sunlight or by a memory of last year's early blizzard on the tundra. But perhaps it is a change in the nutrients in the tundra plants on which they forage. The tundra plants may send their sugars down into the root systems at a predictable time. The geese could tell this by taste, and they might know about the sweet forage in our ponds, prairies, and cornfields down here at 44° North.

When the white-throated sparrows do return next spring, it is quite possible that the pasque flowers will already have withered. They can bloom here as early as the last week in March. Hugging the ground with their lusty purple flowers, they are adapted to the driest and sandiest hillsides. They will emerge from among the brown oak leaves and be assailed by icy winds. The pasque flowers are always among the first on stage in the theatre of spring. But why? Are they adapted to the sudden flush of photons in a spring sun, but not to the shady conditions generated by taller plants later in the season?

The skunk cabbage and the pussy willows, adapted to wetter environments than the pasque flower, will also make their entrance while we are still hoping for spring. But their opportunistic blooming also quickly gives way to the other species that crowd the second act of our seasonal drama. The earliest blooming plants do seem to have found their route to early spring stardom by avoiding the competition for light from the oncoming surge of awakening species.

As we observe the myriad comings and goings—the peenting of the woodcock in early March, the intense purple stalks of liatris in July, the blue-purple hues of the gentians in September—I realize how intricately associated the biological players are with their physical stage.

Seasons, latitude, and topography are the canvas on which the scenery is painted. Temperature, water, soil, and sunlight provide the text of the play. Nature's cast of plants and animals fills the stage to overflowing with their arias and their soliloquies.

The early spring blooming of the pasque flower doesn't seem logical at all from a human perspective. Why enter and leave the stage so quickly? The migration of the geese seems more logical. I certainly envy them as they migrate south. But I also have the urge to put down roots on a piece of land and to stay around for all four of the seasonal acts. And we humans alone

Purple Aster

indulge ourselves in a critical review after the annual closing curtain. We seem almost lonesome in our concerns with fate.

THE PHENOLOGY OF HUMANS

I've known about the relationships of sunlight, water, carbon, oxygen, and hydrogen since the concepts were presented in freshman biology. That was enough to set in motion a curiosity about natural science.

And yet, on this lazy October afternoon, there is something more. What are the phenological expressions of humans? Do we have any? Humans might easily conclude that phenology is the contemplation of all those other species. In that process, it might even occur to us that human phenological expressions are somehow blasphemous, given our ability to reason. And yet, here in this place in October, I do feel immersed in sunshine and content with the season.

It occurs to me that consciousness is really a thin veneer on the surface of life. There is surely willful expression, but the concept of free will remains circumscribed by fixed-action patterns and patterns of learning.

It seems mighty risky for humans to assume that we are the audience, are merely observers and critics, and not phenological players. It is true that we can stand aside and analytically applaud or criticize the performance. We do, from time to time, get caught up in it emotionally: we shout with joy, weep a tear, applaud what we see. We are amazed at the return of the little brown bats.

Are such emotions merely a critic's reaction, or are they also phenological behavior? Which of my behaviors, which of my thoughts, are fixed-action patterns? Probably more than I am willing to admit, even on such a clear afternoon as this. Perhaps I worry too much about reason and logic. Perhaps it sometimes fails me.

WINTER IS COMING

And now, just a week later, October is coming to a close. The sky is dull gray. Snow is falling north of here, across the southern shore of Lake Superior. We can hope there will be an inch or so on the local prairie before morning.

We're ready. The root cellar is full of russet potatoes, carrots, parsnips, winter beets, and celery root from the vegetable garden. The sauerkraut has fermented to perfection.

The woodpile is high, and the odor of new-cut oak flows through the back door every time I open it. The compost has been turned for the final time this year, and the storm windows are up.

Beth has taken down the hummingbird feeder and put up the suet. On the Aldo Leopold Reserve, Nina has for-aged the prairie for the last seeds of the prairie plants. She has stored the seeds in paper bags hanging from the rafters on the sleeping porch.

Now it is time for Charles and Nina to sit before the fire and transfer this year's dates to the permanent phenological record.

TIME FOR DREAMING

As the fire dies low and the oak coals glow, I think once more of Earth as a phenological entity. Some distant observers could be keeping track of Earth's expressions this very evening. What observations would they seek to make? Atomic and molecular composition? Temperature? Atmospheric circulation? The existence of life? Variations in all of these from year to year? Would their instruments be precise enough to record the migration of the geese? Would they note the November emergence of the snowplow on County Trunk T?

Then, from outside in the darkness, I hear them. More of the geese are leaving at this very moment. It sounds as if the arrow is flying straight and true, south by west, and they are not hesitating now.

Next March? I'll be outdoors, standing in the face of a chill wind, when I hear the geese, calling again.

. . . The forest landscape is deprived of a certain exuberance which arises from a rich variety of plants fighting with each other for a place in the sun. It is almost as if the geological clock had been set back to those dim ages when there were only pines and ferns. I never realized before that the melodies of nature are music only when played against the undertones of evolutionary history.

CULTURE OF THE LAND

Preceding page: Geese on Center Pond

STANDING BACK, WE REALIZE CLEARLY THAT THIS PRAIRIE AND SAVANNA could only have come to pass through a process of natural experimentation over very long reaches of time. One can be stunned by the length of time involved, and it can be hard to accept the fact that humans are latecomers, just a dot at the end of the scale. There are moments when I am depressed if I compare the amount of time involved to my personal allotment. Humans have a deep ambivalence about time. We long for the fountain of youth even as we enter our personal golden autumns. We struggle to understand the impact of aging on our psyches. There never seems to be enough of time—for us.

However, as the concept of time begins to expand in our minds, we praise its consequences in all the ongoing life around us, including the evolution of species exquisitely adapted to this time and this place. Then, the passage of time becomes a joy. This understanding of time is the real magic revealed in a close examination of the prairie, the savanna, and the woodlands, as the seasons change and decades roll by.

The deep roots of the prairie grasses can also be compared to our own roots in the natural landscape. The persistence of the prairie grass in the sandy soil becomes a metaphor for all life. Aldo Leopold questioned whether we value the inherent physical and biological strengths in our own roots, or whether we cut ourselves off from our natural inheritance in a blind

and advancing confidence with technology:

> The pigeon was a biological storm. He was the lightning that played between two opposing potentials of intolerable intensity: the fat of the land and the oxygen of the air. Yearly the feathered tempest roared up, down, and across the continent, sucking up the laden fruits of forest and prairie, burning them in a traveling blast of life. Like any other chain reaction, the pigeon could survive no diminution of his own furious intensity. When the pigeoners subtracted from his numbers, and the pioneers chopped gaps in the continuity of his fuel, his flame guttered out with hardly a sputter or even a wisp of smoke.
>
> Today the oaks still flaunt their burden at the sky, but the feathered lightning is no more. Worm and weevil must now perform slowly and silently the biological task that once drew thunder from the firmament. (*A Sand County Almanac,* p. 111)

Some argue that there is no loss in the passenger pigeon. The passenger pigeons had their day. Others are bereaved at the loss of the experience of seeing them. But there is clearly something more—a sense of values. In Leopold's words:

> For the first time in the history of the human species, two changes are now impending. One is the exhaustion of wilderness in the more habitable portions of the globe. The other is the world-wide hybridization of cultures through modern transport and industrialization. Neither can be prevented, and perhaps should not be, but the question arises whether, by some slight

amelioration of the impending changes, certain values can be preserved that would otherwise be lost. (*A Sand County Almanac*, p. 188)

So, what are these values? There are aesthetic values in the prairie landscape that are basically sensory. There are intellectual values in understanding the complex relationships inherent in nature. These sensory and intellectual experiences can be profound as cultures graduate from fearing wild things to respecting them. The growing understanding of how human survival is deeply rooted in nature is even more profound. Humans could make a series of fatal mistakes for our species in our attempts to synthesize and control. We could "normalize" our environment to the point where we lose track of where our future really lies. Or perhaps we could engineer ourselves to prosper in a glacial-age climate or

live submerged in a shallow, tropical ocean.

A canny observer in the field, Leopold understood this intuitively 50 years ago, a half-century ahead of most of his compatriots, as he laid out an ethic based in respect for the land. The knowledge we now have about the environment was not as readily available to Leopold as it is to us today. Biologists and physical scientists have learned a great deal more about the natural web of life and about our role in it. There is now a scientifically rational basis for Leopold's approach to our relationships with the land.

This knowledge is at two levels. First, ecologists are gathering empirical evidence of how species interrelate to maintain a stable position in the physical environment. It is the interrelationships of species, more than the success of a given species, that forms a

Bee Balm and Black-eyed Susan

supportive shield. Second, natural scientists are developing theoretical understandings of patterns of complexity in the natural world and how those patterns are interdependent. As the structure is understood, the importance of Leopold's land ethic becomes more apparent and more critical. As humans gain in these kinds of understandings, there will be an imperative to adapt our patterns of development. The issue then is whether humans will embrace the land ethic in their own phenological expressions. The ethic could become a culture.

That requires restructuring the way we think about time and about Earth. To adopt this culture will require embracing time. We do yearn for a personal fountain of youth in the increasing daylight of a dawning spring day. There is also a sense in us that we can refabricate the land. It even seems possible that we can gain security by steadily increasing our control of the environment around us. We certainly try. But on an aging day in summer we retain doubts about the immortality of youth. And we need to nourish some doubts about our skills at fabrication. Such a view is neither pessimistic nor fatalistic. Rather it is an ongoing search for a natural culture based in an ethic of understanding the land.

This part of our account concludes with a story of fantasy—an examination of another world in another solar system. In that world, a sentient species, having evolved through many more millennia than humans on Earth, believes it has conquered its environment, albeit with some help from natural forces. That species has solved all the problems of environmental risk, or at least assumes it has. In that process, it seems to have rejected all ideas of "free will." In that process, the species has also lost track of what is happening beyond its own planet. But nature will have its say, even out in the cosmos.

PRAIRIE TIME

The particular oak now aglow on my andirons grew on the bank of the old emigrant road where it climbs the sandhill. The stump, which I measured upon felling the tree, has a diameter of 30 inches. It shows 80 growth rings, hence the seedling from which it originated must have laid its first ring of wood in 1865, at the end of the Civil War. But I know from the history of present seedlings that no oak grows above the reach of rabbits without a decade or more of getting girdled each winter, and re-sprouting during the following summer. Indeed, it is all too clear that every surviving oak is the product either of rabbit negligence or of rabbit scarcity. Some day some patient botanist will draw a frequency curve of oak birth-years, and show that the curve humps every ten years, each hump originating from a low in the ten-year rabbit cycle. (A fauna and flora, by this very process of perpetual battle within and among species, achieve collective immortality.)

The Romans named February the month of expiation. Of atonement! February can certainly impose upon us a two-dimensional world.

As I look through the window, the February land and sky seem as flat as a monochromatic etching. The trees are glued to a gray parchment. There is no third dimension from here to the horizon. The February temperature is fixed at 20°F, and the cloud cover remains unbroken. Earth is resigned, it seems, to boredom born of uniformity. And February seems the longest month of the year! Why does time weigh so heavily in February?

Across January, the sky had brightened steadily after the winter solstice, and the new year seemed to be accelerating. Snowstorms howled intermittently. But in between, the air crystallized, and the eastern star lingered brightly through dawn. And now it is February, so uniform it seems the product of a technological fix. I seem to march through time that is measured in equal units, from the first to the twenty-eighth. Nature's days seem as uniform as the institutional calendar on the wall. Each one is reduced to a square framed in four right angles.

The clock is also institutional. It is round, with a brown rim, and with a 10-inch diameter. The digits on the face of the clock are clean, black, and ascetic, commanding atonement. Precisely every 60 seconds, the black minute hand comes to attention and moves like a soldier in a platoon, with a click of his heels. Between now and this time tomorrow, the minute hand will snap to attention precisely 1,440 times on the parade ground of time. The hour hand, like the company commander, will demand a response from me, each hour, from reveille to retreat.

But the clock also has a sweep second hand. This hand is thin and light, and blue, and flows along relentlessly, moving across the markers on the clock. The second hand, between now and this time tomorrow, will have flowed without hesitation by 86,400 way stations on the clock's circumference. Is it the chaplain, seeking to purify time?

I stare at the clock. It hangs there, just above eye level on the wall, inscrutable, its face not making eye contact with me, secure in its units of 60 seconds and 60 minutes, of 12 and 24 hours. How regular! How perfect! How predictable! Do we all fall in line, marching along with the clock?

Time is predictable, isn't it? By the clock it is. But somewhere outside this box of a room, time is relative. Time and space have curvature. They yield to the force of gravity and can disappear in a black hole. Outside, the predictions of the clock are not reality. Perhaps we should search for our sense of momentum on this cold February day, somewhere out there, where electromagnetism and gravity take over from the clock.

SHAKING OFF THE FEVER

It's clearly time to shake off the cabin fever and see what's really happening outdoors in the neighborhood. It's time to put on skis and go out.

The four of us ski across the mesic prairie. From somewhere down in the woods, we hear the unmistakable two-note song of spring. The male chickadee is staking out his territory.

As we cross the road and ski down among the levees, breaking trail through the deep new snow, there is the unmistakable odor of a skunk. We smell him. Does he smell spring?

We pause under a young black oak to catch our breath. Last year's leaves still cling to the branches, and they start to rustle—so softly we must stop chatting and hold our breath to hear them. But the cadence of the rustling leaves picks up. A cardinal startles us when he punctuates the air like a solo clarinet.

Down by Helland Slough, the ice has broken away from the bank and brown water is surging through. Farther out from shore, a shelf of ice has crystals on its surface the shape and color of hepatica blossoms. Just upriver, in open water, two goldeneye ducks see us. They take off with a splash of trailing feet and circle out of sight.

The snowbanks along the trail are thick with the tracks of deer and the spots where they bedded down last night. They had made hollows in the snow nearby to paw out acorns. The white-footed mice have left footprints, each set marked by the line of a trailing tail.

Winter Oak

Out here in the woods, in spite of last night's storm, life is already accelerating.

THE NATURE OF BONDING

Humans are the only creatures who have bonded with the calendar and the clock. If we reconsidered a bonding with the land, what would that do to our sense of time?

As we examine the animal tracks in the February snow, it is possible, in the mind's eye, to slow things down enough to examine the relationships between the land and time. I think about it, as we ski back across long blue shadows. Evening is approaching. Night will soon settle in. Morning will follow. Then another, and another.

What then is the nature of time, if it is not a two-dimensional clock or calendar on the wall? It is obvious that nature does not express time in a series of flat circles or rectangles. Rather the expression is four-dimensional. There are the three dimensions of space—on this prairie, on this earth, and in this solar system. There is depth. Time is the fourth dimension. Given time, Earth's days are embedded within seasons, seasons within years, then centuries and millennia, epochs, and eras—each fitting within the next.

The underlying structure of seasonal time is defined by the earth in its rotation and its orbit. I can measure the delightful progress from day to night as I track the sun's chariot. I measure the coming and going of the annual seasonal chapters by four points on the annual Earth-Sun calendar. These points are the vernal and autumnal equinoxes and the winter and summer solstices.

On the two equinoxes, March 21 and September 21, the sun is directly over the equator, so that night and day are equal on those two magical moments. On the summer solstice, June 21, the sun is directly over the Tropic of Cancer, exactly 23 degrees and 27 minutes north of the equator. The sun is directly over the Tropic of Capricorn, exactly 23 degrees and 27 minutes south of the equator, on the winter solstice, December 21.

The earth rotates like a spinning top and orbits elliptically. The behavior of the earth's solstices and equinoxes varies in a series of rhythms that repeat themselves. After understanding the rhythmic variation, I can predict the exact moment of the solstices and equinoxes from year to year, down to seconds on the clock. The time of arrival is not constant, but it is predetermined.

Earth may be an irascible child, but Old Sol is still in control.

THE CHANGING SEASONS

The biological tension zone that is the backdrop for this prairie is thus related to its location halfway between the equator and the pole. And now, in this interglacial time, in winter's atmosphere, the circumpolar vortex of the north is dominant. In winter the polar air commands more of the hemisphere than in summer, with north-to-south meridional patterns. These meridional flows can lock the land in weeks of subzero temperatures. In summer the polar winds retreat northward. In spring, the weather is punctuated by tornadic clashes as the westerlies surge across the continent and draw moisture from the Gulf of Mexico.

It is at this latitude, near 44° North, that the seasonal changes are so remarkable. If we consider our morning hike on December 21, I can imagine that I am in the beginnings of a glacial age. Indeed, in January this year the temperature did not rise above zero for 10 straight days. If I hike the same trail on June 21 the air will be humid, and the place will seem tropical, as if frost were unknown in this land. Spring and fall are periods of exquisite change, swinging rapidly between the winter and summer extremes. The plants and animals respond in spring to the increasing flow of solar energy and the accelerating change in temperature, with great bursts of growth, and they retreat in the fall. However, the story of the plants is really about the beat of glacial cycles, and I must speak of prairie time as defined by millennia, even by geological epochs, because the tension zone is not fixed in place across the millennia.

BIOLOGICAL TIME

The plants can also tell me about time in seasonal terms, especially the time when they emerge in spring, the time they produce their flowers and seeds across summer, and the time it takes for those seeds to migrate and colonize.

Flowering, for some plants like the skunk cabbage, occurs as early as the spring equinox in March at the edge of melting snow. Others, like the gentians, do not bloom until September. These are phenological expressions. The plants have found a thousand opportunistic niches in the soil. Their behavior is interwoven with the behavior of the insects and the animals, both the residents and the migrators.

The actual phenological expressions of life are not as exact as the seasonal calendar, but are predictable within a certain margin of error. The month-to-month and day-to-day patterns of temperature and rainfall, as well as the variable flow of solar energy, circumscribe the rhythms of plant behavior. Sometimes the atmosphere is clear and sometimes opaque. Some years rainfall is heavy, with the sandy soil here water-logged; and sometimes there is a drought and the sand crystals fill the sky. Sometimes a harsh winter kills an overpopulation of deer, and the plants recover. Someday the glacier will return.

In this sandy land, at the vernal equinox, in this interglacial time, spring life is only beginning to stir—but I mark the moment, because it gives assurance that spring's full blush, with the emergence of the ephemeral

Dutchman's Breeches

flowers, is very near. I can tabulate the dates of emergence and of arrival, anticipating the moment of flowering.

When will the pasque flower bloom in defiance of the retreating snow? When will the woodcock peent in the middle of a velvet spring evening? When will the fringed gentian burst forth in a final defiance of approaching winter? And when will the last Canada geese leave Turner Pond for their winter rendezvous in the south?

The charts reveal that the phenology of the Wisconsin prairie is indeed more subtle and more complex than I could possibly imagine if my views were fixed on the clock and the calendar in this room and in this place.

Out there beyond these local moraines is another, very different, world. It is the world of the great sweeping plains, where the prairie is big and bold, and the shining mountains float like a suspended mirage on the horizon. Out west I can chart the summer storms like distant islands, with drifting rain that does not reach the ground, an hour away, surrounded by an ocean of sunshine. The storms seem to be mirages.

I can see and hear and date the arrival of 10,000 snow geese in whirling March echelons on the Nebraska prairies, and hear the mind-boggling calls of 10,000 sandhill cranes on the Platte River bottoms as they arrive at dusk.

ENTER THE CALENDAR

Phenological expression is natural, but phenological measurement is a human contrivance, because we date the seasonal changes on a human calendar of days and months. Phenologists attempt to understand, and even rationalize, the behavior of plants and the animals in human indices of averages measured as means and standard deviations around the means.

As a phenologist, I must first account for the diurnal relationship. Life has developed a metabolic and hormonal response to day and night. Later this evening I will eat a supper of meatball soup and crusty bread, and then paw out a place underneath a down quilt. I will sleep and dream tonight to live and breathe tomorrow— on the last day of February.

I must then account for the reality that March will follow February. But February and March are merely analogs for the changing seasons. The reality is that spring, with its accelerating surge of life, will follow winter. Rain and snow, wind and calm, and the light and dark of the changing seasons have shaped our lives, the old lives and the new.

I, along with all the other animals, harvest and store. I remember my mother telling me that I was born on a stormy November night, with geese overhead, circling in the dark. Am I forever November's child?

Metaphorically, all of life arrives in winter, flourishes in spring, matures in summer, and ages in mellow autumn. February's days come and then they go, and the solstice approaches right on schedule, give or take a moment or two.

Across the centuries and millennia,

Earth's climatological conditions have ebbed and flowed. Drought has followed flood. Glaciers have yielded to thousands of summers. Some species have flourished in the ages of ice, and others have not. Some have dug in and some have migrated. Some species have become extinct. The ecological tapestry—the mix of species—has been woven and rewoven in its place.

The physical forces on Earth have expressed themselves for billions of years. Mountains and seas have risen and fallen. The underworld of plutons and cratons and subduction zones has stirred and batholiths have risen to the surface. Igneous quartz has been transformed to sandstone and quartzite, to be eroded to grains of prairie sand.

The epochs have been punctuated (and some defined) by the collision of comets and Earth, high-speed impacts that could have caused volcanic eruptions and changed climates. Radiation from exploding supernovas 30 light years away may have depleted Earth's protective blanket of ozone, affecting the intricate web of life. Such forces would have likely caused mass extinction of millennial generations of interdependent species, making way for the construction of a new web.

The analysis of fossil records indicates long periods, millions of years, of evolutionary stasis and then short bursts of extinction, with emergence of new species in a matter of millennia.

And then, there are the eras. They span the longest time, from the current Cenozoic of about 70 million years, back through the Mesozoic, Paleozic, the Proterozoic, to the Archeozoic, some 2.5 billion years ago. Human imagination for naming geological eras runs out with the Archeozoic, even though there is a period of over two billion of those "first" years. Geologists haven't named these earlier eras, in part because they haven't found the fossils that would identify them. But in the span of eras, including the early ones still unnamed, it is likely that life did take form, and basic structures of life survived the cataclysms. Life has probably shared in the process from the earth's earliest times. Life has also shaped the process. Without the earliest life, there would probably be little free oxygen, no complicated organisms, and no contemplations of time by a dominant species.

The Earth history becomes obvious here in this place, during this February, these layers imbedded in time, each one embracing tightly the one that lies within.

But what if I turn around and look at the train of time approaching?

Life evolved, and it will also devolve. For it is possible that in another 500 million to a billion years, the temperature of the sun will increase enough to evaporate Earth's oceans. Perhaps the silicon dioxide will return to galactic dust when the sun burns all its hydrogen about seven billion years from now, expanding to a big, red giant that will scorch Earth for another two billion years before exploding.

Do I stand rooted on the clock at noon, trying to stare it down as the future rushes toward me? Or do I try to get out of the way? To deal with that question, I think about that other leaf of time.

According to the theorists, time and space are relative to some mysterious and immense cluster of galaxies, near-by in our galactic neighborhood, that they call the "great attractor." I could experience the relativity of time if I could travel at the speed of light. At that speed, I would have left time behind. Clocks and calendars, and even Februaries, would not slow me down or speed me up.

UNDERSTANDING THE DIMENSIONS

I do not have to accept traveling at the speed of light to escape February before it's over. Nor do I have to live only by the precision of the clock and the regularity of the calendar that so specifically confine the days and the months of Februaries. But when I really understand the dimensions of time, will I accept that I live immersed in eons as well as seasons, millennia as well as Februaries?

I may resist, because there is in me the sense that I can control variations in the environment; I can focus nature's resources to my use; and I can turn time into a commodity. But my time here is so short! And what do I really gain by controlling everything?

As an alternative, in my mind's eye, I examine each time and place, one by one, and I can travel through time without really going somewhere else. I

can stand right here on the crest of the moraine and see it all.

If we all pause for a minute or two on the moraine, just long enough to kindle the spark of a bonding with the prairie, we will realize that today is a special time, although the days and the seasons are really only fleeting moments. The land tells us, when we really look and listen and smell, that security is more than the confidence of spring. High noon on a dusty summer day is not a confrontation with the aging year. Security really lies in the changes as autumn leaves float on the still waters of the pond. Even more, although hard to admit, security comes from the climatic cycles, and those times when winters overrule summers for 50,000 years.

So what do we make of it?

The diurnal changes, the seasonal changes, and the glacial and geological changes on this land force competition, ingenuity, strength, and cooperation. From the sum of these come the possibilities inherent in the return of spring on this sandy land. There is nothing more inevitable in existence than the passage of time. But there is security in the understanding and acceptance of change through time. Thus, we discover the *patience* of time. And it dawns on us that awareness of time may be the most profound of our human discoveries.

Given our growing technological prowess, we might turn our backs on nature, even disdain it. That, I think, would be the most basic of mistakes the human species could make.

Jack in the Pulpit

Let us proceed to grapple with the longer view and work hard in formulating an ethic that respects natural processes. There is more to this earth than consumption. If we accept that, then humankind's most urgent issue is to organize itself, economically and socially, to sustain natural processes.

And besides, March is just around the corner. Three weeks from now, with the arrival of the spring equinox, we will know that prairie time is infinitely abundant. With that knowledge, we can move right along with the gusty winds of spring and the lusty weeks of early summer.

The cowman who cleans his range of wolves does not realize that he is taking over the wolf's job of trimming the herd to fit the range. He has not learned to think like a mountain. Hence we have dustbowls, and rivers washing the future into the sea.
We all strive for safety, prosperity, comfort, long life, and dullness. The deer strives with his supple legs, the cowman with trap and poison, the statesman with pen, the most of us with machines, votes, and dollars, but it all comes to the same thing: peace in our time. A measure of success in this is all well enough, and perhaps is a requisite to objective thinking, but too much safety seems to yield only danger in the long run.

FROM THESE ROOTS

It is a century now since Darwin gave us the first glimpse of the origin of species. We know now what was unknown to all the preceding caravan of generations: that men are only fellow-voyagers with other creatures in the odyssey of evolution. This new knowledge should have given us, by this time, a sense of kinship with fellow-creatures; a wish to live and let live; a sense of wonder over the magnitude and duration of the biotic enterprise.

Above all we should, in the century since Darwin, have come to know that man, while now captain of the adventuring ship, is hardly the sole object of the quest, and that his prior assumptions to this effect arose from the simple necessity of whistling in the dark.

ROOTS IN THE SAND

Perennial prairie grasses probe deeply into this sandy soil, searching for water, gleaning nutrients, and securing the plants against the storms of the seasons. The community of roots expresses the character of the plants just as much as their aboveground structures do, perhaps even more, because the roots persist all year, while the stems and flowers wither in the fading light of October and before the November storms.

The community of roots has characteristics not unlike a city, but the root community may be more complex than the infra-structure of the city. It has had more time to prove itself.

The persistence of the roots becomes a metaphor for all of life. Animals, even human ones, "put down their roots." The geese come home in spring to this place. I too wander afar, but this is my home.

And I put down my roots into what? Into a soil dominated by silicon dioxide, prone to drought? True, but there can be a physical security here, as well as a biological one—if I listen to the sand. And what does it have to say? It too, metaphorically, has roots.

Some geologists assert that the atoms of silicon and oxygen now on Earth were joined together to form these molecules well before Earth's condensation from a cloud of galactic dust. The condensation of our planet, during the gestation of our solar system, occurred more than 4.5 billion years ago.

If this is true, at least some of the

molecules of silicon dioxide under my feet on this warm May evening are older than Earth. They arrived at the beginning, along with carbon, metallic compounds, and molecules of water. In that sense, the molecules are aliens from another time and another place. But they are the precursors of this prairie.

Although the molecules may predate Earth, our planet recast them in their present quartz form about two billion years ago. The grains of quartz, sparkling in the slanted sunshine, were crystallized during Earth's tectonic processes.

We can imagine that the same molecules existed in an earlier world—possibly from a planet that vaporized when its sun swelled to become a red giant, or a planet that was consumed in the flash of a supernova explosion about eight billion years ago, or perhaps one that was thrown out of its orbit in a system of binary stars, and remained there until swept up by another star. Accepting an estimated age of the universe at 20 billion years, the bonding of silicon and oxygen could have survived several planetary cycles.

It was not so at the beginning, when the Big Bang created a lot of hydrogen and some helium. The heavier atoms were created later, in a sequence of solar furnaces, across time since the Big Bang. Every one of those solar furnaces had a limited cycle of existence. At the end of a cycle, that sun condensed to a white dwarf, spewing out many of its ionized atoms into the

ether, or exploded and dispersed its atoms into the cosmic dust clouds.

It is not accurate, then, to call our quartz crystal igneous rock merely because it was melted two billion years ago on Earth and then recrystallized. That's a geocentric view of things. The atomic origin of quartz was probably deep in the center of an ancient sun, perhaps a grandfather of our sun. And that grandfather sun could have given warmth to a planet that had favorable conditions for life.

We may speculate that the molecules might have brought the memories of earlier intelligent life to Earth imbedded in chips of silicon. Maybe the dust that consolidated into Earth also included fullerenes, complex molecules containing carbon, which possibly carried the blueprints of a life structure. Given an environment for life, more specifically fluid water, intelligence is obviously possible. Its existence here proves that.

If we could decipher the language of atoms and molecules, could we prove the existence of those earlier worlds? Is the message of the prairie where I stand this evening rooted in another world that is an ancestor of ours?

Even though we are willing to consider that possibility, we are convinced that the complexity in our world came about over millennia on Earth. If there was an earlier planet, there is no assurance that ours is a duplicate of it. There is so much here—in this prairie and savanna—that can only be a consequence of the relationship between this quartz sand and these emerging blooms of blue-eyed grass scattered from here to the edge of the woods.

THE LOGIC OF ETERNITY

My dictionary states that eternity is the totality of time, from beginning to end. Therefore the logic of eternity seems to lie deep within these simple minerals. Our time on Earth seems not such a fateful limitation if we can conceive of generations of physical worlds.

I have no doubts that my roots are on Earth, and that my beginning and end are well within the boundaries of eternity, but that does not keep me from contemplating my role in this time and this place. My roots do have a temporal affinity with the grasses now breaking the crust of ashes whose minerals were dispersed to the environment only two weeks ago in a prairie fire. Although I see eternity in the sand, I must put down my roots—in this place—in May.

Accepting that, I know I have inherited DNA that links directly back to single-celled bacteria that evolved on Earth perhaps three billion years ago. Earth's life-chain is unbroken. And, because of that, I am inextricably related to the bacteria that now teem in this sandy soil and the countless algae rimming Turner Pond. DNA is transferable across species, from one to the other, and back again. Viruses see to that. These bacteria and I are cousins with even recent genetic ties.

I also have much more than a nodding relationship with the blue-eyed grass poking through the soot. I know that the two geese herding the yellow fluff of nine goslings on Center Pond this evening are even closer cousins of mine than the grass is. Even our behaviors are synchronous with each other.

I sense these relationships deep in my neurons, though species on Earth so frequently react as strangers or enemies to each other. We perceive bacteria as threatening, or as tools, something to eradicate or to manipulate. We plow down the blue-eyed grass because it has no economic value. The Canada geese and I are suspicious of each other. They have a watchful eye on me right now, and we both know that our cousin the snapping turtle lurks beneath the dark surface of the water waiting for a chance at a gosling and maybe my toe.

I OWE IT TO THE CELTS

While I am a citizen of the world today, I realize that I am a recent immigrant to this North American prairie in this moment of bursting spring, when all life that surrounds us this evening is reveling in an environment of creation and procreation.

My most recent roots are in a different part of planet Earth, in spite of my direct molecular kinship with the grass, the geese, and the snapping turtle. My traceable ancestors were Celts in the Highlands of Scotland. They formed the Scottish clans in those rugged hills within the last 10,000 years, in the interim since the last glaciation. They persisted in Scotland, close to the land, as crofters, until the invading English rooted them out just 350 years ago. The English, a lordly lot, had domestication in mind for that rugged land. Correctly judging they could not really domesticate the Scots, and taking advantage of superior military technology, they shipped the Scots out to a wilder place, chained in the holds of wooden galleons.

My roots in the British Isles may be much deeper than the last glaciation. Bones of modern *Homo*, dating from about 500,000 years ago, have been found in a gravel pit along the English coast. Maybe these are the remains of the ancestors of the Celts, who migrated there from the taigas of Central Asia or from the Tigris-Euphrates Valley.

It is interesting that the climatic fluctuations of the two-million-year-old Pleistocene Epoch do parallel the emergence of modern humans, the shift from *Homo erectus* to *Homo sapiens,* leading eventually to the creation of civilizations near the end of the last glaciation. But *Homo* evolved through perhaps a dozen earlier glacial cycles. At least some of our human ancestors were able to put down their roots in sandy terrain and abrasive climates at the higher latitudes in Europe and Asia well before the last glaciation. There is now evidence that suggests *Homo* was making crude tools from quartzite in the north-central regions of Siberia about 600,000 years ago. The species could have advanced and retreated across the taigas, prairies, and savannas through several glacial epochs. A return of the glaciers here, sometime

in the next two thousand years, is thus not an unthinkable catastrophe for our species, although it might be for our cities.

Wherever *Homo* lived—in Africa or Eurasia—it would seem that the Pleistocene has been advantageous for the modernization of the human species, because it is the glacial period in which intelligence and technology advanced. There seems little doubt that Cro-Magnons, and probably our cousins the Neanderthals, rapidly developed their skills in the regions just to the south of the glaciers in Europe and Asia. Because glaciation caused a major southward shift in the world's great deserts, *Homo* must also have had to adjust to immense environmental changes near the equator and in the southern hemisphere.

From the Celts of Northern Europe, whose ancestors struggled with ice, have come many of the hand tools that we take for granted—picks, hammers, saws, chisels; we still use such tools today and hand them down to our grandchildren from our grandfather's workshops. From the settlers of the Middle East, in the centuries after the last glaciation, came the domestication of plants and animals as their subtropical Edens were flooded by the rising seas and the deserts marched north. What an interesting time it must have been as the glaciers melted and the rising oceans flooded the Arabian Gulf.

From these ancestral migrators have come our abilities to survive on the margins and edges at the higher latitudes, something I do surely appreciate in a Wisconsin winter. Life ebbed and flowed in tune with the glacial cycles. The species and individuals that survived won their places against the realities of climatic change.

PERIPATETIC HUMANS

No humans of any strain have really deep roots here on the glacial outwash of North America. This Pleistocene biology evolved without the presence of *Homo*. Their massive intrusions from all the other continents would change things. Human migrators, with tools and biological baggage, came to North America in a trickle from Asia, and then in massive migrations from Europe and Africa, and, now again, from Asia and Europe. Each wave has brought an increasing load of technical skills to radically disrupt the natural societies here.

The earliest hunters did not have the power of the later settlers' moldboard plow—the implement that broke the hold of the prairies on the land—but they did have atlatls, then bows and arrows, and they did modify the biota of the prairies. They very likely selectively harvested Ice Age mammals. Each of the mammal species would have been adapted to its own choice of forage. The forage array would have been in balance with the species array. The Asian humans would change the balance. By a thousand years ago, they had introduced the cultivation of corn from Tennessee to Colorado.

Some argue the Paleo-Indians played a major role in the extinction of many animal and plant species. Certainly the later-arriving Europeans and Africans would prove expert in the skills of extinction.

But this is not the last act. The question remains open as to whether or not hunters, farmers, and urban societies have really displaced the prairie. This sophisticated and undomesticated prairie web has evolved through perhaps 20 glacial cycles over two million years. If we assume five human generations in a century, we have had only between 500 and 600 generations over the last 10,000 years to learn how to survive here.

THE REAL ABORIGINES

The sandhill crane is probably one of the oldest vertebrate species to retain its ongoing identity here. The crane produces perhaps 20 generations in a century. Thus, it has had something like 100,000 generations over those two million Pleistocene years to learn the path to survival.

Each generation of snapping turtles may live 70 to 80 years, but these ancient creatures predate most of their neighbors by millions of years. Bacteria have a reason to disdain all the "higher" orders, for their genetic structures reach far back before the Paleocene. Bacteria survive through cell division, which happens on the order of every 20 to 30 minutes. Their divisions create multitudes of clones in a strategy that is over two billion years old. But they also have a second strategy. They are able to exchange genetic information in a form of mating, and can evolve in a shifting environment. The bacteria may have been around four times as long as any multicelled creature with nuclei. Are they the ones destined for immortality? Do they have the strongest roots?

In a sense, humans are biotic exotics here, from other parts of the world. We shouldn't be downcast about that, because all species arrive in a new place at some discrete time. The more important question for any species is the survival rate after arrival.

It is possible that we humans, such recent arrivals on the North American prairie, are more subject to the mortal forces we ourselves have created here in this tension zone, than big bluestem, which we have so vigorously attacked in the last 300 years. We can conclude that the long roots of the prairie perennial grasses and forbs have reached deep into the prairie sand and formed a community, not closed to outsiders, but tough in its judgments of newcomers.

The perennial grasses may retreat from the plow. The geese, now hiding in the grass at the edge of the pond, may retreat from my gaze, but the immortality of the grass and the geese is linked to the 100,000-year cycles of the ice in this continuing glacial epoch. The Pleistocene has not exhausted itself. The ice will return.

CAN WE ESTABLISH ROOTS?

Can humans establish roots here? Can we learn of the knowledge that flows all around us? Will we survive the return of the wolves?

Perhaps, over the course of the coming millennia, humans will have figured out how to survive through the next glaciation. My descendants will need to learn to migrate. The genetic resilience is surely there. But it would mean adjusting complicated technological structures to a 60,000-year span of ice, with millennia of tundra, punctuated by 500-year spurts of blowing sand plains, washed by great floods of melting water. Could my descendants, 200 generations down the road, survive in a taiga forest at the latitude of southern Illinois? In an oak savanna in Mexico? Will the southerners accept the hordes of immigrants from the north? Humans would also need to learn to replant themselves in this northern land, after long periods of southward habitation. Our ancestors did.

The plovers, flying with the seasons from Antarctica to Wisconsin, have learned to make such migrations on an annual basis! And they do certainly have more stamina for personal migration than humans. They make the trip without sails, wheels, or jets, in a matter of weeks.

Maybe humans are Ice Age mammals, and our technologies will prosper only as long as the glaciers come and go. But surely there is, in our genetic roots, a memory of the warmer Pliocene. In that case, humans could prosper in a world with temperate climates reaching toward the poles and arid deserts at the middle latitudes.

IS OUR DESTINY TO BE FERAL ANIMALS?

Domestication, defined here as a family farm unit, took hold after the last glaciation. Then, in rapid succession, domesticated humans created cities. Now, with vast migrations to urban areas in the last hundred years, farming the land, at least for some societies, has begun to fade as a way of life. In the cities, the forces of domestication might be losing their economic and social importance. We have yet to really prove, however, that domestication is unimportant for the survival of our species, at least for the numbers of us that still exist in a neolithic world.

Like other animals that have reverted to wild behavior after a period of domestication, some urban humans seem to be turning feral. There are places where they have to search for survival in a fierce individualistic state. Anarchy, the absence of any form of political authority, is a consequence. In some situations, humans act like the feral cats that have prowled the Roman Coliseum for two thousand years, surviving on a diet of garbage thrown out by other humans still holding on to some elements of domestication. Ironically, garbage is the fruit of domestication. Human ferals may not even have the family structure of the Paleolithics, who were the Stone Age precursors of all of us.

There is no reason to believe that feral animals have an advantage, let alone the ability to persist. It is almost an oxymoron to say that ferals have roots, even though their populations initially tend to explode. Domestication is full of human trappings and relies on the most basic of cultures, which is agriculture.

It seems we must retain the wisdoms of the wild prairie, at the same time sustaining domestication—in other words the family farm. In that balancing act, we would certainly do our utmost to observe and enjoy, not just manipulate and employ, significant areas of our land surface. We would not insist that all of this land be hunting preserves, pastures, or hydroponic farms devoted to the raising of genetically engineered tomatoes. We would rethink the vulnerability of cities, interstate highways, and international trade in natural resources.

The real message of the prairie lies in the concept of biological sustainability. Which will be more stable for a domesticated species in the long run—understanding and applying the complexity of the prairie or the complexity of our urban lives—central heating, air-conditioning, and skyscrapers with high-rise plumbing—and the economic structure to support them? But that doesn't mean a return to a wild state for *Homo*, or even a paleolithic society.

Our understanding of nature may be close to a point where we can intellectually advance to a nondestructive, sustainable existence.

THE PRAIRIE ECOSYSTEM

This prairie ecosystem does seem very complex to the observing eye, even chaotic. Some scientists are now considering the possibility that there is a single coherent picture of how the complex world really fits together.

That complexity inherently contains a certain amount of randomness and unpredictability, but there is also deterministic expression here. Determinism says that if you have a cause, you have a predictable effect. For example, if water reaches 32°F, it will freeze. Randomness says that, given a cause, there is an array of outcomes. As winter approaches, we know that someday soon Center Pond will freeze over. We can bet on that date, based on our records of previous years. While the temperature of freezing is deterministic, the date of freezing has some level of randomness—albeit with boundaries. There's an element of chance.

With a deeper understanding of natural processes, humans should be able to explain how and when randomness is compatible with a world that is fun-

Fritillary on Butterfly Weed

damentally deterministic. The pasque flower that blooms in mid-April on the sandy hillside is lavender. For that package of genes, the color is definitely not the flame-red of the cardinal flower or the orange of the butterfly weed. But the pasque flower in the Bradley phenological data is bloom-ing, on average, about a week earlier than in the Leopold data from five decades earlier. Perhaps there is a cli-matic warming trend. But then, delib-erate burning of the prairie may also have an influence. If you chart that first-bloom over a period of 60 years, the dates will vary around a mean, and what initially appeared to be a random variation begins to assume a logical form. Even the mean can shift in a sig-nificant way. There are boundaries to randomness, and there are reasons for determinism.

With this understanding, I can ask questions that can probably be an-swered. Why does the plant have laven-der blossoms that appear in spring rather than fall? What forces explain the variation in the exact dates of blooming for these flowers down at my ankles among the ashes of a spring fire? What happens if I prohibit fire? Is there really an expression of global warming right here in our neighbor-hood? These are important questions, but humans have only recently started to ask them.

On a much larger scale, but with the same basic logic, I am virtually sure that the ice will return across the land-scape on which I stand this evening, because the warming and cooling of the earth is fundamentally related to the earth's orbit, which has determinis-tic cycles. The climate will again turn from interglacial to glacial. But I can-not determine with certainty that first series of years without summers, because there are variables within the earth as a heat machine that have ran-dom characteristics and generate mar-gins of error of hundreds of years.

It is the interrelationship between that which is determined and that which is random that becomes a central question. The specific questions that follow are the roots of an emerging dis-cipline centered around complexity theory. Scientists are beginning to develop models of complexity itself. As the theories are tested empirically in the field, there is growing evidence that what we see in the environment is more than the sum of its parts. The basic components—atoms, molecules, and cells—appear simple enough, as their construction is understood. However, as the components interact with one another, new properties emerge.

Complexity theory rests on several straightforward ideas. The first is that complexity is not merely a quality to be noted, but a quantity that can be measured. This makes it possible to study levels of complexity in nature. The relationships among quartz and water and prairie grasses can be mod-eled. How they coexist in a community can be detected. Future changes in the physical environment, along with bio-logical responses, can be predicted, albeit with some margin of error. But that knowledge of error also gives a margin of confidence. Boundaries can be identified. There can be understanding of the boundaries crucial for our own survival. An example of a potential boundary would be the induced global warming that disrupts our ability to produce grain, a form of prairie grass.

The second important property is that complex things tend to give rise to more complex things over time. Humans may or may not be the most complex creatures around. A judgment on that issue, however, is not as important as the fact that humans are very much a part of a complex web.

This concept of increasing complexity seems obvious, if you consider the path of evolution. Yet the Second Law of Thermodynamics would seem to argue against increasing complexity. It asserts that energy is dispersed to a condition where the energy is not available to do *work* we perceive as useful. And yet we see the prairie, concentrating energy to generate increasing complexity over the millennia.

A third key property seems even more profound than the others. This idea is that complex adaptive systems at different hierarchical levels are bound to different units of time. Bacteria can clone in 20 to 30 minutes. The immune system of a complex human organism can respond almost spontaneously to a foreign invader in hours or days. Many organisms are bound to the passage of night and day—the diurnal cycles. Organisms also respond differently to changing seasons. Some migrate. Some develop

deep roots and stay planted in a given locality. Migrators slowly adapt their expressions over the passage of millennia to climatic changes. The community survives across time with hundreds of species in a process that has grown collectively wise, in tune with different spans of time.

Humans think and act in seconds, minutes, and hours on the clock, and weeks, months, and years on the calendar. But why? Why are we so intricately bound to the passage of time? From a deeper understanding of behavior across time, we should be able to develop an understanding of how far we can press in our efforts to condense or bypass the workings of time without a collapse of biological structure. How far can we squeeze a crop season? What is the price of that?

From such concepts, theorists are beginning to build models based in mathematics, physics, and chemistry. The models show that such things as immune responses, evolution, and the stability of community ecosystems have fundamentally similar structures. It now seems possible that human intelligence should be able to tap this complex world's wisdom, and better understand its organization and stability.

But here, in our time and our place, what if our collective intelligence predicts that humans are creating a runaway population explosion, or that we are accelerating Second Law processes? Would we apply the wisdom of natural structure and our understanding of time? Or would we increasingly try to defy the deterministic and random expressions of nature by stifling those expressions? If we do that, we could cut ourselves off from our roots. I think our hope lies in taking time to smell the flowers.

SUMMER IS ARRIVING

As the evening shadows lengthen, the four of us sit on the porch, overlooking the prairie, anticipating what we shall discover. The cream baptisia and the shooting star are blooming. On Center Pond, just down the way, the geese and the goslings have ventured forth again from the sedges in the wet meadow. There is a crisp image of each reflected on the surface of the glassy water. The adults herd the nine goslings across the pond, one goose leading, the other following behind. A yearling goose trails behind. Just yesterday she had succeeded in piloting three of the new babies away from the parents. This evening, the parents have retrieved the wanderers, and it doesn't look as if the goslings will stray again. The parents are clearly irritated with the juvenile and her brash attempt at parenthood, and have warned her to keep a distance. But will all nine goslings survive the night?

In the evening air, we hear the long trill of the bufo frogs. And the rose-breasted grosbeak is singing. The kingbird arrived today, a week earlier than we expected. An oriole announces his arrival at the edge of the pond with his ratchety call. He takes a noisy bath and a robin flies in to see what the fuss is all about. The robin flinches at the spray of water flicked up by the oriole, and quickly departs.

Yesterday, Nina noted in the journal the first bloom of the lupine, and the

Baptisia

phoebe feeding its young. The new ones will fledge in a week, and we hope the blue jays don't pick them off on their first flight toward the protection of the woods.

I know that hope is a human emotion. I felt no sympathy for the insects the mother phoebe brought to the nest all across this sunny day. But the mother now seems as anxious as I feel, as the young birds impulsively take to flight. All but one. It looks too small to make it to the nearest branch, and it does not try, not this evening at least.

The wood ducks have been mating. The female takes about five minutes to lay her daily egg, then emerges from the nest and immediately breeds again until she has a clutch of 8 to 15 eggs. Then, one after another, the hens retreat to their nests. But not all the females nest on the same day. The males concentrate around the remaining receptive females. This morning 15 drakes were squabbling around one young hen. But soon she will also nest,

and all the drakes will go off by themselves and molt. The young mothers, we hope, will stay with the nests until their eggs hatch.

We hear the quiet thunder of a grouse, beating its wings on a downed log. The white-throated sparrows have headed north. We did not hear their calls this morning.

Checking such comings and goings against the phenological records, we note that almost everything is happening 7 to 10 days earlier than it did last year. Why are things happening earlier this year? The phoebe is not asking why, at least in a language I can understand. Do all these creatures understand something I do not? Has consciousness isolated humans from our surroundings?

Am I lonely now?

No, not really. Wisdom is so abundant around here. And, this evening, there is anticipation of a summer teeming with life.

The pine's new year begins in May, when the terminal bud becomes 'the candle.' Whoever coined that name for the new growth had subtlety in his soul. 'The candle' sounds like a platitudinous reference to obvious facts: the new shoot is waxy, upright, brittle. But he who lives with pines knows that candle has a deeper meaning, for at its tip burns the eternal flame that lights a path into the future. May after May my pines follow their candles skyward, each headed straight for the zenith, and each meaning to get there if only there be years enough before the last trumpet blows. It is a very old pine who at last forgets which of his many candles is the most important, and thus flattens his crown against the sky. You may forget, but no pine of your own planting will do so in your lifetime.

EPILOGUE —
OUR COSMIC RELATIVE

Ability to see the cultural value of wilderness boils down, in the last analysis, to a question of intellectual humility. The shallow-minded modern who has lost his rootage in the land assumes that he has already discovered what is important; it is such who prate of empires, political or economic, that will last a thousand years. It is only the scholar who appreciates that all history consists of successive excursions from a single starting-point, to which man returns again and again to organize yet another search for a durable scale of values.

In the essays in this volume, I have only touched on a very small portion of the vast array of phenological expressions that exist on Earth. Beyond observations, I have sought to explore the underlying questions of why. Why do things happen as they do in the Earth environment? Why is Earth the way it is? Why is there any point in searching for the values in such expressions? It is my hope that these essays do reflect the nature of Earth, but also help serve as standards for our own behavior. First, we find that the question of environmental values has spread beyond the world of scholars. Leopold's vision has taken root. But the outcome remains in doubt and my mind remains restless, perhaps because there is a setting larger than Earth, larger even than our solar system, and we also exist in that context.

We are gaining some understanding of the cosmos, but we don't really know if there are other worlds suitable for life, let alone know anything about the phenological expressions that might exist in those worlds. We may never know. But perhaps we can gain some insight into our phenological status, in this time and in this place, through a metaphor of life on another planet. It's worth a try.

BINARY STARS

Astronomers have recently reported that about two-thirds of the stars in the Milky Way galaxy appear to have stellar companions at least 10 times larger than Jupiter. With such mass, these stars would be solar furnaces like our sun. Binary combinations must also exist in the billions of other galaxies that form the cosmos.

These binary, and sometimes trinary, solar systems appear to be more common than solitary stars like ours. Indeed, it has been reported that the merger of binary companions into a single solar furnace may be almost a daily event in the universe.

Our sun has no known stellar companion, although some astronomers have maintained there is a partner out there, which has an orbiting period with our sun of about 30 million years. Believers in a stellar companion suggest that the orbit between the two is elliptical, and when the two stars are closest together, there is enough gravitational interaction to disturb planetesimals and comets that exist in a vast and cluttered "Kuiper Belt" beyond Neptune and overlapping the orbit of Pluto. That gravitational interaction could create a shower of those bodies inward toward our sun, some of them intersecting the orbit of Earth. Collisions with Earth could result in periodic mass extinctions. Other astronomers have argued that the merger of nearby binary suns could cause a shower of radiation that would lead to earthly extinctions.

The idea of a solar companion causing a periodic rain of comets in our system is not widely held. It is possible, however, that an errant comet or meteor could hit Earth and cause such extinctions. Perhaps we do periodically lie in the path of a shower of comets or a blast of cosmic rays, when another independent star wanders close to our sun.

There are two theories for the formation of binary solar systems. One theory posits that stellar companions are produced when a mature sun "captures" another, well after the first star coalesced. A second theory, now with stronger theoretical support, is that binary systems are formed more or less simultaneously out of a common cloud of cosmic dust.

If the astronomers are correct about binary systems, and if there is sentient life in those systems, we humans have a minority view of the cosmos, because it is quite possible that Earth's dialogue with a single sun is relatively rare on the larger scale of things.

Binary systems appear to have widely variable orbital characteristics. Some double stars may be nearly touching each other and circling each other in less than a "24-hour day." These are the ones likely to coalesce. Others can be as far apart as one-third of a light-year, and would take tens of millions of "solar years" to circle each other.

The evidence of binary stars does not mean that planets are restricted to solitary stars, or even that they are rare in binary systems. According to our understanding of gravitational forces, a planet could be formed and survive in a binary system, provided it circled either relatively close to one of the two stars, or in an orbit out and around both stars. It is theoretically possible that life would be able to exist in these worlds. And what would the phenological expressions be in such a world endowed with two suns instead of one?

THE METAPHOR

I thought about this cosmological question on a clear summer evening not long ago. The air was crisp, but warm enough for me to linger outside.

As evening approached and the

breezes of summer quieted down, it became a night to rethink my commitment to the sandy prairie in southern Wisconsin and planet Earth. There was no temperature inversion in the troposphere and thus no smog drifting in from the Chicago megalopolis. There was no jet trail crossing the Big Dipper, and those ghostly cirrus horsetails in the stratosphere had also evaporated. The Dipper and the North Star seemed to lose even their authority as billions of stars emerged from the haze that so often shrouds Earth.

It's easy to believe tonight that the stars I see are nearby, right here in the Milky Way galaxy. But beyond that are billions of other galaxies in great filaments that are accelerating away from our sun in time and space, accelerating so fast that we could never hope to reach them.

I force myself to focus on one star, just off the handle of the Big Dipper, bright enough to catch my attention on this night of brilliant stellar competition. Is it two stars? I think so. They are so close together that I did not at first recognize a separation. But I've been known to claim that I can see the moons of Jupiter with my naked eye. On the other hand, what I see tonight may be an illusion. It is not easy to keep the eye and the mind focused on a single point of light.

No, there are two! The stars could be far apart if their images are superimposed through line of sight. Light travels 5.9 trillion miles in our solar year, so, if the two stars are only 10 light-years apart, they would be separated by 59,000,000,000,000 miles.

But they could also be right next door to each other, only 60 light-minutes apart. Maybe a star, nearing the end of its hydrogen supply, captured another. Or maybe they were formed at the same time, out of a pillared cloud of cosmic dust, and are aging together. How long can they exist before they expand into swollen red giants and implode to white dwarfs? If they have enough mass, would they explode in a violent supernova? Here in Earth's night, in the presence of all the stars, my imagination takes off on a journey into space.

PLANET ORBIT

I imagine a binary system of two stars, nearly the size of our sun, the two stars with very similar mass, but not exactly the same. We shall call them Sun I and Sun II. An Earth-sized planet orbits 25 light-minutes from one of the suns and 35 light-minutes from the other, influenced by both, but not exactly between the two.

The planet rotates on its axis every 23 hours and 56 minutes. Caught between two suns, it is not at all like Earth. Daylight exists around the clock, but there is not perfect synchrony, because this world is not centered between the two suns. Two bands of shadow stream across the planet's surface every day, with a very subtle dawn and dusk when one sun is rising on the horizon and the other is sinking. There is no midnight, but there are two zeniths, when each sun is directly overhead. In each rotational day there are two magnificent sunrises and two glowing sunsets.

The planet has a nearly circular orbit, almost perpendicular to the suns. Thus there are no obvious seasons, no winters, autumns, or springs. A nearly constant temperature hovers around 60°F, plus or minus only a degree or so, just as the shadows race across the surface. The planet is at the right location for liquid water. Interestingly, 60°F is the mean annual temperature here on Earth. But, on Earth the temperature can vary over a range of almost 200 degrees, from 70°F below zero in Antarctica in winter to 130°F in California's Death Valley in summer.

I decide that "Orbit" is a reasonable name for this planet.

Orbit is much older than Earth, and is tectonically quiet now. Like Earth, Orbit condensed from galactic dust composed of silicon dioxide, carbon, oxygen, and all the other elements heavier than hydrogen and helium. But on Orbit now there are no continents jarring against each other, or subducting oceanic plates. Earthquakes don't exist. On middle-aged Earth, internal heat continues to be released to the surface in oceanic rifts or volcanic plumes because of ongoing fission of radioactive elements deep in the interior, elements inherited when Earth formed. The continents and the ocean floors are on the move. On Orbit, fission ran down and the movement of plates ceased long ago, but the steady arrival of

sunlight has been sufficient to keep water from freezing. Because water never freezes, there is no possibility of snowfall, let alone glaciation. Soft sunshine dominates across unending days and years.

There have been no infalling meteors or comets for a billion years. The gravitational forces of Sun I and Sun II long ago swept the solar system clean of meteors, comets, and even cosmic dust. The surface of Orbit long ago eroded to a peneplain. The peneplain is now entirely covered by a shallow sea, with sunlight sifting gently down to the ocean floor of sediments of silicon dioxide sand sparkling with crystals of heavier elements. Iron has sunk to the planet's core. Since there are no continents, there are no rivers, valleys, or mountains. Because the temperature gradient from equator to pole is very narrow, there are no storms raging around the global ocean. There are no blizzards, typhoons, or tornadoes, no thunder in the middle of a summer night.

It has not always been this way on Orbit. When the suns first formed they were farther apart. It was only through the eons that the suns edged closer together because of subtle differences in mass and modest gravitational imbalances. Orbit began its journey next to Sun I and was heavily influenced by it, but not totally independent of Sun II. It was periodically peppered by infalling comets, and its night skies were streaked with meteorites.

Life appeared on Orbit more than 10 billion years ago in the form of prokaryotic cells without enclosed nuclei. Some of the cells developed ordinary bacterial form, and some developed the characteristics of cyanobacteria, or algae. Both had molecules of DNA, the template for their functions and expressions. Initially the bacteria existed in largely anaerobic conditions, but the algae developed the extraordinary ability to convert photons into stored energy through photosynthesis, releasing free atoms of oxygen. The ordinary bacteria then developed the ability to detoxify the oxygen freed by the photosynthetic properties of the algae, creating the possibility of respiration.

Later there appeared eukaryotic cells, with their DNA encased in nuclei, and eventually multicelled organisms. Speciation took hold. A multitude of organisms with respiratory capacity evolved, an interconnected web of life responding to a varying environment on land and sea. Evolution plodded along and, finally about 500 million years ago, there appeared a sentient organism, an organism that could experience sensations and feelings, consciousness, and even conscience. The sentient species became aware of opportunities in the environment and, as it learned to manipulate the environment to its ends, the population exploded.

Fundamental changes in the environment of Orbit began to occur as the suns inched toward each other.

Tectonic movements lessened. As the planet gradually assumed a circular orbit the seasons faded, ever so slowly, and the environment grew more static. Tropical rainforests, savannas, prairies, taigas, and tundras disappeared and so did many species. As the stars converged, the one sentient species inevitably recognized that its planet was a satellite to the two suns. Its members later developed a way to codify and exchange technical information and gave their planet the name "Orbit." From that date on, they never wavered in the belief that their world circled the two suns, like two big gears and one small gear in a great celestial clock with a perpetual motion that wound itself.

The leveling of the planet's environment would have happened without a sentient species. But, more and more, the members sensed opportunity in an environment they interpreted as being increasingly benign to them. They perceived an optimal temperature, the constant availability of solar energy, and an endless supply of water. They perceived disadvantages in a system where consumer species competed for nutrients, but advantages to species that were primary producers of carbohydrates. They discovered the capacity to engineer life, including their own. The cost of building up their own genetic defenses was too expensive, so they proceeded to eliminate other species. Very wisely, algae were not eliminated. They began to simplify their own multicelled structure in consort with the changing natural environment. The algae became the singular source of their food supply.

As this was happening, life on Orbit had advanced to the level where the sentient species became explicitly aware of other suns, and the possibility of planets around them with environments favorable to life. Tentatively they explored their own solar system and considered going beyond. Over the millennia they realized the difficulties inherent in going elsewhere, and the enormous drain on their own environment in reaching such a goal. What would be the gain?

It seems that they spotted Earth about the time of the Cambrian life explosion on Earth 500 million years ago. They speculated about the possibility of life on this clearly habitable planet. Discouraged that life on Earth did not respond to their radio signals, they made an important decision. They decided to permanently encode records of life on Orbit in microscopic silicon chips and to bury the chips deep in the quartzite sandstones of the planet.

They had long ago worked out, in great detail, the evolution of life on Orbit and so they recorded that. Then, they recorded the natural and social history of life, as much as their records could tell them. And, finally, they recorded the blueprints for their amazing technological developments, including their electronic systems of communication. All of this they replicated millions of times and dispersed the records in the sandstones of the planet. In a global colloquium, they assured themselves that the silicon

records would survive environmental changes on Orbit through the millennia, a sort of permanent fossilization. But, more than that, they believed the silicon chips would survive a catastrophic stellar implosion if the twin stars should ever merge, and would even survive the collision of two wandering galaxies with massive stellar destruction and the creation of new stars.

Then as the millennia passed, they lost interest in life on other worlds. They let the radio antennas fall into disrepair and actually tore down the telescopes. What was the point, considering what they had accomplished on Orbit? And, by 100,000 years later, they had completely forgotten about the silicon library buried in the sandstone.

Besides, the stars grew fainter and fainter as nights gave way to a perpetual day.

And 200 million years after that, in my imagination, I see cells with the structure of large neurons on planet Orbit, capable of prospering in saline water. The neurons exist abundantly throughout the shallow global sea. On closer inspection, they show more internal complexity than earthly neurons. But it is not possible now to really discern the features that have evolved and ones that have been engineered. Perhaps even the cells could not sort it out even if they chose to try. What would be the reason for that?

Each neuron has a capacity for storing information and for internal biochemical decisions, but individuality continues to exist. Embedded among the individual neurons is a system of engineered capillaries, veins, and arteries, filled with a constant flow of countless algae that deliver and recycle nutrients, creating an overwhelming interdependence that controls individual behavior. Abetting that commonality is an advanced structural capability of communication among the cells. Communication is what binds them together.

Neurologists on Earth have estimated that a single human brain has more dendritic interconnections than the number of stars in the cosmos. Those interconnections bind together the psyche of a single human. On Orbit, the neurons have interconnections that are orders of magnitude greater than the cells in a human brain. They have developed a global organism with a collective power to perceive and analyze.

Not a single cell is left out of the cybernetic network. The total number of cells is in the trillions, but the population is fixed by the available resources in a steady state that has been engineered to be compatible with the environment. A simple system, it is based on the recycling of hydrogen, oxygen, carbon, and nitrogen, with a cognizance of minor elements such as zinc, magnesium, iron, and with a tolerance for sodium and chlorine. And there is no need for physical mobility, no need to travel.

Ironically, the cells have not succeeded in eliminating the process of individual aging, but they can transfer knowledge from one cell to another.

Thus there is no loss of experience with the digestive recycling of an aging cell. At the same time there is no population explosion, as one new cell is cloned to replace each aging one, and the new cell carries forward the "being" of the older one. With no signals of pending risk and without competition, the cooperation among cells focuses its intellect on maintaining an equitable environment.

The collective intelligence on Orbit does not have to worry about the morality of individuals bent on self-survival. No elite and self-reasoning individuals argue over policies for the allocation of resources, over population control or a society plagued by destructive urges. Even attempts to predict the future have become superfluous. Logic is invariably logical. Calm analysis reigns supreme. There is only one minor concern—those fleeting shadows twice a day.

Wouldn't Orbit seem a very dull place to earthly humans? Mutation, evolution, and mating are not factors with which the cells must contend. The problem of energy exchange among individuals in the community was solved long ago. Hope and fear are irrelevant emotions. There is no stress. There certainly wouldn't be any point in keeping phenological records. Indeed, phenological expression would be threatening. There's really not much need for sensory input—seeing, hearing, smelling, or feeling.

They would not hear the throaty call of a greater sandhill crane from down in the marsh. There would be none of those earthy smells, none of the flickering fireflies that surround me tonight on a warm, summer evening. Real summer on Orbit happened so long ago that even its existence is forgotten. No meteorite would flash across a midnight sky, even if the sky were dark enough to view it. There isn't even a need for a library full of old books. But there is a fulsome confidence emerging from unassailable security.

THE END OF ORBIT

Having lost interest in cosmology, the neurons on Orbit, with all their collective wisdom, did not see it coming. They did not sense their end. Astronomers on Earth would have known. If their telescopes had been fixed on this binary system, they would have predicted this event—down to the time and place it happened.

By the end of the twentieth century A.D., Earth's astronomers knew the fate of such a world after only two million years of dawning awareness of the cosmos. They rightly predicted that planets in a double system can persist in an orbit that circles close to one of the stars, or well beyond both of them. But if an existing planet should eventually edge into a zone midway between the two stars, it would be tossed out of that solar system by gravitational interactions into the monstrous cold of interstellar space. It would quickly lose its atmosphere and liquid water supply, and its surface would be illuminated only by the twinkling light of distant stars.

Across the eons, Orbit had been edging slowly toward the middle zone. And then, quite suddenly, it crossed that critical boundary. Within the time of a single orbit, within the time of one binary solar year, Orbit went spiraling out into the void. The seas froze, and the shadows rapidly darkened into the most profound of nights. Infinity quieted Orbit in the blink of a galactic eye.

A MIDSUMMER NIGHT'S DREAMING

It's now past midnight in this stellar evening, on the prairie, and a bit of a chill is in the air. I'm happy that I have my jacket.

I remember that I had looked up the origin of the word "Earth" in my Oxford dictionary just a week ago. The Oxford dictionary is normally a self-confident source. But the Oxford writers admitted some mystery in the origins of this word, and that was somehow comforting. The word appears to have Teutonic roots and even some Greek. But the dictionary was not really definitive. As I scanned down the long list of adjunct definitions, I settled on this one: "The world on which we dwell." And then I looked up the word "dwell." It means "to live as a resident," or "to exist in a given place or state."

So the questions become: What is existence and what is given? What do we choose now that we have options? We have the ability to learn to live. But we must also live in order to learn. Do we dwell lightly on Earth? Or do we press ahead for a controlled environment? We could not create a world exactly like Orbit, for we follow a solitary star. But we could march forward by adopting the same principles. We will almost certainly continue to "develop" our world, and reduce the risks that we perceive. But we may not perceive all the risks, and in the process, we may relinquish expression in exchange for security. Is that the real Faustian bargain? However, there is no natural guarantee our species will survive as long as the neurons of Orbit.

At last, I think that I understand my fascination with phenological expressions. There is the rather simple satisfaction in tracking the comings and goings of nature's creatures, the more complicated satisfaction in understanding linkages with the physical world, and the true excitement that comes from observing changes in those expressions over the seasons and years. From this there is knowing.

But satisfying the intellect is only the beginning. More profound are the primal senses of seeing, hearing, smelling, and feeling. If I can combine knowing with the senses, there is a blossoming joy in the sheer existence of it all.

Now there is the faintest of light in the eastern sky. At that moment a robin sings from his perch at the top of

Prairie Phlox

the oak. As the early morning light increases, the oak tree casts a slowly moving shadow toward the prairie. A breeze picks up and rustles the leaves on the oak. The white-tailed doe raises her head and melts into the woods. There is, once again, the fresh smell of summer's dew on the grasses in this time and in this place.

There are some who can live without wild things, and some who cannot. These essays are the delights and dilemmas of one who cannot.

Like winds and sunsets, wild things were taken for granted until progress began to do away with them. Now we face the question whether a still higher 'standard of living' is worth its cost in things natural, wild, and free. For us of the minority, the opportunity to see geese is more important than television, and the chance to find a pasque-flower is a right as inalienable as free speech.

These wild things, I admit, had little human value until mechanization assured us of a good breakfast, and until science disclosed the drama of where they come from and how they live. The whole conflict thus boils down to a question of degree. We of the minority see a law of diminishing returns in progress; our opponents do not.

CITIZENS OF THE PRAIRIE & SAVANNA

Preceding page: Lupine

A GRAND PAGEANT OF WILDFLOWERS AND GRASSES ENLIVENS THE SCENE AT the Aldo Leopold Memorial Reserve in southern Wisconsin, from April through October. Birds are a source of delight when identified near nest sites, at feeders, or by their calls. Tracks and sightings reveal the presence of mammals. Questions follow delight. What are their names, and why? How do prairie plants survive a drought? How do bees and butterflies select a flower? Where do bats spend the winter? Where are baby otters born? Why do some plants persist on one spot, but not a hundred yards away? Why do some plants bloom on a certain date one year, but weeks later in another year, or in 40 years?

From the time he was a boy, Aldo Leopold was interested in the seasonal cycles of wild plants and animals. As an adult he recorded the phenology of many species on his Sauk County property from 1935 to 1945. His daughter and son-in-law, Nina and Charles Bradley, have continued the tradition there. The phenological records given here make use of the Leopold dates and the Bradley dates from 1978 to 1992. Statistical comparison of the two sets of dates shows a trend toward earlier blooming.

The following profiles, although not a comprehensive guide, answer questions about many common plants and animals found on the Aldo Leopold Memorial Reserve.

The flowering plants are listed in phenological order, that is, according to the average date recorded for first bloom (determined by the presence of pollen). (Not all species have significant years of observation by both Leopold and Bradley.) The reader may become interested in recording species dates for another location, comparing seasons and observing patterns.

The heading for each description includes the Latin names for genus and species, common name, family name, the average date of first bloom, the typical height of the plant, and the width of the flower. The second paragraph describes the plant and its growing habits. Genus and species derivations, folklore, and human uses constitute the last paragraph.

Grass descriptions, following the flowers, begin on page 164. If the flowers are the stars that cross the summer stage, the grasses are the chorus that upstages them in autumn. A walk through a prairie in fall, submerged in swaying, whispering big bluestem and Indiangrass, is a thrilling experience. Both of these tall-grass species, as well as the early-blooming hardy short-grasses, are native in southern Wisconsin, where the prairie, oak savanna, and woodland ecosystems merge.

Bird species were chosen by their presence in the savanna and woodland settings, and sometimes by their presence in the writings of Aldo Leopold. Although there are dates connected with some of them, they are listed in alphabetical order, beginning on page 169. The common name is followed by the Latin name, then by the length of the species. A physical description of the species completes the first paragraph. The second paragraph describes some habits of the species, followed by a paragraph on mating and nesting behavior, and a statement about the status of the species.

The format for animals is similar to that for birds. The descriptions begin on page 182.

The Aldo Leopold Memorial Reserve encompasses a microcosm of the southern Wisconsin prairie/savanna/woodland complex. The areas of woodland are mostly deciduous trees with some evergreens. The flower species that grow under the trees tend to bloom early, before the trees leaf out and shade them. The savanna includes clusters of trees, typically oaks, and expanses of prairie with flowers and grasses.

There are mesic prairies that receive medium amounts of moisture, with gradations to wet prairies and dry prairies. There is water, too, on the Aldo Leopold Memorial Reserve, including a section of the Wisconsin River and its floodplain, and numerous ponds. Some plants are tolerant of varying soil and moisture conditions. Others are particular about where they grow, and are good indicators of the conditions that prevail where they are found.

Well over half of the mass and depth of the prairie plants is underground, buffered against drought, fire, and erosion. "Break the prairie" is an apt term to describe the task that faced the early settlers. A thousand miles of resistant roots must be one reason the prairies were among the last parts of the country to be settled. Even after many years under the plow, if farmland is left uncropped, the long-dormant prairie species reappear.

Today, the classic savanna landscape is but a remnant of its presettlement extent. Most of the species, however, persist. So this small corner of the region, part of the Leopold legacy, reflects the past, and is a repository for the future.

SKUNK CABBAGE

Symplocarpus foetidus
Calla family (Araceae)
Average first bloom: Leopold, April 1 /
    Bradley, March 27
Height: 2–3 feet
Flower arrangement: 4½ inches

The first herbaceous plant to bloom in spring, skunk cabbage pops up in marshy places, even in ponds of snow melt. The warmth of the flower head can thaw surrounding frozen earth and snow enough to allow it to push out of the ground. The visible hoods (spathes) range in color from mahogany to green, speckled with white. Hidden inside each is the spadix, a fleshy spike covered with hundreds of tiny flowers. At the time of bloom, the leaves are rolled tightly. They later grow long and somewhat resemble cabbage leaves. Skunk cabbage is named for the odor that comes from crushed leaves, the spadix, and the roots. This smell attracts carrion-eating flies, which pollinate the flowers.

Black bears eat all parts of the skunk cabbage. Native Americans dried the starchy root, ground it into flour, and cooked it. Skunk cabbage is related to taro, a staple in Polynesia. Both plants contain calcium oxalate crystals which cause a burning sensation in the mouth unless the plant is thoroughly dried or cooked. The calla lily is a more elegant relative of skunk cabbage.

HEPATICA

Hepatica acutiloba
Buttercup family (Ranunculaceae)
Also called liverleaf, mayflower
Average first bloom: Leopold,
    April 15 / Bradley, April 9
Height: 2–6 inches
Flower: ½ inch

This tiny beauty is the first woodland flower to bloom. Watch for it when tree leafbuds begin to swell, lest it go unnoticed in the duff. The silver-furred buds emerge with bowed heads. The flowers appear as if by magic one day, facing straight up toward the spring sun. Hepaticas have 5 to 12 petal-like sepals, which may be blue, pink, or white. In the center, many white stamens surround a cluster of pistils. The flowers have a clean, new look, befitting the new season. Behind each flower are three little green leaves. The stems are fuzzy like the buds. *Hepatica* means "liver" in Latin, a name given the plant for the mottled three-lobed leaves that last through the winter. New leaves come only after the flowers bloom in spring.

PASQUE FLOWER

Anemone patens
Buttercup family (Ranunculaceae)
Also called wild crocus, prairie
   anemone, windflower, April fool
Average first bloom: Leopold,
   April 19 / Bradley, April 12
Height: 4–10 inches
Flower: 2 inches

The pasque flower is the first prairie flower to bloom. Its welcome flowers appear fragile, but it grows on rocky slopes and ridges, blown by the cold winds of early spring. On some plants the five to seven petal-like sepals are white. Others shade to delicate lavender. The sepals surround a cluster of deep gold stamens and pistils. The undersides of the sepals, the stems, leaves, and buds are all covered with long silky hairs. After blossoming, the plant produces deeply cut new leaves. The buds, nicknamed goslings, form in late fall. Each seed develops a long feathery tail.

Although the pasque flower contains alkaloids that are toxic, deer sometimes eat this early, fresh food, curtailing the number of pasque flowers. Powdered, dried pasque flower plants have been used to promote healing, and to treat a variety of conditions, including sterility. The Dakota Nation celebrated this earliest flower with songs and ceremonial smoking. Seeking out pasque flowers is still a joyous rite of spring for all those who roam the out-of-doors.

BLOODROOT

Sanguinaria canadensis
Poppy family (Papaveraceae)
Average first bloom: Leopold,
   April 25 / Bradley, April 13
Height: 3–6 inches
Flower: 1¾ inches

The furled leaves of the bloodroot spear up through the dry leaves on the woodland floor. Each rolled leaf protects a single, immaculate white flower, which opens as the wide green leaf unfurls. Bloodroot flowers have 8 to 12 gracefully pointed petals, and many yellow stamens. The leaves continue to grow taller and larger into midsummer. Bloodroot grows from thick rhizomes that, along with the roots and aboveground stems, have red-orange juice. Bloodroot plants tend to grow in drifts, each group from one parent rhizome. The shape of the lobed leaves in one group often differs slightly from that in plants connected to a different parent rhizome. The many seeds in each pointed pod have crests called elaiosomes. Ants carry off the seeds to eat the elaiosomes, dispersing them.

The red sap of the bloodroot is bitter and contains a toxin that affects the heart, nervous system, and muscles. When part of the plant is cut, the sap flows freely, and the cut part quickly wilts. Native Americans have used the red liquid of the bloodroot to dye basket fibers, and to decorate their bodies for ceremonies.

DRABA

Draba reptans
Mustard family (Brassicaceae)
Average first bloom: Leopold,
   April 16 / Bradley, April 20
Height: 2–10 inches
Flower: ⅛ inch

Aldo Leopold's description of draba as "the smallest flower that blows" in "sand too poor and sun too weak for bigger, better blooms," can't be improved. Alas, like the botany books Leopold searched, we have no portrait of draba either. The little white flowers bloom on a short stem rising from small basal leaves. Stems and leaves appear to be white because of their dense mat of white hairs. If you search, as Leopold recommends, with your knee in the mud, you may be rewarded with a look at the modest draba some cold, windy day in early spring.

PUSSY TOES

Antennaria neglecta
Aster family (Asteraceae)
Also called cat's foot, everlasting,
   ladies' tobacco
Average first bloom: Leopold,
   April 19 / Bradley, April 17
Height: 1–8 inches
Flower: ¼ inch

Unobtrusive pussy toes form mats in sunny, sandy places. They do this by means of stems called stolons that loop along the ground, periodically putting down roots. A patch covering several square feet may be just one plant. These stolons come out of a basal rosette of leaves covered with cobwebby white hairs. Clusters of small, pearly-white flowerheads form on erect stems. Each little "toe" is actually made up of many small flowers. The male and female flowers are produced on separate plants (dioecious).

Country people formerly packed dried flower heads from pussy toes with their woollens to discourage moths, and added them to shampoo to get rid of lice. Native American children chewed gum made from the stalks of pussy toes. Some Native Americans made a tea from the leaves that new mothers used as a tonic. Pussy toes, primarily made up of papery bracts, keep well for dried bouquets.

DUTCHMAN'S BREECHES

Dicentra cucullaria
Fumitory family (Fumeriaceae)
Average first bloom: Leopold,
   April 23 / Bradley, April 19
Height: 8–10 inches
Flower: ⅝ inch

Dutchman's breeches bloom before the forest canopy leafs out. They resemble Hans Brinker's pantaloons hung upside down to dry, as many as 10 miniature pairs to a stalk. Two white-to-pinkish, inflated, winged petals join two smaller creamy petals. A cluster of gray-green lacy foliage at the base of the plant frames the graceful stalks.

Dutchman's breeches give true meaning to the term "ephemeral." Look in the woods at the first sign of spring or you will miss them! In a few weeks both flowers and foliage are gone. In their brief appearance, Dutchman's breeches have stored enough of the sun's energy to bloom again another spring. What remains is a cluster of small white bulbs that are high in starch and resistant to cold.

The nectar is deep within the flower. Queen bumblebees, just coming out of hibernation, are able to reach the nectar, in the process pollinating the flower. Some insects "steal" the nectar without pollinating the flower by chewing a hole in the tip of a winged petal. Oval capsules contain the tiny, shiny-black seeds of the Dutchman's breeches. Evolution has provided these seeds with a white protruding ridge that is delicious to ants. The ants carry the seeds to their underground homes and eat the part they like, leaving the remainder buried and ready to grow.

VIRGINIA BLUEBELL

Mertensia virginica
Borage family (Boraginaceae)
Also called Virginia cowslip, lungwort
Average first bloom: Bradley, April 23
Height: 12–16 inches
Flower: ½ inch

The color contrast between pink buds and blue trumpet-shaped flowers is a striking feature of Virginia bluebell. The flowers bloom in clusters at the tip of arching stems with limp leaves along them. Each flower has five crinkled segments. The flower cluster uncoils from the tip down the smooth stem. Virginia bluebell grows in showy colonies in moist woods and meadows. Soon after the seeds are set, the above-ground parts of the plant disappear until the following spring. Hardy and adaptable, Virginia bluebell grows successfully in home gardens.

The name "lungwort" comes from an early belief that the plant was therapeutic for lung disease. Virginia bluebell provides an example of the value of Latin names in identifying plants, as entirely different plants also go by the name "bluebell" and "cowslip."

MARSH MARIGOLD
Caltha palustris
Buttercup family (Ranunculaceae)
Also called cowslip
Average first bloom: Leopold, May 1 /
   Bradley, April 24
Height: 8–24 inches
Flower width: 1 inch

Mounds of intense yellow marsh marigolds rise up out of watery places to light the early spring. Five to nine lustrous, golden sepals form a cup around a cluster of yellow stamens. The sepals have a waxy surface that repels water. Vivid green, glossy, heart-shaped leaves provide a stunning background for these sunny flowers. The stems are hollow and branched. The aboveground parts of marsh marigold plants disappear by summer.

Native Americans referred to the marsh marigold as "the flower that opens the swamps." In the Middle Ages, people decorated churches with marsh marigolds for a festival honoring the Virgin Mary, for whom they are named. The marigolds commonly grown in gardens are composites, and are not related to marsh marigolds. It is not advisable to pick wild flowers because many are rare, but the young leaves of marsh marigolds, if well-cooked, may be eaten like spinach, and the buds pickled and used as capers. Raw marsh marigolds contain a poison that has reportedly killed cattle.

PRAIRIE SMOKE
Geum triflorum
Rose family (Rosaceae)
Also called long-plumed avens, grand-
   pa's whiskers
Average first bloom: Leopold, May 5 /
   Bradley, April 25
Height: 4–6 inches
Flower: 1 inch

The intense rose-colored flowers of the prairie smoke face downward. The bell-shape you see combines sepals and bracts. Tiny cream petals are hidden inside. As seed heads form, they turn upward and the "smoke" appears. This dusky cloud is made of two-inch-long trailing filaments attached to the seeds. In addition to spreading by wind, the seeds are "stick-tights" that catch in animals' fur. Prairie smoke seed heads have inspired other names, including "war bonnet" and "feather duster." Look for prairie smoke on dry hillsides. The leaves are deeply cut and mostly in a rosette near the ground. The entire plant is fuzzy.

A tea from the roots of prairie smoke has been used by Native Americans. An astringent, the tea was used to treat a variety of ailments, including indigestion, eye infection, and fever.

PURPLE TRILLIUM
Trillium erectum
Lily family (Liliaceae)
Also called wakerobin, prairie trilli-
um, stinking Benjamin, red trillium
Average first bloom: Bradley, April 25
Height: 8–16 inches
Flower: 1½ inches

Not as showy as white trillium, the purple trillium lives up to its name of trillium, which means three. It has three crimson-to-maroon petals, three alternating green sepals, and six yellow-tipped stamens. The petals arch backward. There are yellow and white forms of the flower also. The fleshy fruit is dark red with small brown seeds. The sturdy rhizome is brown, has stringy roots, and may be deep beneath the surface of the soil. Purple trilliums thrive in prairies and in woods with deep leaf mold. Slow to germinate from seeds, young purple trilliums do not bloom until they are several years old.

The attractive nickname "wakerobin" may be given to this trillium because it blooms when the robins return north in the spring, although the phenological date for robins in southern Wisconsin is earlier. Less attractive, but more easily explained, is the name "stinking Benjamin." Some of the purple trillium's flowers smell like rancid meat, thus attracting a major pollinator, the big green fleshfly.

BELLWORT
Uvularia grandiflora
Lily family (Liliaceae)
Also called merrybells
Average first bloom: Leopold, May 4 /
Bradley, April 27
Height: 8–20 inches
Flower: 1⅛ inches

Bellwort is a modest yellow lily of medium-dry woods. Its haphazard bell-shaped flowers hang down, partially hidden by an abundance of rather droopy spring-green leaves. The stems seem to pierce through the leaves. Like those of all lilies, the bellwort flower parts are in threes—three petals, three sepals that are almost like the petals, three styles, six stamens, and the fruit is a three-lobed capsule. Bellwort grows from a short rhizome. After blooming, the plant straightens up and develops new leaves.

If the plants are plentiful, and you find them growing on your own property, you can boil and eat the young shoots, rather like asparagus.

WILD BLUE PHLOX
Phlox divaricata
Phlox family (Polemoniaceae)
Also called woodland phlox
Average first bloom: Leopold,
    May 10 / Bradley, April 28
Height: 6–24 inches
Flower: ¾ inch

Masses of lavender-blue phlox brighten the ground layer of wet woodland edges in early spring. A rosette of leaves stays green all winter. With the first warm days, sticky-haired stems grow quickly, producing a flat cluster of flowers on the top. Each flower has five petals, spread like the vanes of a windmill. The lower part of the stem reclines on the ground. The leaves are oblong. The stickiness of the stem prevents crawling insects, which do not serve as pollinators, from getting to the pollen.

"Phlox" comes from the Greek word *phlegein,* which means "to burn." There are other species of phlox quite similar in form to the wild blue phlox.

PUCCOON
Lithospermum canescens
Borage family (Boraginaceae)
Also called gromwell, hoary puccoon
Average first bloom: Leopold, May 1 /
    Bradley, May 14
Height: 6–24 inches
Flower: ½ inch

Deep-yellow clusters of puccoon flowers make vivid splashes of color on dry prairies, about the time speckled fawns are hidden in the grass by their mothers. The top flower in each cluster blooms first. Each tube-like flower has five lobes and is surrounded by bristly bracts. Neither the flowers nor the leaves have stalks, but are attached directly to the stem. The stems are covered with white hairs. Several species of puccoon are native to Wisconsin. A close relative is *Lithospermum caroliniense.* The small ruffled puccoon (*Lithospermum incisum*) is named for the rippled edges of its light-yellow petals.

"Puccoon" is a Native American word for plants that produce dyes. The roots of puccoon, including the deep taproot, produce a reddish-purple dye. The Latin word *lithospermum* means "rock-like seeds," referring to the four hard, flat, white seeds of each puccoon flower. These seeds were made into ceremonial beads by the Menominees. Shoshoni women have used a solution made from the seeds as a contraceptive. Lab tests have confirmed this effect in rats and rabbits.

BIRDFOOT VIOLET

Viola pedata

Violet family (Violaceae)

Also called pansy violet

Average first bloom: Leopold, May 2 / Bradley, May 4

Height: 3–6 inches

Flower: ⅝ inch

The flowers of the birdfoot violet are flat, with two side petals that droop slightly, giving them the look of a small, comical pansy. Colors range from lavender to pale blue or bicolored, accentuated by a deep yellow pistil. Deeply cut leaves give the plant its name. The leaves disappear in summer and develop again in fall. Look for birdfoot violets on dry prairies.

Violet leaves are rich in vitamin C. The flowers, fresh or candied, may garnish salads and desserts. Since the time of Pliny, a first-century Roman naturalist, parts of the violet plant have been used medicinally. Pliny suggested using a garland of violets to treat headaches.

LARGE TRILLIUM

Trillium grandiflorum

Lily family (Liliaceae)

Also called white trillium, great trillium

Average first bloom: Leopold, May 8 / Bradley, May 4

Height: 8–16 inches

Flower: 2–3 inches

The three wide-open, wavy petals of the white trillium seem welcoming, and they are truly a welcome sight in rich woods in midspring. Other parts besides petals are in threes—three green sepals, three leaves in a whorl, three stigmas, and six stamens. The large, almost diamond-shaped leaves grow atop a single sturdy stem, and the flower is on a 1–3-inch stalk above the leaves. The bloom lasts several weeks, turning pink as it ages. The leaves stay green throughout the summer. Many tiny brown seeds are in the fruit, produced without benefit of fertilization. Although large numbers of trilliums may be found growing in a colony, often in sugar maple woods, they are a protected species, and like most other wildflowers, should not be picked. If the trillium flower and leaves are picked, the plant dies, as the thick rootstock has no way to make food.

The Menominee Nation has used wet dressings from freshly dug trillium rhizomes to heal eye infections. Pioneers sometimes ate the leaves when food was scarce. Although trilliums are a native North American species, they have long been cultivated in English gardens.

JACK IN THE PULPIT
Arisaema triphyllum
Calla family (Araceae)
Also called Indian turnip
Height: 1–3 feet
Flower arrangement: 4 inches

Like a minister ready to perform a wedding, Jack, the spadix, stands within the hood-like pulpit, or spathe, that surrounds him. The first signs of Jack in the pulpit in spring are the tightly rolled leaves that emerge rapidly from the moist woodland floor. They unroll into wide three-part leaves that flank the flowers. The tiny flowers bloom at the base of the spadix, enveloped by the cup of the spathe. In young plants the flowers are male, but with storage of sufficient nutrients, next year's may become female. The spathe, the pulpit part, has a top flap that protects the flowers from rain which would otherwise collect in the bottom of the spathe. The spathe varies in color from light green to dark reddish-brown, depending on the amount of sunlight it receives. It is marked by vertical stripes. The showiest time of year for Jack in the pulpit is fall, when the leaves yellow and die, leaving bright red clusters of berry-like fruit standing.

All parts of Jack in the pulpit contain tiny crystals of calcium oxalate, which produce a painful burning if eaten raw. Native Americans dried the bulbs, and then cooked them for a peppery-tasting staple food.

COLUMBINE
Aquilegia canadensis
Buttercup family (Ranunculaceae)
Also called rock bells
Average first bloom: Leopold, May 19 /
  Bradley, May 9
Height: 1–3 feet
Flower: 1¼ inches

The graceful columbine is a familiar flower on rocky ledges and in dry woods in late spring. Salmon-red and yellow flowers nod in clusters near the top of the plant. Most of the lacy compound leaves are grouped near the ground. Spurs on the tubular petals are the most noticeable flower part. The tops of the five petals are creamy yellow, shading into brick-red at the base of the spur where the nectar is. Hummingbirds and bumblebees collect the nectar and pollinate the columbine. Paler red sepals squeeze between the petals, and almost conceal their tops. A brush of yellow stamens protrudes beyond the sepals and petals. Columbine is hardy, partly because of its deep taproot.

By late June pods full of tiny black seeds have formed. The Omaha Indian Nation has used these seeds as love charms, rubbing them on their hands, and then shaking hands with the one admired. Columbine leaves have been eaten as salad greens.

BLUE-EYED GRASS

Sisyrinchium campestre
Iris family (Iridaceae)
Average first bloom: Leopold, May 17 /
　Bradley, May 13
Height: 4–16 inches
Flower: ¼ inch

Tiny bright flowers of blue-eyed grass wink between the stems of true grasses on the spring prairie. Its long, grass-like leaves of light green account for its name, although blue-eyed grass is actually an iris. Search the prairie in early morning to find the clear blue blossoms, for they close as the sun gets high, or if they are picked. One or two flowers at a time bloom from a cluster of buds that emerges from two uneven bracts on the winged flower stem. The sepals and petals are alike, so each flower appears to have six oval petals. Each petal has darker blue lines, converging toward a tiny spike at the tip. Pistils and stamens are yellow. The seed heads contain many tiny black seeds.

Tea made from blue-eyed grass is said to cure stomach cramps. The Menominees have used cuttings of blue-eyed grass in their homes and on their persons to ward off snakes. A mixture of blue-eyed grass and oats was used to make horses fat, and brave in battle. Blue-eyed grass is said to have been one of Thoreau's favorite flowers.

WILD GERANIUM

Geranium maculatum
Geranium family (Geraniaceae)
Also called spotted cranesbill
Average first bloom: Leopold, May 14 /
　Bradley, May 13
Height: 12–28 inches
Flower: 1 inch

The cheerful lavender-to-pink colors of wild geraniums are a welcome sight in woodlands, along roadsides, and in home gardens in spring. Five is the number for geraniums—five spiked sepals, five rounded petals, and five or more parts to each toothed lobe of the leaves. All the parts are covered with fine silvery hairs. Fine lines down the petals lead pollinating insects to the yellow stamens and tiny green pistil in the center. Most of the leaves are basal, but there is a pair of leaves where each flower stem branches near the top.

The five-sectioned seed pod is pointed like a crane's bill. (The name "geranium" is derived from the Greek word *geranos,* which means "crane.") When the pod is ripe, it springs open from the bottom, propelling the seeds outward, sometimes for many feet. Deer and black bear feed on wild geraniums.

LUPINE

Lupinus perennis
Pea or bean family (Fabaceae)
Average first bloom: Leopold,
    May 20 / Bradley, May 15
Height: 8–24 inches
Flower: 1 inch

Lupine thrives in sandy open woods and prairies, often in showy patches. A clump of stems grows from a coarse, branching root crown. Spikes of blue pea-like flowers rise above sturdy, palmately compound leaves of bluish-green. The lupine flower has two fused petals called a keel, which contains the stamens and pistil. When a bee lands on the keel, its weight depresses these petals, squeezing pollen collected in the bottom of the keel onto the bee. Lupine seeds are extremely durable, as demonstrated with some seeds researchers removed from a 10,000-year-old lemming burrow in the Yukon. These lupine seeds germinated within 48 hours after being planted.

The name "lupine" comes from the Latin word *lupus,* meaning "wolf," given to the plant in the mistaken idea that it wolfed nutrients from the soil. To the contrary, it adds nitrogen to the soil, through a symbiotic relationship with nitrogen-fixing microorganisms called rhizobia. Lupine is believed to be poisonous, although deer sometimes eat the blooms.

SHOOTING STAR

Dodecatheon meadia
Primrose family (Primulaceae)
Also called birdbill, Indian chief,
    American cowslip
Average first bloom: Leopold,
    May 22 / Bradley, May 15
Height: 8–24 inches
Flower: ⅞ inch

Tall, smooth stems rise from dry tree leaves at the edge of the oak woods in May, with all the promise of arcing fireworks. They explode into hanging clusters of delicate pink and white flowers. The tip of each flower, consisting of a cone of stamens pointing downward, is dramatically marked with yellow and black. Five thin, curvy petals sweep skyward like the tail of a falling star. Later the stem straightens so that the seed pods develop upright. There is a basal rosette of spatula-shaped leaves, reddish at their base. The roots are fibrous.

Shooting star is one of just a few flowers pollinated by bees that does not have a landing platform. Bumblebees hang upside down from the bottom of the flower, depositing pollen from other flowers on the protruding pistil. At the same time, the bee's beating wings shake the flower, so that new pollen drops to the lower surface of the bee's body, ready to be deposited on another flower.

CREAM BAPTISIA

Baptisia leucophaea
Pea or bean family (Fabaceae)
Also called cream false indigo, prairie
 wild indigo
Average first bloom: Leopold, May 15 /
 Bradley, May 16
Height: 3–6 feet
Flower: 1 inch

A plant of cream baptisia develops as a single, many-branched stem, giving it the appearance of a small shrub, taller than the early summer grasses. Many creamy, pea-type blossoms grow in showy racemes that protrude outward and tend to droop all the way around the leafy plant, so it looks like a large bridal bouquet. Later 1–2-inch seed pods draw attention with their fuzzy, inflated appearance. The leaves are hairy and appear to have five leaflets. In the fall the leaves and pods turn dark brown. The entire plant breaks off at ground level, tumbling in the wind, and spreading seeds as it goes.

Cream baptisia sap becomes purple (indigo) on exposure to the air. Steeped and fermented, the leaves make dye. "Baptisia" comes from the Greek word *baptizein,* which means "to dip." Medicinally, Native Americans have used prairie wild indigo to treat cuts and fevers. The Pawnee Nation made an ointment of buffalo fat and pulverized wild indigo seeds. Livestock will not normally eat cream baptisia.

PRAIRIE PHLOX

Phlox pilosa
Phlox family (Polemoniaceae)
Also called downy phlox, hairy phlox,
 pink prairie phlox
Average first bloom: Leopold,
 May 28 / Bradley, May 21
Height: 6–24 inches
Flower: ¾ inch

The splash of bright pink that catches the eye in May is often prairie phlox. Variations in color may shade to white. The phlox is one of the plants that may be much more abundant the year its tall-grass prairie habitat has been burned. Each flower within the loosely branched cluster has five petals, and a slightly fuzzy stem. The prairie phlox flower looks cheerful, in a shape a bit like a child's pinwheel. The petals fuse into a tube at the base, from which hummingbirds drink the nectar. The stiff narrow leaves of prairie phlox are set in opposite pairs, wider at the base, tapering to sharp tips. The seed capsule has several sections, each with one to four seeds. These capsules when dry seem to explode, scattering the seeds up to several feet away from the plant. Although some phlox are annuals, prairie phlox is a perennial. It should not be confused with the blue phlox of the woodlands.

The species name, *pilosa,* means "hairy" in Latin. Native Americans have used a tea from phlox leaves to cure eczema. The root, used in combination with other herbs, was regarded as a love potion.

CANADA ANEMONE
Anemone canadensis
Buttercup family (Ranunculaceae)
Also called crowfoot, Canada
   windflower
Average first bloom: Leopold, June 2 /
   Bradley, May 27
Height: up to 2 feet
Flower: 1½ inches

A single Canada anemone flower blooms elegantly atop a slender stalk. It has no true petals, but five pure-white sepals, and many pale yellow stamens and pistils. The leaves have five to seven deeply cut parts, and are arranged in whorls. Canada anemones are common in moist prairies throughout eastern North America and Canada. They are often found growing in disturbed soil, or on the edges of potholes, where there is less competition from taller prairie plants.

The name "anemone" is related to the Greek word *anemos,* which means "wind." The tall, limber flower stems bend gracefully with every breeze. Canada anemone seeds are small and flat with a little hook that may stick to fur or feathers; however, anemone plants are more apt to spread by their slender rhizomes. A Greek myth tells that an anemone plant sprang up wherever one of Aphrodite's tears fell, as she mourned the death of the handsome Adonis. Some Native Americans made a tea of the roots for treatment of headaches or dizziness.

INDIAN PAINT BRUSH
Castilleja coccinea
Figwort family (Schrophulariaceae)
Also called painted cup
Average first bloom: Bradley, May 28
Height: 5–24 inches
Flower: 1 inch

Romantically named, Indian paint brush could have been the result of an early artist's dropping some paint brushes after painting a sunset. The brush-like part of the plant, which varies from yellow to scarlet, is made up of a dense cluster of bracts at the top of an unbranched stem. These bracts cover the true flower, which is tubular and yellowish-green. The leaves are long and narrow. Paint brush adds bright splashes, even masses, of color to open meadows and moist prairies. Indian paint brush is a semi-parasite. Its roots grow into the soil until they touch other roots. Then the paint brush roots attach to, and draw nourishment from, the other plant's roots.

SPIDERWORT

Tradescantia ohiensis
Spiderwort family (Commelinaceae)
Also called widow tears, blue jackets
Average first bloom: Leopold, June 2 /
  Bradley, May 28
Height: 1–3 feet
Flower: ¾–1 inches

Spiderwort flowers are three-petaled, and bluish-violet to pink or white in color. Clusters of many flower heads rise above long, leaf-like bracts. Only a few of the flowers bloom at a time. The five yellow stamens are feathered like tiny boas. The leaves are long and narrow, forming prominent bumps where they join the stem. The stems have a white, waxy coating that can be rubbed off. Spiderwort grows in a variety of habitats, from sandy prairies to dry meadows. With time, the spiderwort spreads into a colony with a tangle of tough fibrous roots. In morning sunshine a patch of intense blue spiderwort is beautiful to see, but around midday the blossoms close. If you press the closed flowers, blue liquid oozes out, which accounts for such common names as "widow tears."

Once thought to be a cure for spider bite, the leaves were eaten by Native Americans. Some environmental groups use spiderwort as an indicator for the presence of radiation, which may cause the flowers to change color. The name *Tradescantia* is derived from John Tradescant, the gardener to Charles I of England, who took spiderwort from America to England in the seventeenth century.

WILD IRIS

Iris virginica, var. *shrevei*
Iris family (Iridaceae)
Also called blue flag, poison flag
Average first bloom: Bradley, May 30
Height: 1–3 feet
Flower: 1⅞ inches

The showy, blue wild iris thrives in wet meadows and on streambanks. It has three upright petals, three stamens under protective petal-like branches of the style, and three showy sepals. The sepals are veined, and have some white and a hairy yellow patch at their base. Bumblebees force their way between the petal-like style branches and the sepals, depositing pollen from other blooms on the pistil, and picking up more from the stamens as they search for nectar. Papery bracts cover the buds. The leaves are sword-shaped. Iris grows from rhizomes that are poisonous. The fruit is a three-lobed capsule about one and one-half inches long. If eaten, the black seeds cause a strong, burning sensation in the mouth and throat.

The name "flag" comes from Old English and means "reed" or "rush." In Greek mythology, Iris was the rainbow goddess. The French stylized the iris into the heraldic fleur-de-lis. Native Americans took small amounts of the powdered root as a cathartic. Some tribes have used the root in mixtures to poison arrows. Pioneers used a paste of the root to relieve swelling and pain from bruises and sores. The etymology indicates the wide-ranging love for iris.

WILD QUININE
Parthenium integrifolium
Aster family (Asteraceae)
Also called feverfew, American fever-
  few
Average first bloom: Bradley, May 30
Height: 20–40 inches
Flower head: ½ inch

Wild quinine has flat-topped clus-ters of white flowers. On close exami-nation, what appears to be a single flower is seen to be made up of many smaller flowers. These composite flower heads have five ray-flower petals, like tiny, round ears of white mice. The flowers of the center disk are sterile. The fertile flower is in two or three rows of small bracts. The black seeds produced by wild quinine are less than one-eighth-inch long. Wild qui-nine has rough, hairy basal leaves that are undivided, but that do have coarse teeth. Additional leaves are on long stems attached to the stalk, and may be up to 12 inches long. They alternate along the stem, becoming progressive-ly smaller toward the top.

Tea made from wild quinine leaves was an early-day treatment for fevers. Some Native Americans put the fresh leaves over burns to soothe them.

WILD ROSE
Rosa carolina
Rose family (Rosaceae)
Also called pasture rose, meadow rose
Average first bloom: Leopold, May 31 /
  Bradley, June 1
Height: 6½ feet
Flower: 1½ inches

With its delicacy of color, fragrance, and form, the wild rose seems to epit-omize the sweet, simple side of life. Its flower has five petals, ranging from almost white to deep pink. Numerous yellow stamens surround a cluster of yellow pistils in the center of the blos-som. Wild rose shrubs grow, often in profusion, along the edge of woods and on prairies throughout Wisconsin. The branching root systems spread readily. There are several species closely related to *Rosa carolina.* They hybridize easily, making it difficult to identify them, but the thorns vary from tiny prickles to thick spines, and the number of leaflets may be from three to nine.

Wild rose seeds are clustered in a shiny, red fruit called a hip, relished by birds and animals. Seeds that have passed through a bird's digestive sys-tem germinate readily. The Chippewa Nation has used a liquid prepared from the inner root bark of the wild rose to soothe sore eyes. Rose hips make pretty jelly, rich in vitamin C and several minerals.

PALE SPIKE LOBELIA

Lobelia spicata
Lobelia family (Campanulaceae)
Also called spiked lobelia, highbelia
Average first bloom: Leopold, July 5 /
    Bradley, June 14
Height: 8–40 inches
Flower: 1 inch

Pale spike lobelia's light blue flowers are arranged along a single stalk. They are irregular, with an upper lip, cleft so it looks like two little ears, and a lower lip divided into three larger parts. The center one is pointed; the other two are rounded. As with the cardinal flower (*Lobelia cardinalis*), there is a beard on the tip of the stamens. The pale spike lobelia is an interesting and unusual little flower. These lobelias bloom through most of the summer, and thrive in almost any kind of prairie— from rich meadows to dry sand. The leaves are oval and hairy. They get smaller toward the top of the stalk, and finally become merely bracts.

Native Americans and others know lobelias as emetics and purgatives. They contain alkaloids that are similar to nicotine. Indian tobacco (*Lobelia inflata*) is sometimes used to cure people of tobacco smoking, however. Other lobelias that grow in Wisconsin include the great blue lobelia (*Lobelia siphilitica*) and the brook lobelia (*Lobelia kalmii*). The family is named for a sixteenth-century herbalist, Matthias von Lobel.

BLACK-EYED SUSAN

Rudbeckia hirta
Aster family (Asteraceae)
Also called poor-land daisy, yellow ox-
    eye daisy, deer eye
Average first bloom: Leopold,
    June 22 / Bradley, June 16
Height: 1–3 feet
Flower head: 2–3 inches

With its bright yellow rays and deep brown disk of tiny flowers in the center, crowds of black-eyed Susans epitomize summer on the prairie. The blooms are abundant and long-lasting. Black-eyed Susans have large basal leaves, and smaller leaves on the stems. The stems and leaves are covered with short bristly hairs. Black-eyed Susans are pioneers, much more prevalent on new or disturbed prairies than on older prairies.

The Potawatomi Nation has used boiled disk flowers to dye rushes yellow for basket-making. Early settlers brewed tea from the dried leaves as a kidney stimulant. The name *Rudbeckia* memorializes the Rudbecks, father and son, who were Swedish botanists.

BUTTERFLY WEED
Asclepias tuberosa
Milkweed family (Asclepiadaceae)
Also called orange or yellow milk-
    weed, pleurisy root, Indian posy
Average first bloom: Leopold, July 5 /
    Bradley, June 21
Height: 1–3 feet
Flower: ⅜ inch

The flat-topped, brilliant orange clusters of flowers atop a patch of butterfly
weed are a striking sight on dry prairies.
Rough leaves up to six inches long alternate on the stems. Butterfly weed does
not have the milky sap common to most
milkweeds. The branching taproot
grows strong and deep.

Pollination of butterfly weed can be
completed best by one of the larger
flying insects. The pollen found between the five prongs of each tiny
crown-shaped flower can trap a small
insect, making it unable to pull away.
This happens because the insect's feet
become tangled in a thread that joins
two "saddle bags" of pollen. Fortunately, monarch butterflies are drawn
in flocks to butterfly weed, where they
lay their eggs and pollinate a few of the
many flowers. Only one or two flowers
on each plant develop into seed pods.
Each long, bristly pod holds many
plumed seeds that disperse in the
autumn breezes. Birds do not like
butterfly weed, nor do they like the larvae of the butterflies that acquire dis-
tasteful toxic chemicals from the plant.

Butterfly weed was considered to be
a cure for pleurisy, accounting for the
common name "pleurisy root." Unlike
common milkweed, butterfly weed is
poisonous.

CUP PLANT
Silphium perfoliatum
Aster family (Asteraceae)
Also called rosinweed, Indian cup
Average first bloom: Leopold, July 2 /
    Bradley, June 22
Height: 3–8 feet
Flower head: 2½ inches

One of the dominant yellow, summer sunflower-like plants on moist
prairies, the cup plant is named for an
interesting feature. Its pairs of toothed
leaves form cups around the square
stems. The water that collects in these
cups provides refreshing drinks to
insects and small birds. The cup plant
has narrow ray flowers around the
composite center disk of flowers.

A part of the original prairie, cup
plant was plowed under by the early
settlers. Now University of Wisconsin
agronomists are considering it as a
possible forage crop. It is comparable
to alfalfa in protein and bulk, and has a
much longer life span. Cup plant can
grow for 20 years, but alfalfa thrives
for only three to six years. Cup plant's
spreading, fibrous roots would slow
soil erosion, a problem with corn cultivation. Adapted to wet areas, cup plant
could trap runoff nutrients, minimiz-
ing its need for fertilizer.

MILKWEED

Asclepias syriaca
Milkweed family (Asclepiadaceae)
Also called common milkweed
Average first bloom: Leopold, July 2 /
  Bradley, June 22
Height: 1½–6 feet
Flower: ⅝ inch

Everyone notices the common milkweed in fall when the large, rough pods open, and the shiny, white mass inside escapes, filling the air with little parachutes carrying brown seeds. This robust plant, with its large, smooth leaves, blooms in midsummer. Balls of little mauve flowers hang from the top of the milkweed. Like those of other milkweeds, these flowers are highly evolved. The sepals and petals turn back, and a corona of five hoods stands atop the flower, each hood concealing a stigma and stamens. Only a few of these flowers are successfully pollinated to become pods. It is surprising that such large pods can grow from such tiny flowers. Milkweed stems contain sticky, milky-looking fluid.

Many milkweed parts are edible, but authorities recommend boiling them in several changes of water to get rid of bitterness. The young shoots look something like asparagus. The flowers and buds have been prepared and eaten by the Chippewa Nation. The Sioux extracted juice from the flowers to make a kind of sugar. Some Native Americans cooked the young pods with buffalo meat. Euell Gibbons, a modern-day proponent of wild foods, recommended the broccoli-shaped buds and very young pods. Gather the pods in autumn for dried arrangements. The whorled milkweed, with slender leaves from three-quarters of an inch to an inch and a half long attached to the stem, is another abundant milkweed.

COMPASS PLANT
Silphium laciniatum
Aster family (Asteraceae)
Also called rosinweed, turpentine
  plant
Average first bloom: Leopold, July 15 /
  Bradley, June 23
Height: 5–9 feet
Flower head: 3 inches

The blooming compass plant looks much like a very tall sunflower on the summer prairie, but it is easily identified by the basal leaves which give it its name. They grow up to 20 inches long, and are deeply divided and oriented north and south. This orientation may be useful in conserving moisture, by reducing exposure to midday sun. The taproot of the compass plant can grow 15 feet deep. The number of sturdy, bristly flowering stems depends on the age of the compass plant and the availability of moisture.

Early settlers and Native Americans used concoctions of the roots and leaves of compass plants to cure a variety of ailments from rheumatism to bad breath. The upper parts of the stem exude a gummy material chewed by Native American and pioneer children. Cattle graze heavily on compass plant. This fact, and the use of the plow, explain why Aldo Leopold celebrated finding a single compass plant blooming in the corner of a fenced country graveyard in the 1940s. Leopold would no doubt be pleased that the number of compass plants is increasing, along with renewed interest in the prairie landscape.

MARSH MILKWEED
Asclepias incarnata
Milkweed family (Asclepiadaceae)
Also called swamp milkweed, silk-
  weed, water nerve root, white
  Indian hemp, rose milkweed
Average first bloom: Leopold, July 6 /
  Bradley, June 25
Height: 1–4 feet
Flower: ⅜ inch

Follow the butterflies to this rosy-red member of the milkweed family. Wear boots, as marsh milkweed grows in wet areas. The flowers grow in clusters one to three inches across. Each tiny flower is intricate and highly evolved. When open, the petals turn back, and five fused stamens and a pistil are protected by little hoods with curved horns. The leaves are narrow and pointed, arranged in pairs along the stem. Stems and leaves are smooth. The seed pods are two to four inches long and contain many plumed seeds.

The Latin genus name comes from Asclepios, the Greek god of medicine. Canadian Native Americans drank a tea made from the root of milkweed to become temporarily sterile. Some tribes burned away the plumes from the seeds, steeped the seeds, and used the liquid to draw poison from rattlesnake bites. Europeans have tried the plume fibers for stuffing material. Goldfinches line their nests with them. During World War II Americans tested the milky sap as a rubber substitute. The fibers make good twine, and good nesting material for birds.

GRAY-HEADED CONEFLOWER
Ratibida pinnata
Aster family (Asteraceae)
Also called yellow coneflower, prairie coneflower, drooping coneflower, weary Susan, Mexican hat
Average first bloom: Leopold, July 14 / Bradley, July 1
Height: 1½–4 feet
Ray flower: 2 inches

With petals folded back and a center like a brown gumdrop, the gray-headed coneflower can easily be told from the black-eyed Susan. These droopy-looking petals are really ray flowers, with the true flowers in the disk, which is dull gray in bud, and deep brown when the flowers bloom out. This cone has an anise-like fragrance when crushed, making it easy to identify the seed pods. The ray flowers are a clear, bright crayon-yellow. Gray-headed coneflower leaves alternate on the stem. They are deeply cut and serrated, becoming smaller and simpler near the top of the plant. The stem, which has fine hairs pointing upward, sometimes branches, producing two or more blooms. Gray-headed coneflower is perennial, grows from rhizomes, and tends to grow in showy clumps.

Gray-headed coneflower grows easily from its tiny, flat, winged seeds. It survives in prairie conditions where most other native species have died. Native Americans have used a tea from the flower heads and leaves. Some tribes used the root to treat toothache.

HOARY VERVAIN
Verbena stricta
Vervain family (Verbenaceae)
Average first bloom: Leopold, July 4 / Bradley, July 2
Height: 16–40 inches
Flower: ¼ inch

Small vivid lavender flowers bloom up a cluster of stalks on hoary vervain. The numerous flower stalks grow up to eight inches in length. Blue Vervain (*Verbena hastata*), a related species, is bluer and more branched. Hoary vervain leaves are toothed and hairy with almost no stem. Only a small circle of flowers blooms at any one time, which makes the plant look as if it may be just beginning to bloom. Vervains can become a weed in pastures, partly because cattle do not eat them.

One species of vervain was used in ancient Greek and Roman ceremonies, and the plant's name comes from the Latin *verbenae,* the term for sacred boughs and foliage.

PURPLE CONEFLOWER

Echinacea purpurea
Aster family (Asteraceae)
Also called black Samson, red
    sunflower
Average first bloom: Bradley, July 2
Height: 2–5 feet
Ray flower: 2 inches

Showy purple coneflowers bloom among an array of yellow prairie composite relatives. They are beyond the northern edge of their range in Wisconsin, but thrive in new prairies. The long petal-like ray flowers are more magenta or pink than purple, and surround the raised center of true flowers. Lower leaves have toothed edges, but upper leaves are smooth-edged. All the leaves are rough. In the fall the center dome becomes a spiny ball carrying the seeds, and give the plant its Greek genus name, *Echinacea,* which means sea urchin.

Plains Native Americans had many medicinal uses for the purple coneflower. The dark ridged roots provided poultices for snake and dog bites, enlarged glands, and toothaches. Prairie natives learned that bathing body parts in the juice enabled them to endure extreme heat. Medicine men rubbed the juice on their hands and then took meat out of boiling stew, or rubbed it in their mouths before putting in hot coals. Smoke from burning the plant was a treatment for headache, or for distemper in horses. Some modern doctors use extracts of purple coneflowers for treating wounds and sore throats. *Echinacea* is a popular product in today's health-food stores.

RATTLESNAKE MASTER

Eryngium yuccifolium
Carrot family (Apiaceae)
Also called button snakeroot, rat-
    tlesnake weed
Average first bloom: Leopold, July 22 /
    Bradley, July 4
Height: 2–4 feet
Flower arrangement: 1 inch

Not showy, but interesting, the rattlesnake master has yucca-like leaves— long, thick, and blue-green with sharp, spiny edges. Most of these leaves grow from the base of the plant. The edges of the leaves have tough fibers, which protect the plant from insect damage. Smaller leaves clasp the tall flowering stems that are topped by globe-shaped heads of prickly flowers on short stems. Each head is made up of many tiny flowers, each with five petals hidden under whitish bracts. The seed heads have a honey-like fragrance.

Related plants have been used medicinally since early Greek times. There is a catalog of curative claims for rattlesnake master roots, ranging from being an aphrodisiac to a snakebite cure (from which it gets its name). Chewing the roots does cause saliva to flow. The cords from the leaves provided Native Americans with fiber for twine.

CULVER'S ROOT
Veronicastrum virginicum
Figwort family (Scrophulariaceae)
Also called Culver's physic, Bowman's
    root, high veronica, tall speedwell
Average first bloom: Leopold, July 4 /
    Bradley, July 6
Height: 3–6 feet
Flower arrangement: 6 inches

Flower stalks of Culver's root are eye-catching on moist summer prairies. Some look like candles, some like candelabra. One to nine tapered spikes, crowded with tiny white or pale lavender flowers, grow out of the top of each stalk. Sometimes the stalks are bent (Salvador Dali chandeliers). Close examination shows that each flower is trumpet-shaped, with two stamens and the pistil protruding beyond the four lobes of the trumpet. Whorls of serrated, pointed leaves grow at intervals along the stalk. The fibrous roots are yellow. Later, double-chambered capsules develop, each containing many minute black seeds.

The roots of Culver's root have powerful cathartic and emetic qualities, and the fresh root was used as an uncertain and drastic means of inducing abortion. Culver's root was long used by Native Americans for a variety of complaints. Members of the Menominee Nation have used tea of Culver's root for purification when they had been touched by a bereaved person.

LEAD PLANT
Amorpha canescens
Pea or bean family (Fabaceae)
Also called prairie shoestring, wild tea
Average first bloom: Leopold, July 8 /
    Bradley, July 29
Height: 18–36 inches
Flower: ½ inch

Tiny, dark-purple flowers occur on the lead plant in dense spikes two to seven inches long. Each flower has only a single petal and 10 golden stamens, but the flowers are so densely packed on the spikes that lead plant is conspicuous. The compound leaves are made up of numerous pairs of leaflets approximately one-quarter inch in length. By early June these hairy, gray leaves give a leaden color to little bluestem prairies, a favorite habitat for the lead plant. Mature stems are woody. Like most prairie perennials, lead plant has a deep root system, often extending 10 to 12 feet into the ground. A few inches underground the roots may also spread laterally to four or five feet from the crown. The settlers' plows broke them with a snap, hence the common name "prairie shoestring."

Native Americans have smoked the dried leaves of lead plant and also made tea to treat such varied ills as worms, eczema, and rheumatism. The Omaha Nation called lead plant "buffalo bellow plant," probably because it blooms during the bison rut.

BERGAMOT
Monarda fistulosa
Mint family (Lamiaceae)
Also called bee balm, horsemint
Average first bloom: Leopold, July 12 /
   Bradley, July 10
Height: 2–3 feet
Flower arrangement: 1–2 inches

Lavender bergamot flowers add contrast to the dominant yellows and golds of the summer prairie. The rounded flower heads are ragged-looking. Each is made up of many asymmetrical tube-shaped flowers with projecting pistils and two stamens. Their minty fragrance pervades the prairie, and lasts after the plants are dried. Bergamot has the square stems and paired, lance-shaped, and toothed leaves typical of the mint family. It grows from dense rhizomes in all types of prairie. Butterflies and hummingbirds are attracted to the bergamot nectar more than bees are despite the common name "bee balm."

Bergamot leaves make a strong tea said to be soothing to an upset stomach, although leaf-eating insects leave bergamot alone. The Ojibwe Nation has extracted the mint oil to use as a disinfectant. It was heated and inhaled for bronchitis. The Latin genus name honors Nicolas Monardes, a sixteenth-century Spanish physician and horticulturist.

PRAIRIE DOCK
Silphium terebinthinaceum
Aster family (Asteraceae)
Also called elephant ear
Average first bloom: Leopold, July 12 /
   Bradley, July 10
Height: 2–10 feet
Flower head: 2½ inches

Prairie dock is easily distinguished from the other tall yellow silphiums that dominate the summer prairie. It has heart-shaped basal leaves that may be as large as 12 × 16 inches. These intensely green leaves are translucent, and, with the sun behind them, they create beautiful patterns of light and shadow. Prairie dock leaves are smooth on the top and fuzzy on the underside. The leafless, smooth flower stalk has a number of short branches with flower heads at the top. Although prairie dock is not a true sunflower, the flowers do resemble sunflowers, with 25 or so yellow rays. The true flowers in the center have black specks among the yellow. Prairie dock requires deep soil for its long taproot.

In early times the root was steeped to treat a variety of ailments, including "female complaints."

PURPLE PRAIRIE-CLOVER

Petalostemum purpureum
Pea or bean family (Fabaceae)
Also called thimbleweed, red tassel
　flower
Average bloom: Leopold, July 11 /
　Bradley, July 10
Height: 1–2 feet
Flowers: ¼ inch

Tiny purple prairie-clover flowers, vivid rose in color, are borne on cylinder-shaped heads. They bloom in rings starting from the bottom of the flower head. A group of 8 to 10 tall stems grows from deep perennial roots. All along these stems are leaves shaped like fine evergreen needles, and at the top of each, one flower head. When they are midway through their summer-long bloom, imagination can turn a patch of waving purple prairie-clover heads into a corps de ballet in pink tutus.

Early Americans used all parts of the purple prairie-clover. Native Americans steeped the leaves to make a tea to heal wounds. Pulverized roots flavored a beverage. Settlers mixed the flowers with oak bark and made a tea to treat diarrhea. The Irish and Scottish people baked a nutritious bread from ground clover seeds. The sprouts are tasty but small. Finally, Native American women gathered the stems of what they called broom weed, to make brooms.

IRONWEED

Vernonia fasciculata
Aster family (Asteraceae)
Average first bloom: Leopold, July 21 /
　Bradley, July 15
Height: 2–6 feet
Flower arrangement: 8 inches

The red-violet flowers of ironweed provide waves of color on wet meadows in midsummer. Each loose flower head has 20 to 30 individual florets on short stems. These little flowers are tubular with five lobes, giving a fringed effect. Under each flower head are dark-colored bracts with slender tips. Ironweed leaves alternate along the stem, and are lance-shaped with fine sharp teeth. The stiff main stems of ironweed are tough, fibrous, and bitter. Wildlife and cattle avoid them. Bees, however, enjoy the nectar from the flowers. Ironweed is propagated by pollination, or by spreading rhizomes.

The Latin genus name, *Vernonia*, is for William Vernon, English botanist and seventeenth-century explorer.

SPOTTED JEWELWEED

Impatiens biflora
Jewelweed family (Balsaminaceae)
Also called touch-me-not
Height: 2–6 feet
Flower: 1 inch

If you walk in marshy areas or along streambanks in late summer, you may see bright orange flowers with red spots, dangling like earrings from slender stalks. They sway in the slightest breeze, and glisten in the sun. These are spotted jewelweed, and the ruby-throated hummingbirds know all about them. The coloring of the wide upper petal and the two below lures these birds to thrust their bills deep into a long, curved spur for the sweet nectar there. Delicate, egg-shaped leaves alternate along the limber main stem. They are gently toothed. The plants often grow in dense clusters. By September, slender, green seed pods appear. These provide the name "touch-me-not," for at the slightest touch the pods seem to explode, scattering seeds in all directions.

The Potawatomi Nation has used the watery sap that flows from the stems when they are broken to relieve the itch of poison ivy rash. The remedy is still used by people who find themselves exposed to poison ivy and in the company of jewelweed.

PARTRIDGE PEA

Cassia fasciculata
Senna family (Caesalpiniaceae)
Also called golden cassia, wild sensitive plant, prairie senna pea
Average first bloom: Bradley, July 18
Height: 4–36 inches
Flower: ½–1 inch

With bright green foliage, and copious canary-yellow flowers, partridge pea adds a background of spring-like color for late summer show-offs like blazing star and purple coneflower. The height of partridge pea varies. Its preference is for dry prairie or meadow soil. As many as 15 pairs of oval leaflets grow on each leaf, as in some members of the bean family, to which it is related. The leaves alternate on the main stem. Partridge pea flowers grow at the base of the leaves. The five petals are uneven in size and give the flower a floppy appearance. There are 10 unequal stamens, six of which have dark tips or anthers. These show as a purple-black center in the flower. When ripe, the flat, hairy seed pod splits open and spreads the seeds. They grow readily, so the partridge pea patch may be quite large.

The drug senna comes from related plants in the Middle East. The foliage of partridge pea is somewhat toxic, but white-tailed deer may browse on it. Quail and small rodents eat the seeds.

BLAZING STAR

Liatris aspera
Aster family (Asteraceae)
Also called button snakeroot, rough
   blazing star
Average first bloom: Bradley, July 21
Height: 16–48 inches
Flower head: 1 inch

Blazing star in bloom makes a colorful wash of rose-purple on dry prairies. The composite flower heads have short stems, and are spaced out along the stalk. This spacing is a way to tell blazing star species from gayfeather species. Cup-shaped bracts behind each flower are often rounded, and white to pink along the edges. Blazing star has narrow leaves, which conserve more moisture than the same number of wider leaves would. The knobby buds lower on the stalk are white and button-shaped. These buds and the tubers may have been used by Native Americans to treat rattlesnake bites, probably accounting for the common name "button snakeroot."

Early Americans dug the corms and stored them for winter food. *Aspera* in Latin means "rough," which describes the leaves. Tea from these leaves was thought to ease stomach aches.

GAYFEATHER

Liatris pycnostachya
Aster family (Asteraceae)
Height: 2–4 feet
Flower head: ½ inch

Crowds of tall, magenta spikes of gayfeather wave in the breezes across damp prairies and meadows throughout August, providing credibility to their common name. As many as 100 flower heads are crowded together on each spike. Slowly blooming from the top down to the bottom, they resemble torches. A flower head consists of five to seven tiny flowers. Each flower consists of a tube of five joined petals that flare open to a star shape at the top. The pistil and stamens protrude beyond the petals, giving the flowering plume a fuzzy look. Below the flowers, the stiff and narrow vertical leaves crowd the stem. At the bottom of the stalk the leaves may be four inches long, but they become progressively shorter higher up the stalk.

A perennial, the plant grows from a corm, which is said to taste something like carrots. Native Americans harvested and stored this corm for various medicinal uses, including treatment for urinary trouble and diarrhea. Some of them mixed the flower heads with corn to feed race horses for improved stamina.

JOE-PYE WEED
Eupatorium maculatum
Aster family (Asteraceae)
Also called purple boneset
Average first bloom: Leopold, July 22 /
    Bradley, July 23
Height: 2–7 feet
Flower arrangement: 7 inches

Joe-Pye weed grows in profusion in summers with plentiful moisture. Its flowers are a light shade of red-violet, and the plant is often found in a colorful mix with darker-toned ironweed. Hundreds of tiny flowers make up the flower heads of Joe-Pye weed. Clusters of these flower heads are relatively flat-topped. The slender toothed leaves grow in whorls around the stems, which may be purple or have purple spots. Colonies of Joe-Pye weed grow in moist meadows.

Joe-Pye weed may have been named for a Native American who brewed a tea from the plant to treat typhus. Pioneers considered it a diuretic. Some Native Americans used the leaves as a love potion.

BONESET
Eupatorium perfoliatum
Aster family (Asteraceae)
Also called thoroughwort
Average first bloom: Leopold, July 29 /
    Bradley, July 25
Height: 2–4 feet
Flower arrangement: 6 inches

A rather flat inflorescence branches from the top of the main stem of boneset. This inflorescence is made up of hundreds of tiny dull-white tube flowers, grouped in heads of 9 to 23 flowers. Boneset's wrinkly leaves are gray-green, and grow in pairs fused around the central stem. Both leaves and stem are hairy. Boneset grows in wet prairies. Its underground parts make up for any lack of drama in the aboveground plant. The root system of boneset can go to depths of 16 to 17 feet, enabling the plant to reach water during dry periods. The taproot may be more than an inch thick near the top, with a bark-like covering indicating that it doesn't absorb moisture in the top two feet of soil. The deep roots are shiny white.

Early settlers used tea made from the dried leaves of boneset as medicine. There was an old belief that placing boneset leaves in bandages around broken bones would help them heal, accounting for the name. The other common name, "thoroughwort," means "through the leaves," referring to the stem that seems to pierce the pairs of leaves.

POPPY MALLOW

Callirhoe triangulata
Mallow family (Malvaceae)
Average first bloom: Bradley, July 30
Height: 3–24 inches
Flower: 1¾ inches

The poppy mallow has eye-catching cerise flowers that bloom atop leafless branched stems. The basal leaves are somewhat the shape of a maple leaf. The flowers have five fragile-looking petals. In the center, the white pistil and stamens are on a short stalk.

Relatives of poppy mallow include hollyhocks, cotton, and okra.

CARDINAL FLOWER

Lobelia cardinalis
Lobelia family (Campanulaceae)
Also called scarlet lobelia
Average first bloom: Leopold,
    August 2 / Bradley, August 2
Height: 2–5 feet
Flower: 1 inch

The most intense red imaginable is that of the cardinal flower of mid to late summer. It is the scarlet tanager of the flower world. This eye-catching color is artfully accented by a tiny blue beard on the tip of the stamen. The cardinal flower grows in wet areas such as the edges of ponds and streams or wet meadows. The petals form a tube, opening into an upper lip with two lobes, and a lower lip with three larger lobes. The fused pistil and stamens protrude through the top two lobes. The flowers grow up a spike, with a small leaf beneath each flower. Hummingbirds commonly pollinate cardinal flowers, but sometimes bumblebees make small holes in the tube to gain easier access to the nectar. The roots are white and extensive. The plant has many shiny brown seeds with fluted projections on them.

GERARDIA
Gerardia tenuifolia
Figwort family (Scrophulariaceae)
Average first bloom: Bradley, August 2
Height: 3–26 inches
Flower: ½ inch

Down among the heavy prairie grasses, the bright pink flowers of the gerardia find a place in damp meadows or along the banks of streams and ponds. The bell-shaped flowers have five somewhat irregular lobes. Easy to overlook, this pretty plant doesn't have a common nickname. Delicate in form, gerardia is a striking contrast to the sturdy golden-flowered plants that dominate the season. Part of its dainty look is due to the long thin stalks that hold each flower along the stem. The leaves are thin and pointed, adding to the effect.

STIFF GOLDENROD
Solidago rigida
Aster family (Asteraceae)
Also called rigid goldenrod, hard-leaved goldenrod
Average first bloom: Leopold, August 27 / Bradley, August 11
Height: 1½–3½ feet
Flower arrangement: 4 inches

Goldenrod species provide showy golden tones in autumn, and none is more typical than the stiff goldenrod of the dry prairie. Other species of goldenrod have flowers in columns along the stem, or in arching sprays. The tiny individual flowers of the stiff goldenrod are bright yellow, and close together in clusters. Adding to their effect, the plants tend to grow in clumps. Leathery leaves alternate on the stiff stalk. The lower leaves have their own stalks, but at the top of the plant they clasp the main stem. These leaves are hairy, which causes them to appear light green. The fibrous roots of the stiff goldenrod compete well with the grasses, growing as deep as five feet.

Monarch butterflies feed on the stiff goldenrod in preparation for migrating. Goldenrods are not responsible for hay fever, as their pollen is spread by insects, not wind. People have used goldenrod flower lotion as a treatment for bee stings, and a tea of goldenrod leaves for swollen throats. Goldenrods contain a small amount of latex, which led Thomas Edison to try to make a rubber substitute from them. Fishermen sometimes harvest larvae for bait from galls on goldenrod. Showy Goldenrod (*Solidago speciosa*) is another species prominent on the prairie. Its flowers are in columnar spikes, and its stems are smooth and reddish.

NEW ENGLAND ASTER

Aster novae-angliae
Aster family (Asteraceae)
Average first bloom: Leopold,
    August 21 / Bradley, September 6
Height: 1–7 feet
Flower head: 1 inch

As the greens of summer lose their brilliance, New England asters bloom in profusion, continuing to lend their deep lavender color in piquant counterpoint to the yellows and oranges of fall foliage. The flowers are clustered at the top of tall stems, each with several whorls of ray flowers and deep yellow-orange flowers in a center disk. There are many long, pointed leaves clasping the stems, which are covered with bristly hairs. New England asters grow in colonies in their preferred habitat of mesic to wet prairie. There are many species of fall asters in different colors, including white, blue, pink and purple. They also vary in shape and style, but can be difficult to identify, as they often interbreed. The hardy New England aster blooms from coast to coast throughout temperate zones.

Some Native Americans call the aster "the flower that brings in the frost." *Aster* is the Latin word for "star." Plains Indian tribes ate the young leaves as greens. They burned aster plants for the smoke, used to revive a person who had fainted.

TURTLE HEAD

Chelone glabra
Snapdragon family
    (Schrophulariaceae)
Average first bloom: Bradley,
    August 20
Height: 2–3 feet
Flower: 1⅛ inches

Somewhat rare, and looking amusingly like its namesake, the turtle head is an interesting flower to find. It grows along streambanks and in wet meadows, often almost hidden in the grass. Usually only one flower stem grows from each fibrous root stock, and never more than a few plants grow in a group. A cluster of creamy white flowers blooms at the top of the stem. An inflated upper lip arches over a lower lip, which achieves the turtle look. Bees force their way between the two lips, and disappear inside to get at the sweet nectar. Fortunately for the turtle head, pollen rubs off on the bees to pollinate the next flower they enter. The long, lance-shaped leaves are in pairs. Their edges are finely toothed. Late in the season, the fruit capsule appears, containing many flat, winged seeds.

BOTTLE GENTIAN
Gentiana andrewsii
Gentian family (Gentianaceae)
Also called closed gentian, blind gentian, cloistered heart
Average first bloom: Leopold,
   August 31 / Bradley, August 27
Height: 1–3 feet
Flower: 1¼ inches

Bottle gentian has five medium-blue petals that are fused by lighter-colored segments to form the bottle-shaped flower that appears closed. However, bees are able to wiggle their way into the flowers for nectar, in the process providing pollination. Hidden inside are five fused stamens. Small clusters of flowers bloom around the reddish stem with about three-inch-long leaves under each group of flowers, forming a kind of nosegay. The largest cluster of flowers and the largest leaves are at the top. The simple, stalkless leaves are in opposite pairs lower on the sturdy stems. The fruit capsule contains hundreds of tiny seeds. Bottle gentian blooms throughout early hard frosts. It thrives in wet to mesic meadows.

Native Americans used the root of the gentian to treat snakebite, backache, and other ills. Pioneers believed the root aided digestion. Juice of the gentian root is used today in concoctions to aid digestion. In Switzerland and Sweden, a species of gentian is used to make alcoholic beverages. The family is named for Gentius, king of Illyria from 180 B.C. to 167 B.C. He attributed medicinal qualities to the roots of some 800 species of gentian. The Latin species name *andrewsii* honors Henry Andrews, a nineteenth-century English botanical artist.

FRINGED GENTIAN
Gentiana crinita
Gentian family (Gentianaceae)
Average first bloom: Bradley,
   September 2
Height: 12–32 inches
Flower: 1⅛ inch

With deep, sky-blue blossoms, the fringed gentian is one of the loveliest wildflowers. It thrives in moist areas such as streambanks. The petals are joined in a tube at the base, separating at the top into a flat whorl with fringed tips. The flowers open only in sunshine. Unlike the ephemeral flowers of spring, gentians bloom for a long period in the fall. Oval, pointed leaves grow in pairs along the stem. Fringed gentian is an annual or biennial with a mass of white fibrous roots.

STIFF GENTIAN

Gentiana quinquefolia
Gentian family (Gentianaceae)
Also called ague-weed, gall-of-the-earth
Average first bloom: Bradley, September 16
Height: 3–16 inches
Flower: ⅝ inch

Smaller and less showy than the fringed or the bottle gentian, the stiff gentian is usually the last flower to come into bloom on the Bradley's prairie. The flowers are a soft red-violet in color. Stiff gentian has more flowers per plant than the bottle or fringed gentians. They occur all along the stem, and are open at the top. The four triangular lobes that flare out at the top of the tube-shaped flower have bristles at the tip. The stiff gentian grows in the shade of the tall, dense autumn grasses.

BIG BLUESTEM

Andropogon gerardi
Grass family (Gramineae)
Also called turkeyfoot, red hay
In bloom: late July
Height: 7–8 feet
Seed heads: 2–4 inches

Big bluestem is the symbolic grass of the prairie. To the pioneers, the prairie grasses in late summer resembled the waves of the ocean, and big bluestem was dominant. The stalks grow up to eight feet tall and have heads which resemble a three-toed turkey foot and become reddish in color. There are many linear leaves, growing as tall as three feet. Young stems have a blue cast. Where there are thick stands of prairie grasses, such as big bluestem, there is little erosion. The plants grow in clumps up to two feet across, with an extensive system of roots and rhizomes reaching 7 to 12 feet down into the earth. These deep roots make big bluestem drought-resistant. In a year of severe drought, the grass may not bloom, but it will bloom again when moisture returns. Plants with good underground storage can afford to be patient. Eventually big bluestem shades out most other grasses.

Mature big bluestem is tall enough to hide buffalo and cattle. Foot travelers could lose their way. Young grass makes excellent forage and hay. Settlers made paths through the heavy grass by dragging a log behind a team of oxen. Big bluestem was a favorite material for making sod houses. Settlers cut blocks of sod two feet by one foot in area. They laid the base of the wall two blocks thick, and the second row at right angles to the first. The resulting house was warm in winter and cool in summer; however, the roof usually leaked. Native Americans used big bluestem for many medicinal purposes, especially for treatment of fevers. Most of the best land for big bluestem is now the best corn land.

CANADA WILD-RYE
Elymus canadensis
Grass family (Gramineae)
Also called nodding wild-rye, Canada lyme grass
In bloom: July and August
Height: 2–5 feet

Arching, bearded seed heads up to 10 inches long are the most conspicuous part of Canada wild-rye. The seeds are covered with stiff hairs, and end in a slender awn as long as the seed itself. In spite of the seed's large size, it takes about 100,000 dry seeds to make a pound. The seeds persist through the winter. A coarse bunch grass, Canada wild-rye grows in dry sandy soil. The 12-inch-long narrow leaves are rough to the touch. They tend to curl gracefully near the tip.

Large and small species of wildlife find winter food in Canada wild-rye seed heads. It is a welcome component in grassland pasture. Native Americans ate the seeds, but the yield is scarcely worth the effort of the harvest. Dense spreading roots make Canada wild-rye a good ground cover.

INDIANGRASS

Sorghastrum nutans
Grass family (Gramineae)
Also called wood grass, wild oatgrass
In bloom: late July and August
Height: 4–9 feet
Seed head: 4–8 inches

In the fall, waves of bronze Indiangrass ripple in the prairie breeze, glossy and sensuous. Indeed, the Latin species name, *nutans*, means "swaying." Like most prairie grasses, Indiangrass depends on the wind for pollination. In general, grasses have inconspicuous flowers that do not attract insects. The flower heads of Indiangrass have numerous branches. Spikelets containing the seed develop along each little branch. Each spikelet has a twisted awn, or bristle, about three times its length extending from its tip.

Spring growth of Indiangrass resembles its frequent associate, big bluestem. Indiangrass prefers a little more moisture than big bluestem, however, and its shoots are lighter green. Like big bluestem, Indiangrass is a dominant prairie species. The stems are stout and unbranched. Its narrow leaves are stiff, rough, and usually less than two feet long. There is an identifying claw-like ligule near the node where the leaf joins the stem. Indiangrass has a tough, tangled root system.

A nutritious forage, Indiangrass is a common constituent of prairie hay. A warm-weather grass that ripens in the fall, Indiangrass is most prolific on southern prairies.

JUNEGRASS

Koeleria cristata
Grass family (Gramineae)
Also called crested hairgrass, Koeler's grass
In bloom: late May to early July
Height: 1–2 feet
Seed head: 1–6 inches

Sturdy, dark-green clumps of Junegrass grow among the other prairie grasses, adding to the beauty of the early summer prairie. Grasses that flower in early summer, like Junegrass, are considered cool-weather grasses, most prolific on northern prairies. Junegrass seed heads are dense, shiny cylinders at the top of slender stems. This grass thrives in a wide variety of soil conditions. New seedlings of this perennial are so fine they are almost invisible. The leaves of Junegrass rise from the base of the plant. When green, the leaves are stiff and flat, but as they dry they curl into papery spirals.

The combination of its fibrous root system and its adaptability make Junegrass suitable for use in soil conservation. Young Junegrass is good forage for cattle, deer, and elk. Junegrass is decorative when planted in yards, but the drawback is that it may cause hay fever during its blooming period. The genus name *Koeleria* honors George Ludwig Koeler, a late-eighteenth-century German scientist who studied grasses.

LITTLE BLUESTEM

Andropogon scoparius
Grass family (Gramineae)
Also called prairie beardgrass, wire-
  grass, bunch grass
In bloom: August and September
Height: 2–4 feet
Seed head: 1 inch

Little bluestem was at one time the most abundant grass in mid-America. Hardy and long-lived, it is a midsize grass that grows best in semidry areas between big bluestem and the dry-land grasses. Its dense root system goes from five to six feet deep. The stems are pithy, rather than hollow like most grass stems. Stiff and hard, the stems appear to be lightly powdered. A bluish tint may appear in the flattened young shoots and stem nodes. The stems branch toward the top, giving the plant a vase-like shape. Leaves of little bluestem appear somewhat folded down the middle, distinguishing it from big bluestem, which often grows intermixed with it. Each hairy node on the loose seed head has two spikelets—one fertile and one sterile. In the fall, little bluestem seed heads are fuzzy and white, contrasting with the wine-red stems, which continue to add warm color to the prairie scene through the winter. A prairie of little bluestem tends to be showy with many bright flowering plants. Little bluestem's relatively short, bunchy nature allows light to reach these broad-leaved forbs, and also makes them easier to see.

Deer feed on the nutritious little bluestem, and songbirds eat the seeds. The Comanche Nation treated sores with the ashes of little bluestem.

PRAIRIE DROPSEED

Sporobolus heterolepis
Grass family (Gramineae)
Also called northern dropseed, bunch
  grass
In bloom: August to October
Height: 1–2 feet

A clump of prairie dropseed in summer is like a grounded, green skyrocket—stiff, narrow leaves on wiry stems, shooting out in all directions. About eighteen inches in diameter, this display is anchored by a dense root system. Prairie dropseed flower heads emerge from a sheath, and grow up to 12 inches in length. Delicate spreading branches are lined with spikelets, each containing one seed. The seeds drop quickly, hence the name. Tiny, hard, and shiny, they may not germinate for years. By autumn, prairie dropseed leaves and seed heads have turned a pale pinkish gold. In early spring shaggy, tan tufts of dead grass remain. Prairie dropseed has spread north from more southern origins. It grows best in well-drained prairie.

The seeds of prairie dropseed are fragrant and tasty. Ground-feeding birds eat them. Some Native Americans have parched the seeds and ground them into flour.

PRAIRIE THREE-AWN

Aristida oligantha; also *Stipa spartea*
Grass family (Gramineae)
Also called needlegrass, white grass,
    doghair grass, poverty grass
In bloom: June and July
Height: 1–2 feet

Danger may lurk on a dry hilltop in the summer. This is the impoverished habitat and the ripening time for prairie three-awn, named for the three, protruding bristles, each about five inches long, on each seed. These awns are so stiff and sharp that they can do physical damage to the unwary. The awns catch in animal hair, spreading seeds far and wide. Changes in humidity cause the awns to spiral and "screw" the seeds into the ground, or into the flesh of an unlucky animal. Only a few seeds develop on each loose seed head. Prairie three-awn stems branch freely, and the narrow leaves grow from the base, making tough, wiry tufts, which turn white when they mature. Prairie three-awn roots are fine and shallow. It is an annual, a rarity among prairie grasses.

Only young prairie three-awn plants provide forage for animals, as the awns on the mature plant can harm any animal that eats them. Rodents eat the seeds.

SIDE-OATS GRAMA

Bouteloua curtipendula
Grass family (Gramineae)
Also called tall grama grass, mesquite
    grass
In bloom: July to September
Height: 1–3 feet

The purplish seeds of side-oats grama all hang to one side of the seed head, like a fringe, although they are attached all the way around the stem. There are as many as 50 spikelets on the long seed head. The oat-like seeds are so light that it takes about 500,000 to make a pound. Dry prairie, such as side hills, rocky areas, and well-drained uplands, is side-oats habitat. It is a common grass, growing with other midheight grasses. The smooth erect stems of side-oats rise above a dense root system of scaly rhizomes. The leaves, which emerge at ground level, have hairs along their sides and a flat bristle on the tip. Dried leaves are whitish and tend to curl.

Tasty and nutritious, side-oats grama makes good meadow hay or forage. A commercial variety is planted for these uses. The plant is named for Claudio Boutelou, a nineteenth-century Spanish botanist. *Curtipendula* means "short-hanging" in Latin.

SWITCHGRASS

Panicum virgatum
Grass family (Gramineae)
Also called Wobsqua grass, blackbent,
    thatch grass
In bloom: August to September
Height: 3–6 feet

Switchgrass is most easily identified by its lacy, open, and many-branched bloom stalk. The flower head may be 6 to 20 inches long, with branches 4 to 10 inches long. The flowers have a purplish color. Switchgrass grows in moist areas of the prairie, often alongside big bluestem and Indiangrass. Its stout rhizomes send up many shoots so that it forms colonies and dense sod. A collar, called a ligule, found at the bottom of the leaf where it joins the sheath, provides a way to identify switchgrass before it blooms. Switchgrass is yellow in the fall.

The *Panicum* genus contains about 500 species, including millets, an important cereal crop. Many kinds of birds and animals feed on switchgrass. Pheasants and cottontail rabbits make nests in stands of switchgrass. Buffalo hunters on the prairie avoided switchgrass when dressing out a carcass because if its seeds got into the meat, their tiny spikes might stick in the throat of anyone who ate it. The spikes are also irritating if they catch in hikers' clothing.

AMERICAN WOODCOCK

Scolopax minor
Length: 8¼ inches
Average spring arrival: Leopold,
    March 26 / Bradley, March 19

The American woodcock has a heavy body for the length of its legs, and a long bill. There are several black bars across the top of its head, and white chevrons on its mottled tan back. Its breast is a peachy tan.

The woodcock is not rare, just rarely seen, because it is nocturnal and lives in moist woodlands and swamps. One is more apt to hear, rather than see, the woodcock. It allows close approach, and then explodes out of a thicket with a whir of wings. A woodcock's wings whistle because of modified primary feathers. Woodcocks eat more than their weight in earthworms every day. If worms are scarce, woodcocks eat other invertebrates. Stamping their feet helps woodcocks locate their prey. The holes they make in the ground with their long bills are a telltale sign of their feeding areas.

Woodcocks are perhaps most famous for the aerial courtship display of the male. Aldo Leopold has written lyrically about this "sky dance," in which the cock spirals high into the air, then descends like a falling leaf. The woodcock lands and parades to the female. The nasal sound it makes is called a "peent." All this usually takes place at night. The woodcock's nest is apt to be of leaves and among leaves, not more than 100 yards from the display ground. The female lays from three to five eggs that are the peachy color of her breast. Woodcocks are one of a few species observed transporting their young in the air. Woodcocks winter in the southern United States.

Pesticides and sport hunting threaten the woodcock populations.

BALD EAGLE
Haliaeetus leucocephalus
Length: 32 inches

Because of its keen eyesight, powerful wings, and imperious looks, the eagle has been the symbol of the United States government since 1782. The sight of an eagle alertly upright in a tree, or soaring in the air scouting for food, makes a permanent impression on a viewer. Young eagles and female eagles have brown plumage mottled with some white, especially under the wings. Four-year-old males develop the dramatic white heads and tails that characterize the species as popularly portrayed. In flight, the eagle carries its wings level, rather than raised like the turkey vulture.

Eagles frequent the Leopold Reserve in winter as long as there are fishing areas on the Wisconsin River that are free of ice. The remainder of the winter they fish in open water below dams and scout fields for carrion. To fish, they perch high in trees, then dive to catch the prey in their talons, returning to a perch to eat. When most of the waterways are frozen or fish are migrating through an area, eagles gather in large flocks to fish. Eagles also eat some birds and small mammals.

Monogamous, eagles build loosely constructed nests high in tall trees or on cliffs. They return each year to the same nest, adding more sticks and finer materials until nests grow so large that some have been known to weigh as much as a pickup truck. The female lays one to three dull white eggs in slight depressions on the nest platform. Usually no more than two chicks survive the competition for food. The parents carry food to the young eagles for 70 to 100 days.

Bald eagles, once classified as endangered, were declassified in Wisconsin in August of 1997. Eagles and most songbirds are still protected from harm by federal migratory bird treaties with Mexico and Canada. In the summer of 1997 there were 632 pairs of nesting bald eagles in Wisconsin; they produced a total of 739 young birds. The largest single cause of the earlier decline was the use of DDT and other pesticides. Eagles, at the top of the food chain, ingested the poisons in high concentrations. The young could not be hatched because the shells of the eggs were too thin to withstand damage during the incubation period.

BALTIMORE ORIOLE
Icterus galbula
Length: 7 inches
Average spring arrival: Leopold,
    May 7 / Bradley, May 4

The flaming orange and black colors of the male oriole make it one of the most beautiful North American songbirds. There is a pattern of white in the wing feathers. Females and both sexes of immature birds are mostly gray with a hint of orange. A few years ago the Baltimore oriole lost its name when ornithologists decided that it and the Bullocks oriole should be combined as one species, which they called the northern oriole. But they've recently determined that the two species are really separate, and each has its name back again. Under any name, the Baltimore's song is the same—a series of rich whistles.

The main diet of orioles is nectar and fruit. They will come to hummingbird feeders, but there are nectar feeders available specifically for orioles. A half-orange nailed to a tree also attracts them. When orioles gather flower nectar, they generally pierce the flower and get the nectar without pollinating the plant. Orioles also eat some insects. In autumn, Baltimore orioles migrate to northern Mexico for the winter.

With wings spread, a courting male oriole alternates stretching tall with bowing low. The distinctive oriole nest is a basket of grass and bark strips, which increases in length as it is reused by birds season after season. Four or five blue-white eggs with brown squiggles hatch in about two weeks. The parents feed the nestlings by regurgitating nectar. At two weeks of age the baby birds fledge.

BELTED KINGFISHER
Ceryle alcyon

Average spring arrival: Bradley, April 3
Length: 12 inches

The outline of a kingfisher is unmistakable as it sits above a river or pond. Its head is large, the legs and tail are short, and it has a crest that gives it the appearance of anger. The dominant feather color is gray. The male kingfisher has a white band around his neck, a gray one below that, and a white breast. The female has an additional band of buff lower on her breast. The belted is the only kingfisher species north of Texas and Arizona.

Kingfishers fly with irregular wing beats, often uttering their raucous, staccato calls. Like terns, they can hover as they look for prey, then dive head first into the water. A kingfisher will grab a fish with its sharp beak and slowly swallow it, aided further by rapid digestion. Kingfishers later regurgitate the indigestible parts of fish in pellet form, as do owls and some other birds that swallow entire prey. Kingfishers often winter along temperate coastlines, but they may migrate as far as northern South America.

The kingfisher nest is built in a burrow in a sandy bank over water. Both male and female work to dig the hole, which usually slopes slightly down toward the entrance and is three to six feet deep, and occasionally considerably deeper. The nest is a saucer of grass or leaves. The female lays an average of six or seven white eggs. The parents feed the baby birds regurgitant until they fledge about three to four weeks later. Then the adult kingfishers teach their young how to fish, often by dropping dead fish into the water under the perched fledglings. In 10 days or so the young can catch live fish and begin life on their own.

Clean, healthy waters are vital for kingfisher habitat.

BLACK-CAPPED CHICKADEE
Poecile atricapillus
Length: 4½ inches
Average first winter song: Bradley,
    January 18

The chickadee, pert and neat in its uniform of gray with black bib and cap and its white cheek patches, adds cheer to southern Wisconsin throughout the year. Male, female, and young birds all look the same.

In the summer, chickadees eat insects, including spiders and spider eggs. In the winter they feed on pine seeds, and frequent backyard bird feeders, where they eat suet and sunflower seeds. They become quite tame, and have been known to eat from an outstretched hand. The agile chickadee seems as happy eating head down as head up. Because of the dangers of freezing during severe winter nights, chickadees spend as much as 20 times the amount of time feeding in winter as in summer. This provides them with enough energy to survive the night. Often chickadees travel in small flocks and with other species of birds on their winter feeding forays. On cold nights they sleep in empty nest cavities or in conifers.

A first phenological sign of spring is that date when the chickadees begin to sing a distinctive two-note song with the second note a full tone lower than the first. Their name is an imitation of another song pattern they employ.

Chickadees nest in tree cavities and nest boxes. The nest is lined with soft plant material. The female lays six to eight eggs, white with reddish brown marks, which are incubated for 12 to 13 days. During the first days after hatching, the female stays in the nest and the male brings food. The chicks stay with their parents for about three weeks and then disperse to fend for themselves. Black-capped chickadees can live as long as 12 years. There are seven species of chickadee in the United States, most with discrete territories.

CANADA GOOSE
Branta canadensis
Length: 16–25 inches
Average spring arrival: Leopold,
    March 22 / Bradley, March 1

In early spring, flocks of Canada geese converge on northern marshy areas and ponds, including those in the Leopold Reserve. With their honks and V formations, they bring a sense of wildness to grounded onlookers. Although most continue north, a small number stay to breed. This, our best-known goose, is identified by its black head and neck, accented by a wide white chin strap. The wings and back are mottled shades of brown, and the breast is lighter colored. The range in size is accounted for by the fact that there are as many as 11 subspecies of Canada geese.

During the breeding season, Canada geese stay near fresh or brackish water and in meadows. Their summer diet consists of shoots, seeds, berries, and insects. They also dabble in the water for crustaceans, mollusks, and tubers. In the fall, geese gather in large flocks and eat the grain left in farm fields. One bird seems to be appointed sentinel. Its neck is erect, and its head turns from side to side, as it watches for trouble that might come in the form of a coyote or a human hunter. Every evening the birds fly to water for the night. Geese often become semidomesticated, living in city parks and golf courses. As local waters freeze, most geese migrate to Mexico for the winter.

The mating display of the male

Canada goose includes lowering his head almost to the ground and hissing loudly at the female. Then he entwines his neck around hers. Their bond is long-term. The nest is shallow, made of dry grass and sticks and lined with downy feathers. The hen lays 4 to 10 white eggs. Families generally migrate together.

Large numbers of waterfowl have been killed by lead pellets from hunters' shotguns, which geese ingest as if they were seeds. One pellet can kill a bird the size of a duck. Lead shot is illegal in many places today.

EASTERN PHOEBE
Sayornis phoebe
Length: 5¾ inches
Average spring arrival: Leopold,
    April 7 / Bradley, March 26

The eastern phoebe, a relatively hardy flycatcher, is a small gray-brown bird with a white underside, black bill, and no eye ring or wing bars.

Although the phoebe is not flashy in color, its feeding habits are eye-catching. One may perch on a dead tree limb, repeatedly dip its tall tail, and look about for insects. Then it darts out, snaps up a bug, turns in midair, and returns to its perch. Phoebes like to feed near water, swooping near the surface. Their call sounds like their name, and they vary the accent. Phoebes also have a shrill one-note call.

The female phoebe builds a large well-constructed nest of mud and grasses, often on a projection of a manmade structure, such as a bridge or a shed. On the Leopold Reserve, phoebes nest under the eaves on the deck of the study center, where they are easy to observe. They lay an average of five eggs, white with a few brown spots. There may be two broods a year. Phoebes have been known to build a new nest floor over the eggs of a lazy invader cowbird. In late fall, the eastern phoebe migrates to the southern states. In March or April it returns north.

Beginning in the 1980s, the numbers of eastern phoebes seem to have declined in many of the eastern and midwestern states.

GREAT HORNED OWL
Bubo virginianus
Length: 20 inches

The same owl of children's picture books who says "who who," the great horned owl lives over most of North America in all seasons. It has a heavy body, short neck, and eyes that are fixed in their sockets. Owls' necks rotate, so they can see to the side. Their plumage is mottled tan to gray with horizontal bars on the breast. The facial disk is set off by specialized feathers bordered by a black edge. The owl's ear tufts are not actually its ears. The ears are located at the side of the head, and covered with feathers.

Owls hunt from dusk to dawn, locating prey by specialized hearing mechanisms. Their ears are asymmetrical, enabling them to determine the direction of sounds. The feathers of the facial ruff help to catch sounds and refer them to the ears. Owls fly silently because they have serrated primary feathers that break up the airflow over their wings. Their diet consists of rabbits, rodents, and whatever other meat they find, including small birds, fish, snakes, and amphibians. They dive on their prey, grabbing it with strong talons. During the day, owls roost near the trunks of dense trees. They must sometimes endure "mobbing" by flocks of small birds, a behavior not well understood.

Great horned owls nest in deserted hawk or crow nests, or in crevices, stumps, or among rocks on the ground. In courtship the male feeds the female, and makes an aerial display. While spring snowstorms are still a threat, the female owl lays two or three dull white eggs. They hatch in about a month. The young are in the nest about one month before fledging, and are fed for several additional months thereafter.

NORTHERN CARDINAL
Cardinalis cardinalis
Length: 7¾ inches
Average first song: Leopold,
    February 27 / Bradley, February 11

The cardinal is a source of cheerful color all year in southern Wisconsin. A sighting is always beautiful, whether against snow-covered winter branches, or the leafy green of summer. The male has black around his beak and eye. The female is a more subdued olive, tinged with red. Both have heavy reddish beaks. Immature birds are still more subdued in color. All have pointed crests. Cardinals are common in suburbs and on the edge of woods throughout the eastern United States. A separate population occurs in wooded ravines of the southwest.

Cardinals whistle a number of different calls. It is common to hear several males sitting on the top branches of trees, whistling back and forth to announce their territories. During late fall and early winter, cardinals do not sing. The first cardinal songs of the new year are one of the earliest phenological dates to note. A cardinal's diet consists of insects, seeds, and fruit. The birds prefer to feed on the ground, but will come to bird feeders for seeds.

Like teenagers of the Big Band era, courting cardinals sway back and forth, singing softly. They use all manner of materials for their cup-shaped nests, and usually raise two broods a year. The male cares for the first brood while the female incubates the second hatch of three or four eggs. The male juveniles get their red feathers before their first winter. Cowbirds often lay their eggs in cardinal nests.

RUBY-THROATED HUMMINGBIRD
Archilochus colubris
Length: 3 inches

The ruby-throated hummingbird, tiny and fast, is the only hummingbird east of the Great Plains. These birds have green backs and white breasts. The species is named for the male, which has a red throat patch that is iridescent when the light catches it.

It is easiest to observe hummingbirds when they are feeding at yard feeders or on nectar from flowers, usually red. They can hover and fly backwards, enabling them to feed on tubular flowers where there is no place to perch. They also eat some insects, and in spring may rely on sap where sapsuckers have drilled holes. Hummingbird wings beat up to 75 times a second, producing the hum. Ruby-throated hummingbirds also make a feisty, short, squeaky chirp. Hummingbirds need to be aggressive, as they are always within a few hours of starvation. To get enough nourishment they may void 75 to 85 percent of their body weight a day in liquid. Hummingbirds winter in Mexico and Costa Rica.

As a mating display, the male flies back and forth, and up and down, in front of the female, as if displaying his maneuverability. The tiny nests are often positioned over water, and are made of such fairy-like materials as bud scales and lichen, bound with spider silk and lined with plant down. Two white eggs hatch after about two weeks. Males do not help raise the chicks, and seem to migrate before the females.

RUFFED GROUSE
Bonasa umbellus
Length: 14 inches

The most notable feature of the ruffed grouse's plumage is its wide color-banded tail, which the male spreads into a fan, peacock-style, during the mating display. There are gray phase and red phase grouse, the latter having a reddish tone to the small crest, and the color bands of the tail. The outer tail band and the ruff are strikingly dark. The soft breast feathers are mottled with tan and white. The grouse is well-camouflaged against the floor of the forest.

Habitat for ruffed grouse is deciduous and coniferous woods, especially aspen, across northern North America, where it is a year-round resident. Ruffed grouse browse on foliage, including buds, leaves, flowers, seeds, and fruits. A small portion of their diet is insects. They are usually solitary in winter, when one method of roosting is diving and burrowing into snow.

Hearing the sound of a solitary ruffed grouse drumming, in April, is the most likely way of noticing one. As a mating display, the male grouse chooses a high spot, usually a log, and produces a resounding, hollow sound by rapidly beating his wings. The beating accelerates and decelerates. The grouse's tail is spread, his ruff and crest erect. Then he struts before the female. She lays 9 to 12 buff eggs with brown streaks in a nest hidden under branches, at the base of a tree, or beside a log. The nest is a hollow in the ground lined with leaves, pine needles, and feathers. The diet of the young birds is primarily insects. The female will aggressively defend the young birds, and will perform a distraction display to lead intruders away from the nest. The young birds stay close to their mother until late fall.

There is a fall hunting season for ruffed grouse in Wisconsin, with a bag limit of five per day in most of the state.

SANDHILL CRANE
Grus canadensis
Length: 37 inches
Average spring arrival: Bradley,
    March 10

The crane's size, grace, life story, and historic age catch the imagination as perhaps no other bird's does. The wild calls and stretched silhouettes of the first sandhills to migrate north to the marshes on the Leopold Reserve trumpet the arrival of spring as well. Most of the population arrives in March and April. Adult sandhills are gray with a bare red cap and white cheeks. Immatures are brown all over. In flight the rapid upstroke of the wings is notable. The birds alternate gliding and flapping. Often they migrate in large flocks.

Cranes are at home in meadow and marsh near fresh water. Their varied diet includes insects, small mammals, bird eggs, grass, seeds, berries, bulbs, and aquatic plants. Sandhill cranes winter in southern Texas and Mexico.

Cranes mate for the long term after an elaborate courtship dance that includes calling, bowing, leaping, running with wings outspread, and throwing grass. They build loosely constructed nests of sticks, reeds, and grass. At dawn and dusk a pair may perform its famous unison call over the nest. In this call the birds share notes to produce a complex song. In 28 to 32 days two buff-with-brown eggs will hatch. Usually only one chick survives the battle of the fittest. Cranes stay together as a family group until the next spring, when the young, with much squawking and complaining, are thrown out on their own.

Crane migration is made more difficult by the draining of wetlands, and by power lines and pollution. After years of declining numbers, these birds are now being monitored closely, partly through the work of the International Crane Foundation of Baraboo, Wisconsin. The number of sandhill cranes is rebounding.

WHITE-THROATED SPARROW

Zonotricia albicollis
Length: 5¾ inches
Average spring arrival: Bradley,
    April 17

The white-throated sparrow appears in the phenological record four times. It arrives in southern Wisconsin in April and leaves in late May to summer farther north. It returns in September and stays until November before migrating south.

This sparrow has a neat white bib, but is often easier to identify by the bands of black and white (or buff in some strains) on its head, with a yellow spot over its beak and eye. Young birds may not have the yellow spot, but can be distinguished from white-crowned sparrows by the white-throat's shorter neck. White-throated sparrows have pale gray breasts, brown backs, and white wing bars.

White-throated sparrows live in thick undergrowth, where they eat insects from foliage. They also consume spiders, seeds, and some fruit. Some people interpret the white-throated sparrow's song as "Old Sam Peabody, Peabody, Peabody." Sometimes these birds sing at night. White-throated sparrows winter in the southern and eastern United States, where they often form flocks with other sparrows.

During courtship, the female sparrow flutters her wings and trills. Females with white-striped heads seem to prefer to mate with males with tan-striped heads, and vice versa. The nest is cup-like, built in a low shrub, and made of coarse grasses, twigs, and pine needles lined with finer materials. Four to six eggs are laid; they have reddish-brown markings. The eggs hatch in less than two weeks, and in another eight or nine days the baby birds have fledged.

WOOD DUCK
Aix sponsa
Length: 13½ inches

The male wood duck, in breeding season, is a stylish member of a well-dressed group. His large head is iridescent green with a swept-back crest, white lines, and chin strap. He has a red bill and eye. The front part of his body is chestnut brown with white dots. Behind a belt of white and black, his breast is buff and his back and wings are bands of gray and brown. In flight, the duck can be identified by the square tail. The young, females, and winter males have dull plumage. The females have white eye rings.

Wood ducks require wetlands and woods, nesting in deep cavities in trees. They dabble for aquatic weeds, insects, and invertebrates. They also eat some seeds and berries. When alarmed, wood ducks give a shrill, rising whistle. They fly rapidly and skillfully maneuver between trees. Wood ducks winter in Cuba and the Bahamas.

Courtship and pairing begin in the fall and continue into spring. Ten to 15 creamy white eggs are average. Sometimes wood duck females lay eggs in other wood ducks' nests. The eggs hatch after 28 to 37 days. Within two days, the ducklings use their sharp claws to scramble out of the nest made of wood chips and down.

At the beginning of the twentieth century, wood ducks were almost extinct. They were killed for their plumage and for food. Hunting was prohibited from 1918 to 1941. Loss of habitat due to draining of wetlands and logging also contributed to the low numbers. Wood ducks have made a comeback, partly because of the construction of wood duck houses by conservationists. The ducks adapt well to nesting in these houses.

BEAVER
Castor canadensis

The beaver is the largest rodent in North America, adults weighing from 30 to 60 pounds. Beaver bodies are compactly rounded, and are covered in two layers of brown fur for waterproofing. The inner layer is soft and thick; the outer layer is long and lustrous. A beaver's front paws are hand-like and capable of manipulating logs and sticks. Its hind feet are large and webbed for swimming. The hind feet have special split nails for grooming fur to keep it waterproof. The most conspicuous part of the beaver is its flat paddle of a tail, which is scaly, oval, and 10 to 12 inches long. It has many uses, including rudder, sail, paddle for dam-building, prop for sitting up, and warning device—its slap on the water resonates for up to half a mile.

Beaver teeth are legendary. There are four, orange front teeth shaped like chisels that can cut a three-inch-wide aspen in 12 minutes. In a year a single beaver might cut down 200 trees. Thick molars in strong jaws grind the beaver's vegetable diet, which includes tules, sticks, and bark.

Beavers live near lakes or streams in aspen or cottonwood habitats. Some live in lodges in dams they build; other beavers live in tunnels as long as 50 feet, dug into the banks of streams or rivers. On the Leopold Reserve beavers live in both the river and ponds. All beavers work hard in autumn, anchoring logs and sticks underwater for food during the long winter. Holding a length of log in its forepaws, a beaver can eat the bark in the same way that people eat corn on the cob. A beaver's lips can close behind its big front teeth, allowing it to gnaw under water. Beavers are most active at night. Although beavers must breathe above water, they are expert swimmers who can stay under water for as long as 17 minutes and cover distances up to one-half mile.

Beavers live in family groups of six to ten. Sometime between April and July, two to six kits are born in a grassy nest in a lodge or tunnel above the waterline. They weigh about a pound at birth, and can soon swim on their own. Beaver kits sound almost like human babies, uttering whimpers, mumbles, and cries. Female beavers have four mammae on their chests. Usually the young stay with the family about two years before they must get out and form households of their own.

At the time of settlement, beaver ranged over all of Wisconsin. By 1900 the numbers were down to as few as 500. By 1996 the beaver population in Wisconsin had recovered to about 100,000. People are the greatest enemy of beavers. Besides beaver fur, castoreum used in the manufacture of perfume is a valuable commodity. This musky-smelling substance comes from glands in the groins of beavers, especially the male. Trapping beavers requires a permit and is limited to a winter season.

Although the numbers of trappers and the beavers they may trap is not limited, the population of beavers continues to increase. Their activities create settling basins for silt, provide havens for waterfowl, enhance the food chain for trout, and build prairies. On the downside, beavers can flood grazing areas and highways, and destroy pulp trees.

GRAY FOX
Urocyon cinereoargenteus

The gray fox is less numerous in the Great Lakes area than the red fox. Its size is about the same, but the gray fox has longer legs, and may weigh slightly less. It is less curious and playful than a red fox, and not as good a runner. The undercoat is buff with mixed gray and white guard hairs. There is a black line down its back, and black tips the tail and feet. There is often orange color on its legs. Gray foxes live throughout the United States except for the northern Rocky Mountains. Their range goes as far south as Central America.

A striking difference between red and gray foxes is that the gray fox can climb trees. It has long front claws that help it climb the trunk like a cat; it can also jump from branch to branch. Gray foxes prefer to live in the woods near water. Quiet animals, they carry on most of their vocal communication by low growls and contented grunts. They also communicate by means of scent posts.

The gray fox den is usually a stump, hollow tree, or rock crevice in the woods. The kits are born blind and nearly naked. The male starts to bring food to the den when the kits are about three weeks old. The family stays together until autumn.

Gray fox fur is not as valuable as red fox fur, so the grays are trapped less often than the red foxes. Enemies of young foxes include coyotes, bobcats, and great horned owls. The size of fox populations seems to evolve over about a 10-year period. Foxes are prone to tularemia, rabies, and parasites.

LITTLE BROWN BAT
Myotis lucifugus

The only mammals that fly, bats need special equipment. A membrane connects a bat's fingers, arms, sides, legs, and tail. Only its thumbs are free. Bats are capable of rapid flying and diving. A specialized larynx enables a bat to utter as many as 50 squeaks per second, which are too high-pitched for humans to hear. Bats have short, hairless ears that can hear echos of these squeaks. Like sonar, this allows them to locate insect dinners and to navigate in the dark. Bats also squeak in another range that is audible to people.

Little brown bats are about two inches long, with black beady eyes. They roost in colonies during the day, hanging by their hind feet in dark places such as caves, hollow trees, mine shafts, or buildings. At dusk they fly out to catch insects in their mouths, or by scooping them up in their tail membranes. Bats cannot take off from land or water. They probably range one or two miles; however, bats released many miles from home have returned within a week. Little brown bats do migrate, but probably not long distances. In the fall they seek a cave or deserted mine shaft where the temperature remains a constant 40°F to 50°F. The bats spend the winter living on stored fat. In the spring they return to the same nesting sites. Bats are pugnacious when disturbed, but among themselves seem to live in relative harmony.

Although bats mate in the fall, fertilization takes place toward spring. One or two babies are born between May and July. The infant bats may "hang out" in the roost or cling to the mother when she flies. They can fly on their own in five to six weeks. The life span of a little brown bat in the wild is about seven years.

Bats have few enemies. One hazard is cold weather in spring that limits flying insects. Bat colonies should be encouraged because of the number of insects they destroy, and many bird specialty stores sell bat houses.

RED FOX
Vulpes fulva

The sly, clever, and curious red fox is a staple in literature from Aesop to the one that "went out on a chilly night." Red foxes live in favorable habitat throughout North America. They generally have a bright orange coat with black feet, eyes, and nose. Other colors are black or silver (hairs of black edged with white). Red foxes have pointed ears and bushy tails always tipped with white. The tail gives balance to a running fox. In cold weather, it serves as a muffler, covering the feet and nose of a curled-up fox. The foot pads are densely furred in winter. Red foxes have keen senses of smell, sight, and hearing.

Red foxes prefer to live in combination woodland and open country, such as the Leopold Reserve. They have become adapted to living near people, although few raid farmyards. Their diet consists mostly of cottontail rabbits, with some rodents, snakes, large insects, ground birds, and fruits. Red foxes do their hunting between dusk and dawn. They move at a graceful trot and range about a mile. Their tracks form a straight line, on which they may double back to escape, or spy on, pursuing dogs and humans. Red foxes prefer to follow paths or roadways. In daytime they curl up in sheltered places. On the occasions when a red fox makes a noise, the male yaps, ending in a guttural sound; the female yaps more shrilly, ending in a screech.

Red foxes make their family dens in the ground. The hole is usually 15 to 20 feet long, but may be as long as 40 feet! A fox may dig its own hole, or move into an abandoned den. A den has two or more entrances, and other dens nearby serve for escape from predators. After a gestation period of about 53 days, five or six pups, or kits, are born in a grass-lined area of the den. The tips of their tails are already white, but the rest of their coat is gray fuzz. During the nursing period, the male often brings food to the female. When the kits are about three weeks old, they come to the den entrance to play. Here the parents bring food to them, and it often gets quite messy with leavings. One parent always stays on duty. The fox kits leave the den when they are about four months old, and breed the first year.

Red foxes are valuable alive for the large number of rodents and rabbits they consume. Fox fur, especially the black and silver mutations, is prized for its beauty. Humans trap and hunt foxes. In Wisconsin in 1996, there was a four-month winter fox-hunting season with no bag limit. Fox kits are vulnerable to predators, such as coyotes and owls.

RIVER OTTER
Lutra canadensis

Members of the weasel family, river otters can live throughout the United States, except in deserts. They weigh up to 30 pounds. An adult otter's head and body are 30 to 40 inches long. A round, stout, tapered tail adds about 19 inches of rudder. The otter's legs are short, so that its body drags on the ground when it walks on land. The tail and webbed hind feet enable the otter to swim powerfully with style and grace. The short dense fur is brown to grayish above and light gray on the underparts. The otter's face is a winning one, with luminous black eyes and side whiskers. The otter grunts, chatters, chuckles, and makes piercing whistles.

River otters live along the edges of streams and lakes. In the Leopold Reserve they live in the Wisconsin River. They build dens into the bank as deep as three to five feet, and about 10 inches in diameter. They bury their waste in designated spots away from the dens. The diet of river otters includes fish, crayfish, frogs, insects, snails, and some water plants. Their teeth tend to become worn. Otters may travel six miles in a day of feeding. In winter they will travel cross-country to find open water. A male river otter may cover as much as 50 to 60 miles.

People find river otters attractive for behaviors that seem to be pure play. They create mud slides into the water. Entire families will repeatedly run and slide on their bellies. Audubon reported seeing a pair make 22 runs before being startled. In winter the slides are made of snow, and the ride ends under the ice, where river otters may swim a quarter-mile in four minutes. Otters also shoot rapids and play-dive for clam shells, leaving trails of silvery bubbles.

From one to four babies, each weighing less than one-half pound, are born in March or April after a gestation period of 11 to 12 months. The den is near water and lined with vegetation. The babies are blind for several weeks, so one parent stays with them. Often they have to be coaxed to swim. Sometimes the mother will swim into the pond with a baby on her back, and then dive out from under the surprised little otter. The young go out on their own at about eight months, and are fully grown at two years. They may not become parents until they are five or six. Otters have few enemies other than people.

STRIPED SKUNK
Mephitis mephitis

As one writer put it, the skunk's "scent glands are well-developed." Get beyond that famous stink and you will discover a fascinating and attractive little animal. The striped skunk is about the size of a housecat with rather short legs and a heavy rear end. Its front feet have long claws for digging. The skunk has a bushy tail and long, black, glossy fur. A narrow white stripe runs up the face. A white patch on top of the head divides into two stripes down the sides of the back, ending at the tail, which usually has some white in it. The anal scent glands are like little nozzles surrounded by a gizzard-like muscle. With them, the skunk can shoot several fine sprays of a sulfur-alcohol compound up to a distance of 15 feet.

Striped skunks live throughout most of North America in woods, plains, meadows, and suburbs, and are the most common carnivores in Wisconsin. Skunks hunt at night. Around dusk you might see one ambling along, nose to the ground, stopping now and then to dig a shallow hole, looking for insects, which make up about half of its diet. Skunks also eat small mice and even fruit. Apparently realizing their defensive power, skunks seem indifferent to the presence of humans or other animals. They do not climb trees and do not like water, although they can swim. Their main senses are relatively weak, except for touch.

Although striped skunks are not playful, they are slow to anger. They seem reluctant to spray, and do so only if molested. A skunk gives warning by turning its back, growling, stamping its forefeet, and finally raising and flagging its tail before firing. While skunk dens may have the characteristic odor, the smell does not necessarily mean a skunk is nearby. The odor may stay for months on the ground and carries on the wind for up to a mile. The spray stings the eyes but does no permanent damage.

Skunks live in dens, which may be tunnels left by rodents, hollow logs, caves in rocks, or space under buildings. The dens may be about 20 feet long and go three to four feet deep. In a high, wide spot in the den, skunks make a nest lined with grass and twigs pushed into place with their noses. From five to seven babies are born in May or June. Their eyes and ears are closed for about 30 days. Although baby skunks are nearly naked, their skin shows the future color pattern of the fur. Later in the summer, the baby skunks follow their mother single file when she goes out to hunt. When cold weather comes, skunks bed down for the winter, 8 to 12 together, usually one male to a group. Males may venture out on any warm winter day, but the females and young usually stay in the den. Striped skunks have a life span of about eight years.

The main enemies of skunks are large owls and humans. Many skunks are killed by cars, especially before denning in the fall. Skunks are hunted for their fur. The Chippewa Nation prized the high-quality oil from skunks, and the meat is edible. If poultry is not protected, skunks may eat the eggs, but they also consume huge numbers of insects, including squash bugs and potato beetles. Skunks are sometimes kept as pets after the scent glands have been surgically removed.

WHITE-FOOTED MOUSE
Peromyscus leucopus

"Dainty" is a good one-word description of the white-footed mouse. It is about six to eight inches in length, and almost half of that is its long, hairy tail. Its habits of careful grooming are cat-like, and its tracks in snow are like lace—four little prints with a line between where the tail drags. The white-footed mouse has big eyes and ears for its size. It is sometimes called a deer mouse because of the tan-to-gray color of its coat. Its undersides are white. It is as widespread in the United States as any mammal.

The white-footed mouse lives in mixed woods and thickets alongside streams. Its diet includes seeds, berries, nuts, acorns, insects, and even small carcasses. The mouse hunts for food nocturnally by galloping in a zigzag pattern along the ground. It communicates by tapping its toes on a hard surface, making a sharp buzzing sound like a fingernail pulled across a screen.

White-footed mice can climb, and often nest in shrubs as well as burrows. The nest is made of shredded materials with a plug to close the entrance. About four babies are born after a three-to-four-week gestation period. The naked, crinkled infants, with eyes and ears closed, weigh but a fraction of an ounce. They may stay firmly attached to the mother's nipples for hours at a time. The baby mice are weaned before they are a month old, and may breed at 10 weeks of age. Parents average four litters from March until October.

This prolific little mouse thrives in spite of predators such as weasels, skunks, coyotes, foxes, owls, and snakes. White-footed mice store seeds for winter, and in cycles of high population may eat almost all available tree seeds, hampering reforestation. On the other hand, the mice may help the woods by eating white grubs that attack the roots of tree seedlings.

WHITE-TAILED DEER
Odocoileus virginianus

Wisconsin residents are familiar with the alert face of a white-tailed deer as it studies an intruder, and with the white flag of its tail as it bounds away in the next second. The white-tailed deer is the official Wisconsin wildlife animal. It weighs from 150 to 300 pounds, with the does smaller than the bucks. The white-tail's coat is grayish in winter, molting to reddish-brown in the summer. Its underparts are white. Bucks have widely branched antlers, but females normally have none. The antlers drop off in December or January; a new set begins to grow in the spring. A thick skin called velvet covers the growing antlers to nourish them. In three to four months, when the antlers are grown, the bucks rub off the dead skin. White-tailed deer have narrow, pointed, cloven hooves.

Deer spend the day secreted in the wood, coming into the open in the evening and early morning to eat. Their diet includes grass, leaves, and twigs. When they pull twigs off trees they leave a jagged end, rather than the neatly clipped edge a beaver would leave. As the season progresses deer browse on different species; favorites include yew, white cedar, hemlock, mountain ash, and red maple. During a hard winter deer may "yard up," sometimes in tamarack swamps. Speedy runners and excellent jumpers, deer often give three or four bounds followed by a 10–20-foot leap.

Does bear one or two, and rarely three, fawns in April or May. The mother may go off to feed, leaving the odorless spotted fawn curled in a bed of grass. It will not move, and it is not abandoned. When the fawn is about one month old, it will start to travel with the doe. The rut is in the fall, with a gestation period of about 26 weeks. Deer have sharp senses of smell and hearing, but only fair vision. The average lifespan in the wild is about 10 years, but in captivity deer may live 20 years.

White-tailed deer are the most numerous of the three deer species in the United States. The others are the black-tailed and the mule deer. Wisconsin deer populations were low 140 years ago. There were very few in southern Wisconsin, although it is unlikely that they completely disappeared from the Baraboo Hills. Deer have always been hunted and enjoyed for their beauty. They have continued to multiply, and are now a management problem throughout the state. Many deer die in the winter when forage is scarce. Reasons for the overpopulation include increase in summer food and absence of natural predators.

STRIPED CHORUS FROG

Pseudacris triseriata

Length: ¾–1½ inches

Chorus frogs have smooth skin and stripes down the back, one of which goes through the eye. Their back color may be gray, brown, reddish, or green, even for frogs in the same location. There is a white stripe along the upper lip.

Chorus frogs awaken with the first warm rains of spring. During the mating season they sing day and night. A rising trill, which sounds a bit like a fingernail pulled across the teeth of a comb, best describes their voices. The male sings while sitting on floating vegetation, and dives into the water at the first sound of an intruder. Chorus frogs live in grassy areas or woods where there is water—often a temporary spring pond. They are widespread in North America, from southern Canada to the Gulf Coast.

The breeding season varies according to longitude. During mating the frogs' forelimbs enlarge and thumb pads develop. After the breeding season chorus frogs climb into weeds or low shrubs, and are seldom encountered.

During spring nights on the Aldo Leopold Reserve there are a number of frogs and toads that produce a din of croaks, rasps, and tiny, bell-like sounds. The chorus frog is just one representative of these. Some other common species are the American toad, gray tree frog, and spring peeper. In winter frogs hibernate, and in summer and fall they are quiet.

As members of the order Salientia of amphibians, frogs and toads have many things in common. They all have water and land phases. Frogs and toads commonly come down from trees and weeds to breed in water. Clusters of eggs hatch into larvae—tadpoles in the case of most frogs and toads. These larvae live in water for as long as three summer months. When fully developed they enter the land phase of their lives. As adults they have lungs, but most breathing takes place through the skin. Adults have no tails, necks, or outer ears. Well-developed eardrums are located on the sides of their heads. Although the outer layer of skin is kept moist by secretions from the inner layer, they are prone to dehydration. The muscles in their hind legs enable frogs and toads to jump.

Frogs and toads eat a protein diet of mostly insects, spiders, and small worms. The forward portion of the tongue is fixed to the bottom of the mouth, leaving the long rear part mobile. The tip of the tongue is sticky, and a frog or toad can flip it out rapidly to catch prey.

GLOSSARIAL NOTES
NORTH AMERICAN GEOLOGY
INDEX

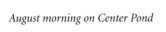

August morning on Center Pond

GLOSSARIAL NOTES

These glossarial notes are intended to serve two purposes. They provide an explanation of various terms relating to the text and also describe the special sense in which some of those terms have been used here and the philosophy behind my interpretations of them. J. R.

Aborigines. Various species living naturally in a particular area or environment. The term is often used to refer to the earliest humans in the area, but, as used here, has a broader meaning, referring, as well, to the other life forms.

Acidic lake; acidic soil. A lake or soil condition characterized by a high concentration of hydrogen ions. Acidic lakes and soils can occur naturally, as they do in northern Wisconsin, with granitic soils and relatively high precipitation. The natural condition in southern Wisconsin tends toward neutral or base because of buffering by limestone formations. Precipitation containing abnormal amounts of sulfuric or nitric acid, "acid rain," can cause contaminated drinking water, and damage vegetation locally and regionally. Symptoms are most obvious in areas naturally acidic.

Aerosol. A gaseous suspension of fine solid or liquid particles. Refers here to particles suspended in the atmosphere, such as dust or water molecules.

Agate. A fine-grained form of chalcedony. *See also* Chalcedony; Quartz

Albedo. The fraction of electromagnetic radiation reflected by the earth and its atmosphere, or by other bodies in the solar system. The amount of a sun's radiation that is reflected by a planet (rather than absorbed and reradiated) is affected by particulates in the atmosphere of the planet, such as dust, and also by water particles in the form of cloud cover. More particles would tend to increase the albedo and thus decrease absorption of energy at the surface. An increased albedo caused by dust from volcanic eruptions will tend to depress ambient temperature on the planet surface as long as the dust remains in the atmosphere. The planet will thus cool until a new thermal balance is reached.

Alluvial bench. A remnant of an alluvial deposit that has been formed by a river, or preserved by a change in the course of a river, or the level of the sea.

Alluvium. A sediment deposited by flowing water, in a riverbed, floodplain, or delta. Some alluvial deposits on the Leopold Reserve are recent, as in stretches in the floodplain of the Wisconsin River; some are much older, dating to the last glaciation. This land is ever changing. *See also* Alluvial bench

Anaerobic. Relating to environmental conditions that are marked by a lack of free oxygen. Certain bacteria can thrive in an anaerobic environment.

Analog predictor. An expression or form used to predict the expression or form of another. An example of an analog predictor is the use of a high pressure symbol on a weather map as a predictor of clear weather.

Angiosperm. A plant characterized by having seeds enclosed in an ovary; flowering plants such as the spring ephemeral plants in the prairie. *See also* Gymnosperm

Anthropomorphism. The attribution of human motivation, characteristics, or behavior to inanimate objects, animals, or natural phenomena. Although some people are critical of anthropomorphic references, it seems to be a common part of human nature to see ourselves reflected in nature.

Anticline. A convex fold in the earth's crust, with strata sloping downward on both sides from a common crest. *See also* Syncline

Antipodes. Any two places situated on exactly opposite sides of the earth; also used for something that is the opposite of another.

Arctic high (pressure). The Arctic is that portion of the earth that is above Latitude 66 degrees, 33 minutes North. High pressure refers to a cell of air with a pressure higher than normal atmospheric pressure that flows downward and outward in a clockwise motion in the northern hemisphere. The arctic high would form at a latitude above 66° North, move southward, and bring colder air into the middle latitudes. A sign of an oncoming high pressure area is a shift of wind from the southwest to the northwest. In the world described in *Prairie Time*, an arctic high in winter is characterized by temperatures at or below zero and by stunningly blue skies. As the high is arriving, those cold winds blow, but, when the high is overhead, the winds calm down.

Astronomical rhythmic dance. A term referring to the Earth-Sun relationship. Rhythm implies a predictable pattern reaching over the millennia that affects Earth's climate. The dance analogy is used to describe the patterns of Earth's orbit in relation to the sun, as affected by the precession in the orbit, and the variable pattern of the elliptical orbit.

Astronomy. As defined in most dictionaries, the scientific study of the universe beyond the earth. I believe that Earth and its relationship to the universe is an integral part of "astronomy," because our planet is embedded within the universe. The astronomical environment, including the force of gravity, the amount of sunlight, the changing seasons, and even the impact on our imaginations of an approaching comet, is the fundamental factor in framing environments on the earth.

Atlatl. A hunting weapon of Uto-Aztecan (Indian) origin; a dart thrower used in North America before (as well as after) the bow and arrow. The atlatl has a pivoting arm, which gave hunters a farther range than was possible with a hand-thrown spear.

Atmosphere. The mixture of gases surrounding a celestial body with sufficient gravity to maintain it. Earth's atmosphere extends up to 100,000 miles. Humans are most intimately acquainted with the first 50 miles or so, which includes the troposphere, reaching out 5 to 10 miles, the stratosphere, reaching to 30 miles, and the mesosphere, reaching to 50 miles. Those three regions contain about 99 percent of the total mass of Earth's atmosphere. *See also* Stratosphere; Troposphere

Basalt. A hard, dense, dark volcanic (igneous) rock, that has solidified from a molten or partially molten state.

Basaltic upwelling. A basaltic upwelling occurs when there is a fissure in the earth's surface and molten rock flows upward and laterally across the land. Such upwellings occur at midocean ridges, and sometimes on continental surfaces, as in the basaltic fields of eastern Washington and Oregon, Siberia, and India. Closer to this region, there is an ancient basaltic upwelling in the western Lake Superior area.

Base. Any of a large class of compounds, including the hydroxides and oxides of metals, that have the ability to react with acids to form salts. Base or alkaline soils occur in regions of light rainfall.

Batholith. A large block of igneous rock that forms below the earth's surface, and may be later uplifted to the surface during tectonic processes such as mountain-building.

Big Bang. A theory which posits that all of the matter and energy in the universe was concentrated in an infinitely dense state, from which it exploded, with the resulting expansion continuing until the present. The explosion may have occurred about 16 billion years ago. Recent observations of ancient stellar explosions suggest that the rate of expansion is increasing, not decreasing, as was suggested earlier.

Binary star. One of two stars that rotate together. Some astronomers now assert that combinations of two or more stars are more common than single stars. Our sun probably has no stellar companions, although some writers hold that there is a distant companion orbiting our sun with a period of about 30 million years. Binary stars are thought to form where a mature star "captures" a companion well after it has matured, or when gravitational coupling occurs between two or more young stars.

Biological tension zone. An area where geological and/or climatic "boundaries" place a strain on the biological inhabitants. Such a tension zone would occur where there are changes in elevation or topography, abrupt and persisting changes in patterns of weather due to a juncture of land and water, or margins of earlier geological processes such as glacial edges. Tension zones can range in size from an entire continent to a few hundred acres. Tension zone locations can shift geographically over time as geological and climatological conditions evolve or cycle. Continental drift would cause a long-term change in the location of tension zones. Glaciation causes shorter change. Human intervention could cause a

shift in a biological tension zone. Burning fossil fuels, for example, could result in global warming by leading to an increase of carbon dioxide in the atmosphere and thus an increase in the proportion of solar radiation trapped in the troposphere before it is reradiated to outer space. Thus the boundaries for the Corn Belt in the United States or the Wheat Belt in Canada might be altered. Another example is found in the Sahelian Zone of North Africa where intensive grazing and well drilling appears to lead to a southward extension of deserts. An early indication of biological tension-zone shifts should show up in the phenological behavior of plants and animals. *See also* Greenhouse effect

Biota. The animal and plant life of a particular region considered as a total ecological entity. Study of the biota leads to such theories as "environmental stability through species diversity." Recent research suggests that a region with diverse biota is stable as a biological "community" but risky for individual species; under this theory, a region with fewer species would be more secure for the individual species.

Blocked meridional flow. *See* Meridional flow

Boreal forest. Forested regions in the northern temperate zone or the Arctic, reaching as far as the northern tundras. The change from boreal to tundra occurs over a distance of a few miles. The margins of the boreal forests shift north and south according to shifts in global temperature, the cycling of glacial epochs, and shorter interglacial climates. The forest-tundra boundary is a biological tension zone.

Braided levee. An embankment formed and reformed naturally in a floodplain where a river has low elevational changes and seasonal or storm-related surges in water. A braided levee may appear as a complex web without an obvious pattern, but the formation is a response to the kinetic, volumetric, and gravitational forces in the flowing water. For a beautiful description of these forces, see Luna Leopold's *A View of the River* (Harvard University Press, 1994). On the Leopold Reserve there are natural braided levees as well as a human-constructed levee. *See also* Levee

Cambrian Period. The early Paleozoic Cambrian Period on Earth occurred from about 570 million to 500 million years ago. With estimates of the age of the earth ranging up to 4.7 billion years, the Cambrian could be considered to be "old-age." Life forms as shown in the fossil record exploded during the Cambrian. *See also* Paleozoic Era

Cambrian sandstone. In this text I refer to Cambrian sandstone that probably washed down from mountains next to a seacoast over 500 million years ago. The sand was buried under additional layers of sediment, and increased pressure and heat lithified the sand into rock. The sandstone can be further metamorphosed into quartzite. *See also* Monadnock; Sandstone; Quartzite

Capillary fringe. The soil zone immediately above the water table that draws water upward because of its molecular attraction to individual soil particles. The capillary fringe (and the water table) fluctuate according to rainfall, river flooding, atmospheric humidity, and the seasons. Water evaporates at a faster rate in summer than in winter. In dry conditions the capillary fringe will drop, especially in sandy soils, which drain quickly. Plants rely on this capillary fringe for their water supply. They will be constrained in a sandy soil through lack of water, and also in a clay soil that is water-logged.

Carbohydrate. Any of a group of chemical compounds, including sugars, starches, and cellulose, that contain carbon, hydrogen, and oxygen only, with the ratio of hydrogen to oxygen atoms usually 2 to 1. Carbohydrates are produced through plant photosynthetic processes. Reduced carbohydrates from which oxygen has been removed are hydrocarbons. Oxidation of carbohydrates and hydrocarbons produces carbon oxides and water. Thus, we talk about the carbon cycle, an underpinning process for life.

Carboniferous swamp. A swamp formed during the Carboniferous Period (the Mississippian and Pennsylvanian geologic periods) from about 285 to 360 million years ago. The time was characterized by sprawling swamps and the deposition of plant remains that were later lithified into coal. Carbohydrates were reduced and converted to hydrocarbons during the process. The climate in the swamps would have been warm and humid over many millions of years.

Chalcedony. A milky or grayish quartz with distinctive microscopic crystals arranged in parallel bands. *See also* Agate; Quartz

Chaos. Any condition or place of total disorder or confusion. Some religious views have argued that the universe is chaotic. It might seem so on a clear night sky with the three-dimensional display of millions upon millions of stars scattered wildly in a vast abyss. But we now know that there is order and form in the universe. I also believe that the same judgment can be made as we view the prairie—there is order in what may appear as a chaotic terrain. *See also* Cosmos

Chemical energy. The potential for action inherent in the structure of molecules.

Energy is released when chemical bonds are broken or changed. For example, the potential energy in a carbohydrate molecule is released when it is oxidized by burning in the metabolism of plants and animals, or a fire in the prairie. *See also* Photosynthesis

Chert. Microscopically crystalline mineral varieties of quartz (silica dioxide); also called agate, chalcedony, flint, and jasper.

Chroma. A variation in color that is affected by the hue and saturation of the perceived color. In a sensory way, chroma is a major force in our perception of the surrounding landscape.

Circumpolar vortex. The pattern of atmospheric circulation that moves outward from the poles in the winter, and tends to be distinct from the air masses that rise over the equator and sink over the lower middle latitudes. The polar circulation expands in winter and retreats in summer, tracing a seasonal path back and forth across the temperate zones. The circumpolar vortex also becomes more dominant over a larger portion of the earth in a glacial period and retreats during an interglacial. The outer edge of the vortex is somewhat defined by the paths of the jet stream.

Cirrus horsetails. High altitude clouds composed of narrow bands or paths of thin, generally white, fleecy "horsetails." The horsetails are actually precipitating snow crystals.

Climate. The set of meteorological conditions, including temperature, precipitation, wind, and cloud cover, that tend to prevail in a particular region or time span. In this text, climate is considered a major defining parameter for the biota. Indeed, it provides a major answer in our search for why things happen the way they do—particularly phenological expressions. The terrain defined in *Prairie Time* is at a major

boundary between polar and equatorial climates, defined by the circumpolar vortex and equatorial circulation. Moreover, the area has been physically shaped by the climate-driven advance and retreat of glaciers.

Clone. One or more organisms descended asexually from a single ancestor; also, a group of genetically identical cells descended from a single common cell ancestor. Identical twins, formed by the division of an embryo, are an example. Biologists have apparently succeeded in "synthetically" producing clones of plants and, in recent years, animals, through laboratory propagation. It is now technically possible to clone humans and theoretically possible to clone parts of humans.

Co-evolution. The process in which two species develop, over time, in a way that enhances the survival of both. Evolutionary processes select characteristics in both that enforce this mutual benefit. They "evolve" together and become dependent on each other, as, for example, milkweed and butterflies are. Accordingly, a decline of one species will then cause a decline in the other. Humans may be intervening in such a process, as with the use of broad spectrum pesticides on agronomic crops such as corn. Pesticides kill a range of insects, some of which have co-evolved with prairie plants. In that case, the prairie plants die out.

Complexity theory. A newly emerging theory that asserts (1) complexity can be quantified, (2) levels of complexity can be defined, (3) complex changes can be predicted over time. In addition, complex things tend to give rise to more complex things over different time scales. In this text, complexity theory provides a basis for understanding the relationships between the physical and the biological worlds. More than that, it is suggested as a logical, empirical basis for protecting the natural world as a means to our own survival.

Cosmic dust. Solid materials of matter in interstellar space. Cosmic dust includes all the elements, often in molecular forms, that constitute our earth. Abundant hydrogen and some helium were created in the Big Bang. All the other elements were created by fusion in stellar furnaces and then spewed out in stellar explosions, creating cosmic dust. This text refers to the likelihood that atoms of oxygen and silicon, now in earth's environment as silicon dioxide, have been circulated through several generations of solar systems, and perhaps planets, since the creation of the universe.

Cosmos. The view of the universe as an orderly, harmonious system; distinct from chaos. *See also* Chaos

Craton. A stable, relatively immobile area of the earth's crust that forms the central mass of a continent, such as the largely granitic Canadian shield.

Cretaceous Period. The geologic period from about 70 million to 145 million years ago, when dinosaurs flourished. The Rocky Mountains rose near the end of the Cretaceous. However, birds and mammals were fairly well established, having emerged in the Jurassic Period, the time just before the Cretaceous. In relation to the age of the earth, these periods are characterized as "late modern."

Cro-Magnon. An early form of modern man (*Homo sapiens*) characterized by a robust physique and known from skeletal remains found in southern France.

Crystal. A solid body that expresses a regular internal arrangement of its atoms and molecules. Particles in the solid have definite geometric relationships to each other. Crystals can be formed when a sub-stance changes from a gas or liquid state to a solid. *See also* Igneous quartz crystal; Magma; Quartzite

Cybernetics. Control systems and communication systems in living organisms and machines. In cybernetics, analogies are drawn between the functioning of the brain and nervous system in animals and a computer or other electrical system. Use of the term in this text refers to the possibility of a cybernetic relationship among species in a specific location, and also the cybernetic relationship between the physical and the biological worlds. Inherent in the concept of cybernetic systems is the possibility of control, with a quantifiable prediction of outcomes. We have spent much effort in temperature control in small spaces—for example, the relationship between a thermostat and the temperature of a room or a refrigerator. Another example is "cruise control" on an automobile or an "automatic pilot" on an airplane. The next step would be to create systems of environmental controls for entire communities—as in habitat experiments.

Deciduous. A term for the temporary shedding of foliage at the end of the growing season, as in deciduous trees. The deciduous trees in our woods and savannas are jungle-lush in the summer. They undress for the celebration of winter solstice and the annual winter epiphany. Each year's leaves die and drop off in autumn, but the deciduous tree can persist as a singular organism for many years.

Dendrite. A branched part of a nerve cell that transmits impulses toward the nerve cell body. The term literally means "tree-shaped," and it is sometimes used to describe patterns in biotic relationships among individuals and species, and even crystalline patterns in minerals. Such usage suggests that this is a universal form that transmits information in physical and biological nature.

Determinism. The theory that states that certain events and reactions are the result of "causing" factors. For example, ice results when the temperature drops below the freezing point of water, and water vapor results when water is heated above the boiling point. Thus, the temperature "determines" whether water is solid, liquid, or gaseous. Although in many cases the phenomena of the natural world reflect such deterministic patterns, there are numerous instances of random, or stochastic, patterns, and the interplay between these different kinds of responses is interesting to observe. This interplay is revealed in phenological expressions, which is one reason phenology is such an interesting "science." Phenologists try to figure out why some expressions appear more deterministic and some appear more random, or stochastic. Actually, both processes are at work in most expressions. At this time in the evolving understanding of biology, the determinists seem to be winning many of the arguments. *See also* Random variation; Stochastic pattern

Detritus. Loose fragments, particles, or grains that have been formed by the disintegration of rocks or organic material. In its derivation, "detritus" is related to "detriment," which carries the connotation of damage or harm, but I believe that such an implication is misleading, because detritus is the raw material for new organization, as nature recycles everything. Detritus also provides a window into the past.

DNA. Deoxyribonucleic acid, the substance present in most living organisms, including all cellular organisms, in which genetic information is coded.

Dolomitic limestone. A magnesium-rich sedimentary rock in the limestone family; in other words, a calcium-magnesium carbonate. A very durable form of limestone, it tends to resist erosion.

Driftless Area. An area in southwestern Wisconsin that escaped glaciation, and is not covered by glacial outwash sediments, or "drift." Repeated glaciations occurring across the two million years of the Pleistocene deposited moraines of drift and debris, but finer materials also blew downwind as the glaciers melted; such deposits are called loess soils. As the impact line of the glaciers is not linear or even smoothly curvilinear, it is not clear why they did not advance into this area. *See also* Loess prairie; Wisconsin glaciation

Ecological restoration. The process of allowing and/or encouraging natural forces to work out a balance between organisms and their environment. One approach is to provide outright protection, such as establishing parks and wilderness areas, or safeguarding endangered species. Another approach involves the reintroduction of natural biota, such as prairie plants, wolves, or even the reestablishment of such areas as oak savannas. An approach of this sort may also involve the deliberate burning of an ecosystem, because fire was a more pervasive natural element before the era of fire prevention.

Ecology. The science of the relationships between organisms and their environment. Recently, the term has also taken on a philosophical and political aspect as a counterpoint to economic development and exploitation of natural resources. The etymological root for "ecology" is *oikos*, which is Greek for "house" or "home." Note the similarity to "home economics."

Econometric discipline. The application of statistical techniques to economics; the study of problems, the analysis of data, and the development of theories of economic behavior. Students of econometrics also seek to predict economic behavior using theories and models that are both stochastic and deterministic. *See also* Determinism; Stochastic pattern

Ecosystem. A basic ecological unit in the biosphere. A community of plants and animals in an environment that supplies them with raw materials for life. Ecosystems vary in scale. An ecosystem may be as small as the reestablished prairie on the Leopold Reserve or as broad as the oak savanna that stretched in a belt across the continent before settlement. *See also* Ecology

Ecotone. An ecological community that shares plant and animal species in the zone of overlap between larger-scale, adjoining communities, or ecosystems. Continental ecotones are those margins created by the junctures of continents and oceans, glaciated and unglaciated terrain, climate boundaries, or hemispheric boundaries between air circulation patterns. Ecotones may be expressed, for example, as changes on the land from forest to savanna to prairie. The gradual change from tall- grass savannas to short-grass prairies on the American high plains provides another example. The Leopold Reserve, at the edge of the glacial terrain in Wisconsin, is an example of an ecotone embedded within the savanna that stretches across North America. *See also* Biological tension zone

Elliptical orbit. An orbit that is in the form of an oval, or an ellipse. The earth has an elliptical orbit around the sun. There is some patterned variation in the regularity of Earth's orbit over time, which is influenced by gravitational pulls of the other planets. This variation affects the amount of solar radiation reaching the earth, and thus has an influence on variable climatic conditions over time. *See also* Orbit

El Niño. A Spanish name for the Christ Child, used to refer to a climatological phenomenon of heavy rain in an arid region, first identified years ago around Christmas on the Peruvian coast, and intermittently repeated since then. El Niño is associated with warmer than normal coastal waters, a blockage of cold upwellings, and a major die-off of anchovies that prosper with nutrients from the rich, cold upwellings. Interestingly, climatological evidence from beach fossils in Peru suggests that warmer coastal waters and higher rainfalls prevailed in that area 5,000 years ago, suggesting a very different climatic regime.

Emian Period. The last interglacial period that occurred about 100,000 years ago. Climatologists increasingly argue that glaciation has been cyclic rather than episodic during the two million years of the Pleistocene. Although the climate of the Emian would have been similar to the present-day interglacial Holocene, there is some speculation that the Emian climate flipped from cold to warm and back again, more frequently than climate in the Holocene has.

Entropy. A measure of the amount of energy in a system that is not available to do work. Energy is "conserved" but becomes unavailable for a given level of work, because the system moves to a lower temperature. It cools off. One physical theory predicts that the universe will expand and cool forever—thus a continuing entropic process. However, Earth, as we know intuitively, seems to have succeeded in countering entropic processes, at least for a time. Thus, we have an example of negentropy, where energy is available to do work. Work such as metabolism is available as a consequence of energy stored through photosynthesis, but negentropy also implies the construction of complex structures, such as a molecule of DNA. I suggest that an understanding of entropic and negentropic processes, in our natural environment, and in the habitat we manipulate, is a fundamental principle in maintaining a sustainable environment. This principle underlies the metaphor in my final essay on the Planet Orbit.

Eonic. A general term that refers to the length of time it takes a revolving galaxy to complete a rotation. Seeming ponderously slow to the human psyche, it is not slow at all when measured against the time and distances involved. The question is whether this galactic "eonic" rotation has a measurable impact, over time, on the earth's environment. Some scientists suggest that the sun and its planets move in and out of dust zones as the galaxy rotates, thus changing climatic conditions on Earth. Our sun is traveling at about 155 miles per second, and it takes about 220 million years for the Milky Way galaxy to complete a rotation.

Ephemeral. As used in this text, a term referring to the flowering plants (forbs) that bloom for only a brief time in spring; for example, the pasque flower. In studying ephemerals, phenologists are curious not only about why they bloom in the relatively harsh conditions of spring—but also about why the duration of their flowering period is so short compared to that of other later-blooming plants.

Epiphany. The name of a Christian festival on January 6 that celebrates the manifestation of the divine nature of Christ to the Gentiles. The term is also used for a sudden manifestation of the essence of something, such as the sudden intuitive realization of the natural beauty in a Wisconsin prairie on a warm day in June.

Equinox. Either of the two times during the year when the sun crosses the terrestrial equator and when the length of day and night are approximately equal, the vernal equinox and the autumnal equinox. Readers of this text will have detected that I have some problems with the usual descriptions of Earth-Sun relationships. For example, the sun doesn't literally cross the equator. Nor does the sun rise in the morning. Rather, the sun "appears" to cross the equator from the perspective of an earthling, and appears to rise at dawn. It is the earth that is rolling around, and we are rolling with it.

Erratic granite boulder. In this text, a rock that was removed from its source area by glaciers, carried in the ice, and deposited as a boulder when the glacier retreated.

Escarpment. A steep slope or long cliff resulting from erosion or geologic faulting, which creates a separation of two relatively level areas, resulting in different elevations.

Eukaryote. A cell that has a well-defined nucleus and a complex structure. Biologists have maintained for some time that eukaryotic cells on Earth followed prokaryotic cells by perhaps up to a billion years, with the assumption that the eukaryotes evolved from the prokaryotes, or that eukaryotes are actually symbiotic combinations of prokaryotes. There is now consensus that eukaryotic cells, with highly specialized functions, did combine to form multicelled organisms. More recently, some scientists are arguing that eukaryotic cells may be almost as ancient as the prokaryotes, having appeared in the first billion years or so of Earth's existence. Eukaryotes may be 10,000 times as large as prokaryotes, but the two are undeniably related, as evidenced in the structure of their DNA. *See also* Prokaryote

Evolution. The theory that groups of organisms, as species, may change with the passage of time so that descendants differ morphologically and physiologically from their ancestors. Evolutionary theories can encompass other levels of organization, including biological and social communities. *See also* Co-evolution

Fauna. Animals collectively; or the animals of a particular region, for example, the American prairie.

Feral. Savage or wild; also having returned to an untamed state from domestication. In this text, I suggest that humans might behave like feral animals if they become detached from a domestic existence based in localized use of resources such as energy and food.

Fixed-action pattern. A genetically prescribed pattern passed on through inheritance; a pattern of biological behavior not easily influenced by variable responses due to environmental conditions. Early theories proposed that some species rely more on fixed-action patterns than others, and that humans are the only species with the ability to respond through cognition. Recent theories propose that all species (and therefore individual organisms) respond to some combination of patterned inheritance and cognition. A phenological example would be bird migration over long distances. The migrator would know innately when to migrate and where to go, influenced by signals from the environment. But it is also apparent that migratory paths, in some cases, are taught by parents to each new generation. Significantly, there seems to be no particular "superiority" in one mode over the other. Thus form, behavior, and expression result from a complex web of nature and nurture. To deny one or the other is to deny existence. However, either can be limiting.

Flint. A hard, very fine-grained quartz that sparks when struck with steel; a variety of chert. Formed and used as a tool by humans.

Floodplain. A plain beside the river course subject to flooding. Humans seem to persist in building on floodplains and trying to constrain floods, often with great costs, epitomized in such events as 100-year floods.

Flora. Plants collectively; also used to describe the plants of a particular region. Flora, in Roman mythology, is the goddess of flowers.

Forb. A herbaceous plant other than a grass.

Fullerene. Named for architect Buckminster Fuller, who worked with geodesic domes, a fullerene is a hollow-caged molecule of 60 or 70 atoms of carbon, resembling a soccer ball in shape. Natural fullerenes were identified in soot in 1985; fullerenes were generated in the laboratory in 1990. Fullerenes show some promise as a superconductive agent.

Gamete. A mature sperm or egg capable of participating in fertilization, containing half the chromosomes required for a developing organism.

Geocentric. Having the earth as the center. Early philosophers believed that Earth was the center of the universe, around which the sun and other planets revolved. Some people—and I among them—believe that the term is still conceptually and philosophically useful because there is security to be had in our understanding of the physical, chemical, and biological systems at work on this planet. Aldo Leopold was also arguing for this concept when he stated that "we should live lightly on the land."

Glacial outwash. The sand, gravel, clay, and boulders that washed away from melting glaciers, or were left behind as moraines during glacial retreats. The authors live on the west edge of Madison in the middle of an outwash of sand, clay, and boulders. Our backyard is sandy, but the glacier left a great muddle of granite boulders just across the way, some of them as big as a Volkswagen. It is possible to stand on this outwash under the black oak tree and imagine the torrents of ice and water that molded this land from 16,000 to 12,000 years ago.

Glacial remnant. In this text "glacial remnant" refers to a biological island on the landscape, something that seems to be from a colder time, the time of glaciation. For example, the dominant biota on the landscape may be prairie and oak savanna, but tucked away in a ravine—as on the North Slope in the Leopold Reserve—there may be a copse of white birch or a cluster of white pines. The area where they continue to persist is colder than the surrounding terrain. They are a living reminder of a glacial climate.

Gley. A sticky, bluish-gray soil layer formed under the influence of excessive moisture.

Granite pluton. A mass of granite that formed beneath the surface of the earth by the crystallization of a magma. *See also* Magma; Plutonic rock

Grass. Any one of numerous plants of the family Gramineae that have narrow leaves, hollow jointed stems, and spikes or clusters of membranous flowers borne in smaller spikelets.

Gravitation. The attractive force existing between any two particles of matter. The force holding us to the surface of the earth is the same as the force holding the planets in the solar system. It is now believed that a massive black hole at the center of the Milky Way is the integrating force that holds the galaxy together.

Gravitational energy. The energy required to maintain gravitation. Scientists still search for a unifying theory that would relate gravitation to electromagnetic force, and to the forces inherent in atomic structure.

Greenhouse effect. A term used to describe the way in which atmospheric gases account for Earth's temperatures that are benign for life. Visible light comes from the sun to Earth, and, upon reaching Earth, much of it passes unimpeded through a blanket of gases, including water vapor, carbon dioxide, methane, nitrous oxide, and ozone. Some of that light is absorbed by the surface of the earth (soil and rocks), and much of that is re-radiated as infrared radiation. Some of the warm infrared is trapped in the atmosphere and reflected toward Earth. This process keeps Earth habitable at a temperature suitable for life— about 60°F, on average. We prosper in a global greenhouse. However, increases in the atmospheric gases can bring about increases in the average temperature by several degrees. Decreases in gases can have the opposite effect. Such changes have occurred in the past and are associated with, for example, the coming and going of glaciation, or the advance and retreat of deserts. Many climatologists now believe that human activities can produce enough change in atmospheric gases to cause global warming and thus major changes in weather patterns. *See also* Biological tension zone

Gymnosperm. A plant species of the class Gymnospermae, which includes coniferous trees and other plants having seeds not enclosed within an ovary; gymnosperms are older, in an evolutionary sense, than angiosperms. *See also* Angiosperm

Helix. A three-dimensional curve that lies on a cylinder or cone; a spiral form or structure. A double helix is the structure of the DNA molecule. The helix is used in this text as an analog to describe an ecological structure of plants and animals, or a sensory impression of natural form in the landscape. *See also* DNA

Hierarchic. Stratified; arranged in a graded series. Used in this text to suggest that one level of complexity is embedded within a higher one, which is in turn embedded in a higher level. For example, individuals on our savanna-prairie are themselves complex. But they are embedded in the populations and species around them. The local ecology is embedded in the regional variables of soil, climate, and seasons—in other words, the prairie and savanna ecotone. The ecotone is embedded in the continental and Earth environment, which is fundamentally influenced by astronomical conditions.

Holocene Epoch. The most recent and current period of geological time, equivalent to the last 10 to 15 thousand years. The name, if interpreted literally from its Greek roots, means "entirely new," which would be an anachronistic term for this, or any other, geologic age. Perhaps the only "new" feature of the Holocene is the emerging dominance of humans as Earth's pervasive predator.

Hydraulic lift. The ability of a plant to take water from the soil and move it upward, against gravitational force, through the plant's vascular system.

Hydrocarbon. Any organic compound, such as methane, ethane, propane, and butane. The compounds contain atoms of carbon and hydrogen, for example, methane—CH_3. Hydrocarbons oxidize, or burn, readily, thus their value as fuels. *See also* Methane

Igneous quartz crystal. Silicon dioxide that crystallized from magma, often with a planar structure that is visible without magnification. *See also* Magma; Quartzite

Infolithic. A term I have devised to suggest that *Homo sapiens* has now entered a time when the storage and exchange of technical information via silicon chips will be the dominant factor in framing our culture. Although the term itself is not used in the text, its relationship to the ideas proffered in the essay on Orbit, pages 119–128 above, is readily apparent. "Lithic" means of or pertaining to stone; anthropologists refer to ages in human development according to the use of stone. Paleolithic is the cultural period beginning with the earliest chipped stone tools, about 750,000 years ago; Mesolithic designates the cultural period between the Paleolithic and the Neolithic that is marked by the appearance of the bow and of cutting tools; and Neolithic refers to the cultural period beginning about 12,000 years ago in the Middle East, and characterized by the invention of farming and the making of technically advanced stone implements. The relationship of "Infolithic" to "stone" derives from the use of the pure silicon "chip" as a medium for the storage of information—in other words, a tool. But I also believe that we have not abandoned the earlier cultural forms. *See also* Synthelithic

Interglacial. That time period between major glacial climates and glaciations, characterized by warmer temperatures. The last continental glaciers started to recede about 16,000 years ago, with the glaciers in full retreat about 12,000 years ago. The present interglacial thermal maximum occurred about 6,000 years ago, and many climatologists believe we are drifting slowly back to the next glacial climate. Whether or not they are correct, the era of fossil fuels—coal, oil, natural gas, and peat—which warm our hearths and contribute carbon dioxide to the atmosphere, would produce but a blip in the long-time climatological record.

Jet stream. A high-speed wind near the boundary of the troposphere and the stratosphere, generally moving from a westerly direction at speeds which often exceed 250 miles an hour. It tends to define the outer margin of the circumpolar vortex, and also "storm tracks." *See also* Circumpolar vortex

Jurassic Period. Geologic period from about 145 to 200 million years ago; life forms included dinosaurs, mammals, early birds, and flowering plants. Dinosaurs persisted throughout the Triassic, Jurassic, and Cretaceous Periods, a time span of about 130 million years. These three periods are considered "late modern," in relation to the age of the earth, which is more than 4.5 billion years.

Kettle bottom. A depression left in a mass of glacial drift, probably formed by the melting of an isolated block of buried glacial ice.

Kinetic energy. The energy associated with motion, equal to one-half of the product of an object's mass and the square of its speed. In nature, there are dramatic displays of kinetic energy all around: for example, the Wisconsin River at flood stage, the appearance of a burning meteorite in an August night sky, or the unanticipated arrival of a comet.

Land ethic. A set of moral principles or values, rooted in conservative and radical principles, that protect and manage Earth's resources in a responsible way. Aldo Leopold's seminal philosophical contribution is that the land ethic should be based in conservation and sharing by all species. Leopold argues that although such an ethic is in the interest of human survival, there is also a deeper, moral obligation, as in right from wrong.

Leguminous forb. A herbaceous plant other than a grass that is a member of the family Leguminosae. Well-known examples are peas, beans, clover, and alfalfa. Many leguminous plants have a symbiotic relationship with bacteria that have the capacity to "fix" atoms of nitrogen with atoms of oxygen and thus make the nitrogen directly available as a plant nutrient.

Levee. An embankment in the riverbed formed by the natural positioning of sand, silt, and gravel by running water. It can also be a barrier erected by humans to control the river "within its banks." Levees can persist over time or can change quite quickly. *See also* Braided levee.

Limestone. A sedimentary rock composed chiefly of calcium carbonate, formed in shallow, tropical seas by marine organisms, especially corals. Limestone formations exist in the geographic area described in this text, on the surface of the Driftless Area, but also below "recent" glacial deposits. They speak of ancient tropical reefs, atolls, and vastly abundant, earlier life forms such as foraminifera, which are microscopic animals with shells.

Linear trend. Because "linear" means resembling a line, having only one dimension, the term "linear trend" is often used to mean a straight line, or an increasing or decreasing slope. The more inclusive meaning, however, is "having only one dimension," as there is also the possibility of a curvilinear line that expresses a linear trend. The linear trend expressed in a curvilinear line may be more descriptive of many natural phenomena than a straight line would be. The trend may have a rhythm. An example might be a pattern over time in the average dates of phenological expressions that form a sloping or wave-like curve, possibly reflecting a result of a rhythm in rainfall or climate.

Loess prairie. A prairie habitat with a mix of grasses and forbs that is rooted in loess, a fine-grained silt or clay sediment carried by wind from the edge of a retreating glacier. European settlers found that some of Wisconsin's loess prairies presented rich soils for agriculture, and they remain so today. The loess prairies are now largely occupied by corn, alfalfa, and soybeans. *See also* Driftless Area; Prairie

Magma. A mass of rock and dissolved gas that forms in the mantle or crust of the earth, and cools and crystallizes into various forms of igneous rock.

Manifest Destiny. An ideological term that was introduced in the nineteenth century to justify the occupation of North America by American colonists. The "opportunity" to expand became a "moral imperative." The term might also be used to rationalize an accelerating rate of economic development in the twenty-first century. But it is susceptible to other interpretations as well. Some environmentalists argue that the way in which we exploit or tolerate the natural environment will reveal our real destiny, one that has not yet been fully revealed. That idea has been conceptualized as "Limits to Growth."

Meander. Used in this text to describe a turn in a river. The word comes from the name of a winding river in Asia Minor. As a verb, "meander" can mean to wander aimlessly and without direction, but meanders in a river have a very fundamental underlying "direction," because the river works to adjust its path to the energy of the flowing water. Meanders can be quite precisely described in terms of kinetic energy and changes in elevation. *See also* Braided levee

Meridional flow. A meridian is a circle on the surface of the earth that crosses both the North and South Poles, and is expressed as longitude. Flow, in this situation, refers to patterns in atmospheric circulation—whether air flows north-south or west-east.

In the winter, at middle latitudes, north-south meridional flows tend to dominate. In summer, the westerly winds are more dominant. In the text I refer to a blocked meridional flow, which is one that tends to persist over days or weeks at a given location. In the winter, a northerly flow results in a so-called cold snap; a southerly flow would bring a January thaw. Blocked flows can also occur in summer, but they are less likely at the equinoxes.

Metabolism. The interrelated physical and chemical processes involved in the maintenance of life for an individual organism. Some ecologists talk about the "metabolism" of an ecosystem.

Metamorphic rock. A rock mass which has undergone an alteration in composition, texture, or structure because of great heat or pressure.

Methane. An odorless, colorless, and flammable gas made up of one atom of carbon and four of hydrogen. The simplest molecular structure of the hydrocarbon family, it is the major constituent of "natural" gas. Settlers called it "swamp gas" because it was emitted from vegetatively rich wetlands. Methane can be formed by the reduction of organic carbohydrates, and also in nonorganic processes.

Midden. A refuse heap, especially of an earlier or primitive habitation.

Miocene Epoch. The name given to the geological epoch from about 5 to 24 million years ago, within the Tertiary Period.

Molecular structure. The relatively stable configuration of atomic nuclei and electrons bound together by electrostatic and electromagnetic forces. The molecule is the simplest "structural" unit that displays the characteristic physical and chemical properties of a compound. For example, the molecular structure of water involves two atoms of hydrogen and one of oxygen.

However, molecules of water can unite to form a more complex structure that expresses many of the fascinating properties of water, such as its unusual capacity to retain heat energy.

Monadnock. A mountain or rocky mass that has resisted erosion and stands isolated in a plain or peneplain. The Baraboo Range is the monadnock featured in this text. The range has the appearance of an elongated bowl enclosing a canoe-shaped depression. It is made largely of quartzite. The hills are the eroded remnants of ancient upheavals that were preceded by sandy outwash from earlier mountains. Their quartzite is one of the oldest rocks exposed in North America, dated at over 1.5 billion years. Those Archean mountains would have been covered by snow, but with an atmosphere greatly limited in free oxygen, thus barren of life. *See also* Quartzite

Mulch. A protective, organic covering lying around plants that prevents the evaporation of moisture and freezing of roots. Applied by gardeners to control weeds and contain moisture, it can also occur naturally. An example in this text is the "mulch" in an old quackgrass meadow that retains the cold of winter well into spring. Fire burns out this mulch, thus allowing the plants to respond to a warming sun earlier.

Neanderthal. A name given to a race of humans who lived during the late Pleistocene age in Europe and Africa and used Middle Paleolithic tools. The name comes from Neanderthal, a valley near Dusseldorf, Germany. The evolutionary relationship between Neanderthals and *Homo sapiens* has not been defined to the point of acceptance.

Neolithic Age. The human cultural period beginning around 12,000 years ago in the Middle East and later elsewhere, char-acterized by the invention of farming and the making of technically advanced stone implements. Some anthropologists argue that humans turned first to animal husbandry and then to cropping, perhaps a thousand years later, because of warmer and dryer conditions after the retreat of the glaciers. Recently, some geologists have suggested that a sudden flooding of the Black Sea basin (as continental glaciers melted) caused agriculturalists to spread out of that basin into Eurasia. *See also* Paleolithic Age

Niagara Escarpment. A ridge of dolomitic limestone that reaches across the northeastern quadrant of North America through the Great Lakes region. In Wisconsin it forms the Door County peninsula and appears above the surface in patches diagonally across the state, with some apparent remnants on Blue Mounds, west of Madison. Some climatologists think the escarpment served to vector the glaciers in a northeast-southwest direction across the state.

Oak opening. A cluster of oak trees (deciduous or evergreen trees or shrubs of the genus *Quercus*, bearing acorns as fruit) surrounded by prairie. An oak opening may include trees of other species. The ecosystem that describes the savanna in this text is the combination of oak opening and prairie.

Oligocene Epoch. The name given to the geologic epoch from about 24 to 37 million years ago, in the middle of the Tertiary Period. It was a time when many mammalian creatures lived and roamed all across the North American continent. Many geologists believe that in the Oligocene, the continent was centered near the current latitude of Central America. It has since drifted northward and westward. Perhaps volcanic tuff, glacial till, and continental drift are the true manifestations of biological destiny.

Opal. A translucent mineral of hydrated silicon dioxide that is softer than quartz.

Orbit. The path of a celestial body or manmade satellite as it revolves around another body, such as the moon around Earth, or Earth around the sun. It also describes the path of an electron around an atomic nucleus. In the text it is used as the name of an imaginary planet orbiting between companion suns.

Orogeny. The process of mountain formation through the folding and faulting of the earth's crust, usually a result of colliding continental or oceanic plates.

Osmosis. The diffusion of a compound through a semipermeable membrane until there is an equal concentration of the material on both sides of the membrane. The term is sometimes used metaphorically to indicate absorption in general, as, for example, in cognitive processes, to learn a language by exposure to it or to personally accept an ethic originally laid out by a single prophetic mind. This idea of osmotic diffusion could be applied to the writings of Aldo Leopold, who argued that the only lasting land ethic will come about through the "osmotic" acceptance of a "land ethic" standard by individuals in a community.

Paleocene Epoch. The name given to the oldest geologic epoch in the Tertiary Period, from about 66 to 58 million years ago.

Paleolithic Age. The human cultural period beginning with the earliest known chipped stone tools, about 750,000 years ago, and ending with the beginning of the Mesolithic Period, about 15,000 years ago. There is now evidence suggesting that the Paleolithic started more than two million years ago. Some anthropologists believe that the use of tools by humans was stimu-

lated by the emergence of the Pleistocene, or Ice Age; humans could thus be defined as Ice Age mammals. Given glaciation, it is likely that the circumpolar vortex would have expanded, and the subtropical convergence, and thus the desert regions, would have been closer to the equator. Hominids, such as *Homo erectus* and *Homo sapiens*, may well have existed at the middle latitudes where climates were colder and existence more harsh than now. Paleolithic sites dated well into the last glacial period have been excavated in Siberia. At that time the landscape was one of tundra—with grasses and low shrubs. *See also* Infolithic; Neanderthal; Neolithic Age; Synthelithic

Paleontology. The study of fossils.

Paleozoic Era. The geological term for an era that stretched from about 570 million years ago to the beginning of the Mesozoic, about 245 million years ago. The earliest period in the Paleozoic is the Cambrian, a time when a great variety of complex organisms emerged. Some scientists argue that these ancient animals and plants were structurally and physiologically as complex as later forms. At any rate, there was ample time for evolutionary change in the Paleozoic, over 300 million years. *See also* Cambrian Period

Passerine. A bird of the order Passeriformes, which includes perching birds and songbirds such as jays, blackbirds, finches, warblers, and sparrows. Many, but not all, make up the migrators that fill the pages of the Leopold and Bradley phenological journals. However, the sandhill crane and Canada goose, which figure prominently in the journals and in our text, are not passerines.

Peneplain. A nearly flat land surface representing an advanced stage of erosion.

Phalanx. Originally, a formation of infantry carrying overlapping shields and long spears, developed by Philip II of Macedonia and used by Alexander the Great. The concept produces raw material for analogic descriptions of natural phenomena, such as the phalanx of trees on the top of the moraine.

Phenology. The study of periodic biological phenomena, such as the flowering of plants and the breeding and migration of animals. The biological phenomena are related to climate, including seasonal, temperature, and barometric changes. Phenological expressions are also almost certainly influenced by such things as magnetic fields, the shifts in seasonal flow of photons reaching Earth, continental structures such as mountain ranges, geologic formations such as soil types, and perhaps even the astronomical variations in Earth's position as related to the sun over time.

Photon. The quantum of electromagnetic energy, generally regarded as a discrete particle, that has zero mass, no electric charge, tends to move freely at "the speed of light," and has an indefinitely long life span, perhaps limited only by the life of the universe.

Photosynthesis. The process by which chlorophyll-containing cells in green plants convert incident light (photons) to chemical energy, and synthesize organic compounds from inorganic compounds, especially carbohydrates from carbon dioxide and water with the simultaneous release of oxygen.

Pleistocene Epoch. The name given to the "glacial epoch" of the last two to three million years. The epoch may have started with the rise of the Himalaya Mountains or the closing of the Isthmus of Panama, which possibly affected global air and ocean circulation patterns and the carbon cycle. One theory is that the increasing erosion from the Himalayas served to transfer carbon dioxide from the atmosphere into

carbonate deposits, thus reducing the "greenhouse effect." The closing of the Isthmus would affect patterns of ocean currents. Glacial epochs have occurred in earlier times as a function of location of continents, land forms, and atmospheric and astronomical conditions. *See also* Greenhouse effect

Plutonic rock. A mass of igneous rock formed beneath the surface of the earth by the consolidation of magma. *See also* Magma

Podzol. A leached soil formed mainly in cool, humid climates, characteristic of glaciated areas.

Pothole. Literally, a hole or pit. In this text, it refers to a pit formed on the earth's surface as a result of glaciation, probably through the melting of a remnant block of ice.

Prairie. An area of flat or rolling land vegetated with grasses and forbs; for example, the high plains of central North America. Toward the western part of the continent, the prairies reach from sky edge to sky edge; big country to the eye. Toward the east, the prairies occupy large areas, and are also defined as oak savannas. The prairie-savannas, I suggest, are locally more sensuous than the big, open landscape to the west. The prairies, it seems, have a major impact on the economies of and the psyches of their human inhabitants, whose intentions have ranged from exploitation to preservation, and whose emotions have ranged from apprehension to affection. It is the relationship between the wild prairies and the wild weather that imprints those most dramatic images in our minds. *See also* Loess prairie

Precession. A complex motion executed by a rotating body subjected to a torque that tends to change the axis of rotation. The precession reveals a conical locus of the axis, as in a spinning top or the spinning earth.

Prokaryote. A cellular organism, such as a bacterium or a blue-green alga, in which the nucleus lacks a limiting membrane. Considered the oldest form of life on Earth, it is still by far the most abundant. Because it has existed for such a length of time, some scientists maintain that it is the most successful cell structure in the earth environment. The cell does contain the universal genetic agent DNA but usually as a single loop. Prokaryotes remain absolutely vital in the structure of the living community. Algae are the original generators of free oxygen and are still the major force in maintaining an oxygen balance in the atmosphere, so vital to eukaryotes and to multicelled organisms. Too little free oxygen stifles respiration; too much can lead to uncontrolled fires. *See also* Eukaryote

Quackgrass. A grass (*Agropyron repens*) that invaded North America in historic times, perhaps mixed in with alfalfa seed imported from Asia, or in the bedding of cattle brought to the New World. It is very aggressive in areas maintained as animal pasture because of its abundant production of rhizomes. It is not well adapted to established natural prairies because it does not have the deep roots of native prairie grasses.

Quartz. A hard, crystalline, vitreous mineral of silicon dioxide found in most rocks, especially sandstone and granite. Varieties include agate, chalcedony, chert, flint, opal, and rock crystal.

Quartzite. A metamorphic rock that is recrystallized quartz sandstone. The Baraboo Range is largely quartzite.

Random variation. A statistical term used to describe a set of values pertaining to phenomena that do not exhibit the same outcomes or consequences every time they occur under identical (or similar) circumstances. Phenological expressions, for example, the flowering dates of spring ephemerals, show a degree of randomness from year to year. The flowering times are not without measurable causes, however, as they reflect the influence of differences in the genes of various plants and in the conditions of weather, fire, soil, and animal grazing. In other words, variations can be predicted with some margins of error. *See also* Determinism; Stochastic pattern

Recessional moraine. Ridges of glacial till left behind as a glacier retreats. There is a series of recessional moraines on the Leopold Reserve that mark a glacial retreat. These moraines may also be deltas between the melting glacier and a large lake that formed south and west of the glacial lobe. The moraines are not exactly parallel, forming curves on the landscape, but they do reveal how the glacier haltingly melted over perhaps two to three thousand years.

Relative humidity. A term used to define the ratio of the amount of water vapor in the air at a specific temperature to the maximum capacity of the air to hold water vapor at that temperature. The warmer the air, the greater the capacity to hold water. Thus, a relative humidity of 35 percent at 80°F holds much more moisture than a relative humidity of 35 percent at 30°F.

Rhizome. A root-like, usually horizontal, stem growing under or along the ground that sends out roots from its lower surface and leaves or shoots from its upper surface. A prime example in this text is the non-native quackgrass.

Sand blow. A concentration of glacial sand usually deposited through wind action. The blow is drier and more barren than surrounding areas.

Sandstone. Sedimentary rock composed predominantly of quartz grains cemented by lime, silica, or other materials.

Sandy moraine. A glacial moraine, either recessional or terminal, that is predominantly quartz sand.

Savanna. A grassland with openings of trees and shrubs in the prairie terrain. Oak savannas and prairies form the prevailing biotic patterns in the border zone that stretches diagonally across the continent—from southwest to northeast.

Seasons. The four divisions of Earth's year characterized by differences in the relative lengths of day and night and the amount of heat received from the sun. In this sense, at the equator, there is little temperature change, although there are wet and dry "seasons." In high latitudes, spring and autumn are very short. The Leopold Reserve is nearly half way between the equator and the North Pole; thus the four seasons are well defined. However, changes in weather tend to lag behind the calendar dates for the seasons. The seasonal changes are a defining characteristic for this text. For the reason why Earth has seasons, *see* Tilted axis

Second Law of Thermodynamics. A theory in physics defining a spontaneous process that results in an increase in the total entropy in a system. The Second Law theory predicts that the universe is inevitably cooling down after its explosive origin, and that the energy in the system will be dispersed and the temperature drop to near absolute zero—unless the universe starts to coalesce and the entropic process reverses. *See also* Entropy

Sedge meadow. A tract of grassland that contains any of numerous plants of the family Cyperaceae, which resemble grasses, but have solid rather than hollow stems.

Sedge meadows normally have a high water table and mucky soils, and are poor cattle pasture.

Sedimentary rock. A rock that has formed from sedimentary material such as sand, clay, silt, gravel, or organic compounds transported by water, wind, or ice.

Short-grass prairie. A natural prairie dominated by short-grass species, common in the western parts of the great prairie/savanna region of North America. Grass species and individual plants found there are relatively "short" as compared to those in tall-grass prairies in the eastern zone. The composition is a function of amounts of moisture and elevation, the western regions being more arid and higher. Characteristic species include little bluestem, side-oats gramma, prairie dropseed, needle grass (porcupine grass), and buffalo grass. *See also* Tall-grass prairie

Silicate. Any of numerous rock-forming minerals that contain silicon, oxygen, and a metallic or organic radical.

Silicon dioxide. A usually white or colorless crystalline mineral containing one atom of silicon and two of oxygen (SiO_2); commonly called quartz, sand, flint, agate, or chert.

Silurian Period. A geologic period from about 410 to 440 million years ago, characterized by the presence of fishes, vascular plants, mosses, and perhaps seed ferns.

Solar constant. The amount of solar radiation that strikes a unit area perpendicularly at a distance of one astronomical unit from the sun (defined as the distance from the sun to Earth) in a unit interval of time. The solar constant has an average value of 1.94 calories per minute per square centimeter. Implied in this definition is the idea that the sun's average energy output is maintained over time. Some astronomers argue for variable or cyclical solar activity, for example as expressed in sunspot cycles of 11 years. A "constant" sun gives us some measure of confidence about the future existence of life, at least for the next four billion years, more or less. However, some astronomers have argued that the sun could become unstable as soon as 500,000 years from now, its radiation expanding outward enough to sear the earth and the other inner planets.

Solstice. Either of two times of the year when the sun has no apparent northward or southward motion, at the most northern or most southern point of the ecliptic. Here the summer solstice, when the sun is in the zenith at the Tropic of Cancer, occurs about June 21. The winter solstice, when the sun is over the Tropic of Capricorn, occurs about December 21.

Solvent. That part of a solution that is capable of dissolving another substance. The extraordinary capability of water as a solvent is a feature of this text.

Somatic cell. Any body cell, other than a germ cell, that is part of an individual's tissues or organs.

Steady state. A stable condition or system that does not change over time, or in which a change in one direction is continually balanced by change in another. The term can apply to chemical, physical, biological, or social states, as in the theory of a steady state economy. Some environmentalists favor such an economy, with a low throughput. In a sense, the idea of a steady-state defies environmental logic. Although there are optimal boundary conditions for life, for example, there appears to be nothing constantly steady in nature.

Stochastic pattern. I use this term in the sense of random; i.e., with regard to phenomena that do not show the same outcome every time they occur under the same circumstances. *See also* Determinism; Random variation

Stolon. A stem growing along or under the ground and taking root at the nodes or apex to form new plants. It is different from the rhizome.

Stoma (plural, **stomata**). A minute pore on the underside of a leaf through which gases and water vapor pass. Stomata are involved in plant respiration, but also serve as a way to control plant temperature through evaporative processes.

Stratosphere. A layer of the earth's atmosphere between 10 and 30 miles above the surface that has dry, clear, and "thin" air. Temperatures range from -30°F to -100°F. Ozone in the stratosphere serves to shield the earth's surface from excessive ultraviolet radiation that is harmful to life.

Subduction zone. A region where one crustal plate descends below the edge of another, often resulting in volcanic activity and earthquakes. The classic example in North America is the sinking Farallon Plate off the Northwest Coast. The volcanic Cascade Mountains in northern California, Oregon, and Washington are the result of subduction processes. There are no active subduction zones in the midcontinental area to which this text relates.

Subtropical convergence. A climatological zone. In this text, it refers to a mass of warm air in the lower latitudes of the northern hemisphere. The warm air has risen over the equator and flowed northward. As the air in the sub-tropics rises and moves, it tends to sink and unload its moisture. The down-welling dry air frames the conditions for the classic deserts of this zone—the Sahara, Saudi, and Rajasthan. (The same thing happens in the Southern Hemisphere—for example, the Australian desert. There are fewer land masses in the South, so the zone is not so obvious.) The zone is not fixed in place over the millennia. With global warming it tends to move north. With cooling it moves south. We now know such changes can occur abruptly, within a matter of decades.

Sun dog. A small halo or rainbow near the horizon caused by the sun's rays reflecting off atmospheric ice crystals. The halo is most visible on the two sides of the sun, thus a pair of sun dogs. Look for sun dogs in the deepest days of winter. Oldtimers who rely on visible signs of weather change say that sun dogs signal the approach of a winter storm, and in the West they say that coyotes howl when sun dogs appear.

Symbiosis. The close relationship of two or more different organisms in an association that may be, but is not necessarily, of benefit to each organism.

Syncline. A low, trough-like area of bedrock in which rocks incline together from opposite sides, sloping downward from opposite directions to meet in a common point or line at the bottom, forming a concave structure. *See also* Anticline

Synthelithic. A term, not used in the text, which I propose to describe a potential future condition in which humans rely increasingly or exclusively on synthetic molecules for their sustenance, habitat, and even for reconstruction of the human organism. The end result would be a radically simplified, but increasingly controlled, environment. For the derivation of the word, *see* Infolithic. *See also* Molecular structure

Taiga forest. The subarctic evergreen forest of North America and Eurasia. The northern and southern margins of the taiga move latitudinally as the climate shifts from glacial to interglacial.

Tall-grass prairie. A kind of prairie characteristic of the savanna region in the eastern half of the North American plains, containing such species as big bluestem, Indiangrass, switchgrass, and Canadian wild-rye. Tall-grass prairies receive more moisture than short-grass prairies do, and this land uses summer rainfall to sustain corn and soybeans. *See also* Short-grass prairie

Talus slope. A sloping mass of loose rock debris at the base of a cliff. Examples of talus slopes in this text are the blocks of quartzite eroded from the Baraboo monadnock. Some of that talus was swept away and ground to sand during the last glaciation. The talus that remains below the cliffs along the preglacial gorge was just beyond the reach of the glacier.

Tectonic process. The internal process that moves and deforms Earth's crust. Although normally a very slow-moving process, it can be revealed suddenly and dramatically by an earthquake, volcanic eruption, or landslide. Over the eons, the crust has been formed and reformed in monumental ways that we have understood only in the last 50 years or so. We now know that rivers are created and destroyed, oceans open and close, continents drift from equator to pole, and mountain ranges rise and fall. Life clearly adjusts to tectonic changes, though the changes are slow and often subtle.

Temperature inversion. A meteorological condition in which a mass of warm air becomes lodged above a mass of colder air, creating an "inversion" in the temperature gradient. This inversion tends to trap pollution, dust, and smoke.

Terminal moraine. An accumulation of boulders, stones, sand, or other debris carried and deposited by a glacier and marking its point of farthest advance.

Tertiary Period. The geologic period from about 2 to 70 million years ago. Epochs within the Tertiary include the Paleocene, Eocene, Oligocene, Miocene, and Pliocene. In general, world climate was warmer in the Tertiary than in the more recent Pleistocene, the glacial period. Mammals flourished and evolved into an array of species in the Tertiary. By the Oligocene, there were many more species of mammals as represented in the fossil record. A prominent example is the subhyracodon, a hippo-like creature. Many of those mammalian species, however, are now extinct. An example of an extinct mammal from the Paleocene is the psittacotherium, a rat/dog-like creature. The Tertiary is known as the age of mammals. Mammals did exist in the earlier Cretaceous period but they begin to really prosper in the Tertiary. Boundaries of geological periods and epochs are often defined by relatively abrupt changes in the biota that are assumed to derive from radical changes in the environment. A popular idea is that the Cretaceous ended with a giant meteor impact with Earth, wiping out most of the dinosaurs. But not all. Birds are now classified as dinosaurs. Possible causes for changes in the biota include meteor impacts, massive volcanic activities, and radical climate changes. Such causes are likely interrelated.

Thermal mechanism. A term referring to the ability of matter to absorb, store, and release heat energy. In the essay on water, I refer to its thermal capacity. Earth's oceans are great energy depositories. Thermal mechanisms in the oceans include currents, upwellings, evaporation, and even solvent capacities, such as, for example, the capacity to absorb carbon dioxide. These ocean mechanisms are fundamental in determining global climate and maintaining temperatures hospitable to life. *See*

also Thermodynamic capacity; Thermodynamic feedback

Thermodynamic capacity. The amount of energy that an object or substance can absorb and store. Water has a comparatively high ability to capture and store thermal energy.

Thermodynamic feedback. A term that describes the relationships between the atmosphere, oceans, and land of energy that is received from outside Earth, absorbed, reradiated, and exchanged. Thermodynamic feedback is a fundamental support mechanism for life, whether in the air, in the sea, or on land. Life prospers within a fairly narrow thermal optimum. Normal human body temperature is 98.6°F. The optimal surrounding, or ambient, temperature for humans is about 72°F. If it is less than that we dress and seek warm shelter; more than that, we undress and seek the shade. Thermodynamics puts boundaries on seasonal extremes and makes Earth more habitable.

Tilted axis. A term used to describe the line of Earth's rotation in relation to the sun. Earth's line of rotation is not at a right angle to the sun; the tilt of the axis is 66.5 degrees. This is the reason for the changing seasons on Earth. In the northern hemisphere when the earth is angled away from the sun we have winter; in our summer the earth is angled toward the sun. *See also* Seasons

Topaz. A colorless, blue, yellow, brown, or pink aluminum silicate mineral, often found in association with granitic rocks and valued as a gemstone.

Tornadic front. An advancing low pressure area that may spawn a number of tornadic funnels. Seen from a weather satellite, the multiples of tornadoes show up as darkened cells with horizontal tails that trail away at the top of the vortex. Not all of the cells reach the ground. Even so, such a front can generate excitement for creatures at the surface of the earth, and some humans—I among them—would like to stand outside to observe the funnels.

Tornado. A rotating column of air usually accompanied by a funnel-shaped downward extension of a cumulonimbus cloud that has a vortex several hundred yards in diameter whirling at speeds of up to 300 miles an hour.

Triassic Period. The geologic period that occurred from about 210 to 245 million years ago; part of the Mesozoic Era.

Trophic structure. A series of higher feeding levels in a food chain of an ecosystem, generally proceeding from vegetation through herbivores, omnivores, and carnivores. One level would be the grasses in the prairie that rely on photosynthesis involving carbon, nitrogen, water, and sunlight for their nutrition. A level above this would be the herbivores that rely on the grasses, such as mice, rabbits, bison, and cows. Next are the omnivores—bears, swine, humans—that feed on vegetation and also on the mice, rabbits, bison, and cows. The final level includes the carnivores that rely on the herbivores and often on the omnivores; examples include the wolves, rattlesnakes, and hawks. Taken together, these creatures in a food chain constitute a trophic structure. A population diagram of the trophic structure is pyramidal in shape, with smaller populations of individuals (and species) at each succeeding level.

Tropic of Cancer. The northern circle on Earth's sphere that is parallel to and at an angular distance of 23 degrees 27 minutes from the equator and is the limit of the apparent northern passage of the sun. It is associated with the summer solstice in the northern hemisphere.

Tropic of Capricorn. The southern circle on Earth's sphere that is parallel to and at an angular distance of 23 degrees 27 minutes from the equator and is the limit of the apparent southern passage of the sun. It is associated with the summer solstice in the southern hemisphere.

Troposphere. The troposphere extends upward from the earth to about 5 miles at the poles, 7 miles in mid-latitudes, and 10 miles at the equator. The air in the troposphere is in constant motion, a condition we experience as wind. Air temperature decreases with elevation and is about -70°F at the boundary with the stratosphere. *See also* Atmosphere; Stratosphere

Tundra. A treeless area between the timberline of arctic regions and the polar ice cap. It has a permanently frozen subsoil and supports low-growing vegetation such as lichens, mosses, and stunted willows. Because the summer days there are long, the tundra provides a biologically rich environment.

Wet mesic prairie. A prairie situated in a low-lying area with relatively poor drainage, usually because of underlying clay, which supports grasses and forbs that can tolerate higher than normal water levels in spring and in years of heavier than normal rainfall.

Wisconsin glaciation. The latest period of glaciation in what is now Wisconsin, but also across North America, occurring within the last 100,000 years and starting to retreat about 16,000 years ago. There is considerable evidence of earlier episodes of glaciation as expressed in glacial drifts. For a complete description, see Lawrence Martin's *The Physical Geography of Wisconsin* (The University of Wisconsin Press, 1965).

Woodland. A land with a covering of trees and shrubs. This region, in the current climatic regime, is naturally characterized by oak savanna–grassland, with "openings"

of oaks and other deciduous trees. Under cultivation for the last 150 years, the land has shifted dramatically toward cultivated fields of agronomic crops and "improved" pasture, but, surprisingly, also toward woodland. The woodlands, typically on sites less desirable for cultivation, have increased in large part through fire suppression. Some farmers have "cultivated" woodlands for timber as a cash crop. Particularly desirable are white oaks to make whiskey barrels.

Xylem cell. The supporting and water-conducting cell in a vascular plant such as a fern or a seedbearer.

Zenith. Technically, the point that is directly above an observer who is standing on the celestial sphere (Earth). The zenith of the day—when the sun is at its highest point in relation to the horizons—is the moment of "high noon." Unless it is cloudy, high noon is most obvious to those of us here in the middle latitudes on the day of the summer solstice, June 21. In that sense, the day of the solstice is the seasonal "high noon." The moment can be emotional, if you think about it. Afternoon becomes symbolic of a fading year, or even of approaching "elder years."

NORTH AMERICAN GEOLOGY

The following geological time chart is representative of North America, including the savanna/prairie described in this volume. We know, however, that Earth has been a very "plastic" planet. Continents have merged and separated. Landmasses have changed in latitude and longitude. Seas have occupied continents and retreated. The oceans have risen and fallen with glaciation. Mountains have been thrust up and eroded away. Climates have changed globally, and also regionally. Plants and animal species have emerged, evolved, and disappeared.

Conditions for our temperate prairie and savanna are geologically very recent. A million years from now the natural prairie and savanna will be measured in the fossil record, if not in reality. Indeed, that record could generate a level for an oncoming epoch, an epoch where the recorders have revised the name "Holocene" to "Homocene."

With all this history, however, there is so far an unbroken life chain organized at the level of cells and their internal genetic maps. Indeed some biologists argue that evolution is framed at the level of DNA more than at the level of organisms and species. Deeper than biology, however, is a continuity in the rocks. It is interesting that geological time charts are defined in both biological and physical terms. What we see today is thus unchanged but changing. This is the grand scope of nature. In this sense our "prairie time" is but an interlude. But it is the interlude in which we are embedded.

Era	Period	Epoch	Millions of years ago	Life
Cenozoic	Quaternary	Holocene Pleistocene		*Homo sapiens*
			—2.0—	
	Tertiary	Pliocene Miocene Oligocene Eocene Paleocene		
			—66.0—	
Mesozoic	Upper Cretaceous	Laramie Montana Colorado Dakota		placental mammals
	Lower Cretaceous	Washita Fredericksburg Trinity Arundel Patuxent		grasses, grains
			—144—	
	Jurassic	Upper Middle Lower		birds flowering plants mammals
			—208—	
	Triassic	Upper Middle Lower		
			—245—	ginkos
	Permian			cycads and
			—286—	conifers
	Pennsylvanian			insects
			—320—	cordates
	Mississippian			reptiles
			—360—	
Paleozoic	Devonian			
			—408—	
	Silurian			amphibians
			—438—	
	Ordovician			seed ferns vascular plants
			—505—	
	Cambrian			fishes mosses
			—570—	
Proterozoic				invertebrates
			—2500—	
Archean				bacteria marine algae
			—3900—	
Hadean				
			—4600—	

INDEX

Page numbers in italics refer to photographs.
Page numbers in bold refer to species descriptions.